DATE DUE			
DEC 01 1995			
DEC 12 1995			
DEC 1998			

A FINE WILL BE CHARGED
FOR EACH OVERDUE BOOK

Realism and the Romance
Nathaniel Hawthorne, Henry James, and American Fiction

by
Elissa Greenwald

UMI Research Press
Ann Arbor / London

Produced and distributed by
UMI Research Press
an imprint of
University Microfilms Inc.
Ann Arbor, Michigan 48106

Library of Congress Cataloging in Publication Data

Greenwald, Elissa, 1954-
   Realism and the romance : Nathaniel Hawthorne, Henry James,
and American fiction / by Elissa Greenwald.
      p. cm—(Nineteenth-century studies)
      Bibliography: p.
      Includes index.
      ISBN 0-8357-1948-0 (alk. paper)
      1. American fiction—19th century—History and criticism.
   2. Hawthorne, Nathaniel, 1804-1864—Criticism and interpretation.
   3. James, Henry, 1843-1916—Criticism and interpretation.
   4. Realism in literature.   5. Romanticism—United States.
   I. Title.   II. Series: Nineteenth-century studies (Ann Arbor, Mich.)
   PS374.R37G7   1989
   813'.3'09—dc19   88-39441
                                                              CIP

British Library CIP data is available.

To My Parents

Contents

Figures

Acknowledgments

I would like to thank my teachers at Yale College for setting before me a model of teaching, scholarship, and humanity. I am grateful to Alan Trachtenberg, advisor *extraordinaire,* for his keen insight, support, and patience. I am also indebted to Richard Brodhead, whose teachings inspired many of my ideas. I have benefited from conversations on American literature with Debra Fried, Kenneth Meyers, Richard Millington, and the Young Americanists at Rutgers. Jonathan Freedman provided helpful criticism and sympathy at an earlier stage.

I am particularly indebted to colleagues at Rutgers University who read parts or all of the manuscript, keen eyes and kind hearts all: Maurice Charney, Alice Crozier, William Galperin, Myra Jehlen, David Leverenz, George Levine, Barry Qualls, Thomas Van Laan, and Susan Wolfson. I have also profited from the very helpful comments of Professor Julian Markels and another, anonymous reader for UMI Research Press. My students at Rutgers provided insights and continual challenges. In particular, I have learned from the students in my Junior Honors Seminars and my senior thesis student Daniel Antonellis.

Many friends provided support during the writing of this book, especially Laura Kendrick, Rosemary Jann, Jackie Miller, Sandy Flitterman-Lewis and Joel Lewis, Judy McCarthy and James Lent, Jeslyn Medoff and Antony Crossman, and the members of the singing group Cantabile.

An earlier version of chapter 6 appeared in *Studies in the Novel* 18 (Summer 1986), 177–92, published by the University of North Texas.

I would like to acknowledge three women whose aid enabled me to write and publish this work: Elaine Showalter, who believed in me; Leslie Mitchner, who gave invaluable advice; and my mother, Fay Teichman Greenwald, whose own career and work on James have provided me with a fine example. Finally, I would like to thank both my parents for re-reading the same stories to me endlessly when I was a child and so developing my appetite for twice-told tales.

Introduction

Romance and realism have frequently been considered opposing strains in fiction. Much criticism of American fiction has classified it as romance, while describing English and European fiction as "realistic novels."[1] American writers have traditionally complained that America lacks the material for novels, an idea voiced most famously by Henry James in his critical biography, *Hawthorne* (1879).[2]

This dichotomy has led to the separation of the study of American literature from that of English literature, emphasizing the insularity of national literatures. In addition, the dichotomy between romance and realism is based on two presuppositions that may be challenged. One is the notion that realism is essentially a mirror of a world outside itself. Indeed, to claim a strong division between romance and realism often entails seeing realistic novels primarily as transcriptions of a society around them, so that the novels are judged on the richness of their details, which is dependent on the milieu in which they were written. The second presupposition is that there is a reality outside representation to which works of art refer. Recent post-structuralist criticism has questioned that assumption, noting that art works do not necessarily refer to a world outside themselves (for, indeed, there may be no such "reality"). Thus the goal of making the work a perfect mirror of "reality" is not only undesirable but impossible to achieve.

To understand the nature of romance and realism in the novel, then, demands a more flexible definition of both terms which will account for their interaction. In this work, I address the larger question of the relation of romance and realism, English and American fiction, through the examples of two writers, Nathaniel Hawthorne and Henry James. The relation between Hawthorne and James challenges the schematic division between romance and realism as American and European genres, respectively. Indeed, James's status as a writer international in both theme and personal situation illustrates his capacity to cross borders of genre as well as nationality.

James's biography of Hawthorne, as well as the writings of both authors on romance, have been used to justify the romance-realism dichotomy. Yet reading *Hawthorne* not according to James's explicit statements but with awareness of his continual defensiveness against Hawthorne reveals the continuity between Hawthorne and James to which James's works of fiction throughout his career also testify. In *Hawthorne,* written for the English Men of Letters series, James emphasizes the lack of novelistic material in the United States primarily to distance himself from his homeland and his principal American predecessor. His often harsh critique of Hawthorne is in some ways a defense against Hawthorne's excessive early influence on him, as well as an echo of Hawthorne's own complaint about the paucity of American materials in *The Marble Faun.* Yet even as James attacks Hawthorne for those aspects of his work associated with romance, notably the use of symbolism and the supernatural, he begins to adapt those techniques for his own use. While attempting to reinforce the dichotomy between romance and realism, then, James is actually revealing his indebtedness to Hawthorne's romance and adapting it for his own creative writing.

Thus in his critical biography of Hawthorne, as well as his other critical essays on Hawthorne, James did not so much escape Hawthorne's influence as transmute it. Indeed, James's novelistic craft, sometimes seen as the ultimate extension of realism, is deeply indebted to Hawthorne's romance. The use of romance to inform realism enables James to use the novel to project imaginative views rather than imitate a pre-existent reality. Thus James depicts a world at once convincing and fantastic, in its extravagant detail and often elevated characters. James's representation is indebted to the heightened drama of romance for its intensity and richness, so that even the convincingness of his portrayals is indebted to this mode; in this way, romance heightens the realism of his works. James's treatments of the International Theme, as he himself frequently admitted, are not the results of documentation or the imitation of ordinary life. Rather, they depend on a strongly projecting imagination which eventually finds its correlates in the material world. Recognizing the romance in James's realism reveals as well the realism in Hawthorne's romance, the way Hawthorne's symbolism and other forms of projection are used to provide accurate and deep analysis of characters (what James called the "deeper psychology") and social conditions. The similarities between Hawthorne and James illustrate not only the continuity of nineteenth-century American fiction but the affinities between American and European fiction.

The focus on romance in the novel illustrates the point that the novel need not, and perhaps cannot, reflect a world outside itself. Every "picture of life" depends on the artist's imagination which shapes the picture. That imagination must draw its materials at least in part from the physical world, if only to produce a simulacrum of them. But the projections of imagination may create a reality constituted by representation itself. In some ways, that reality is especially convincing to us because it incorporates our perceptions in experience. Thus it gives us the world as we experience it internally, and provides intimations that the reality we see may always be a mixture of our own perceptions with the material realm.

The creations of romance are self-consciously artificial and fictive, and so may seem to deviate from reality. However, the sense of a stable reality that coheres outside of fiction may be an illusion. For reality may be as much a construct of our desires and fictions as a separate, pre-existing entity. Thus fiction itself can be seen not as a kind of false world, or a secondary creation, but a form of reality in itself. For the reality which we seem to see reflected in representation may be an illusion created by the work itself. The sense of the presence of an external world in fiction creates the feeling of a reality that would not otherwise exist.

 In some ways, the aims of realism, with its attention to physical detail, analysis of social structures, and psychological complexity, seem opposed to those of romance, in which verisimilitude is sacrificed for imaginative coherence, three-dimensional characterization for allegory. Yet, as Northrop Frye has noted, romance persists even in the form of the nineteenth-century realistic novel, in his view through the continuing presence of archetypal romance plots.[3] Romance is at the very heart of realism in more ways than its often-repeated stories. Every work of art demands the author's shaping presence, and romance dramatizes this presence far more than other genres. Romance's presentation of action as determined by desire provides deep psychological portrayal. Its seemingly two-dimensional characters are the results of projections of inner states. In its focus on such states, romance also provides access to the realm of the unconscious. Indeed, many of the seemingly bizarre events of romance are the products of a plot governed by a logic which resembles that of dreams more than that of cause and effect.

Both Hawthorne and James create the illusion of life by showing a world transformed by romantic imagination. In his last essay on Hawthorne, James describes perception as creative, helping to bring into existence the reality it depicts. In James's late works, reality is not only reflected but constituted by consciousness. For both Hawthorne and James, imagination provides a way not to escape but to know reality. In their works, reality has the aura of romance, as if the world we know were also the one we desire. For reality comes to us enhanced by the charms bestowed by imaginative projections of desire. James's praise for Hawthorne's "deeper psychology" may refer to the capacity of romance's symbolic projections to convey unconscious states. Romance's seemingly "wild" creations, naturalized in James's depictions, enable penetration to the most deeply hidden emotions. Most previous critics of the James-Hawthorne relation have claimed that James, as realist, "perfects" or "completes" Hawthorne's romance, fleshing out his themes, characters, and plots.[4] But acknowledging the full extent of Hawthorne's influence rather shows the interpenetration of romance and realism in James's Anglo-American art.

James conveys the heightened drama of romance precisely by means of a highly detailed representation of European civilization, transforming the cloak of symbolic and supernatural occurrences in Hawthorne's romance into the particulars of social manners. His descriptions of Europe serve not primarily to reflect contemporary manners but to provide signs of an inner drama. By taking an American, "romantic" perspective on Europe, James dramatizes both the richness of European life to an American imagination and the ultimate fictitiousness of that life perceived as representation. In his works, James combines the projective and mirroring tendencies of representation to uncover what lies below the surface of appearances, a necessary strategy to decipher the complex codes of European society. He strikes the "real romantic note"[5] (which he acknowledged in Hawthorne) by showing the mixture of inner states with the world, the horizon along which we become aware of the presence of our perceptions in a world we previously thought of as external to us.

Hawthorne's work demonstrates the subjective aspect of romance not by depicting battles between dragons and knights but by demonstrating how such representations are generated by psychological states: for example, symbolism may be a consequence of repression which suppresses any literal meaning that is threatening or forbidden. Hawthorne dramatizes the essential subjectivity of romance by showing how its projections are frequently the products of neurosis or self-contained introspection on the part of his characters. James's innovation, the center of consciousness, a precursor of modernist stream of consciousness, is in part indebted to Hawthorne's emphasis on subjectivity. Thus, if James's adaptation of Hawthorne's romance forwarded the aims of realism, it also subtly undermined them from within, for romance blurred the line between inner and outer worlds, leading to the modernist undermining of the belief in a stable realm outside the self or even a stable self.[6]

Understanding the role of romance in James and in the nineteenth-century novel generally requires a definition of romance that will demonstrate its links to realism. Traditionally, romance has been seen as an earlier form that was superseded by the novel in the nineteenth century. However, But aspects of realistic representation may be discerned within romance. That is, from the outset, romance is not so much a repudiation of mimesis as a particular way of viewing reality. Despite his general thesis that all American fiction is romance, Richard Chase acknowledges the presence of both romance and novel in American fiction in his landmark work (indeed, his book is entitled *The American Novel and Its Tradition*). But he continues to state that romance is incapable of providing deep analysis of character or social conditions, considering symbolism antithetical to that aim: "the romance can flourish without providing much intricacy of relation. The characters, probably rather two-dimensional types, will not be complexly related to each other or to society or to the past. Human beings will on the whole be shown in ideal relation—that is, they will share emotions only after these have become abstract or symbolic." Chase feels that in its tendency to abstraction, romance turns its back on social and historical reality, and that it is incapable of employing rational principles. Nonetheless, he notes that "the very abstractness and profundity of romance allow it to formulate moral truths of universal validity, although it perforce ignores home truths that may be equally or more important."[7]

The very aspects of romance which Chase sees as leading away from knowledge of reality, such as idealization and abstraction, may enable deeper understanding of moral and social issues. Since romance presents emotions familiar to all, it can indeed formulate "moral truths of universal validity." For example, the rather extreme and unlikely drama of *The Winter's Tale* is made plausible because it presents an emotion every spectator has experienced: jealousy. By revealing emotions that are universally familiar, romance presents truth that is more than only subjective. In another way, romance may heighten understanding of this world by composing it into a coherent pattern. Romance narrative tends to work through symbols and tableaus to create pictorial designs.

Precisely through symbolism, romance may provide insight into character and social conditions, for symbols may represent real things rather than imaginary ones. While a character in romance may seem two-dimensional, her subjectivity may be explored as much through its projection into events as through direct analysis of her personality. In many ways, symbols do not diffuse but focus emotion, as the scarlet letter intensifies while representing the various emotions (shame, guilt, pride) attached to it. Symbolic representation may also provide social analysis, especially of a society that depends on symbols for its very constitution, like that of the Puritans in *The Scarlet Letter*. In both *The Scarlet Letter* and *The Blithedale Romance*, Hawthorne uses symbols (the scarlet letter, the veiled lady) to demonstrate the coercive and manipulative nature of the communities he describes.

Recent critics of American romance, such as Michael Bell, have noted that by the nineteenth century, romance had been so often and variously defined that the term ceased to have any specific meaning.[8] But both Hawthorne and James recognized the force of romance as a genre even as they transformed it. In part working in the context of contemporary definitions of romance and novel, both were also influenced by Renaissance models, as shown by Hawthorne's extensive use of Spenser and James's interest in Shakespeare (*The Tempest* was the subject of one of James's last essays, of 1907). Indeed, understanding the nature of the genre itself requires a combination of diachronic and synchronic, historical and ahistorical approaches.

To some extent, romance preserves the illusion of ~~verisimilitude~~ expectations because it presents a world that is clearly fanciful but nonetheless familiar. The convincingness of romance is emphasized by Northrop Frye, who notes that "the quest-romance is the search of the libido or desiring self for a fulfillment that will deliver it from the anxieties of reality but will still contain that reality."[9] The wish-fulfillment enacted in romance would not be so satisfying if it did not seem to project the illusion of life. Frye's definition suggests the representational function of romance, which, by using symbolism and deviating from ordinary laws of cause and effect, externalizes unconscious desires to project as real the inner structures of the mind. Events in romance which may seem unlikely or bizarre when referred to ordinary causality appear believable and detailed when viewed as externalizations of mental patterns. Frye's definition of romance is difficult to apply to nineteenth-century novels (although he does see romance as an underlying, archetypal pattern in many novels) because he feels medieval and Renaissance romances have been replaced by nineteenth-century realistic and twentieth-century ironic modes.

Frye's view does not account fully for the evolving role of romance in the nineteenth century, the period of our concern. In what way is romance as a genre historically defined, and in what ways is it affected by historical context? The social contexts for romance in the nineteenth century are analyzed more fully in Fredric Jameson's recent *The Political Unconscious*.[10]

In the chapter "Magical Narratives: Romance as Genre," Jameson considers romance an apt paradigm for the Marxist view of history, a quest-like progression towards a Utopian goal. Jameson views romance as "mode" rather than genre, not a set of formal principles but an atmosphere that can easily combine with other modes. For Jameson, romance is characterized especially by a kind of action, featuring "transformed states of being, sudden alterations of temperature, mysterious heightenings, local intensities, sudden drops in quality, and alarming effluvia, in short, the whole semic range of transformation scenes whereby, in romance, higher and lower worlds struggle to overcome each other" (p. 112). In Jameson's description, the typical romance battle of good and evil becomes virtually a struggle between life and death. In a sense, romance dramatizes the struggle of meaning to realize itself.

Jameson's definition of romance as mode allows him to see its characteristics as present even in situations where its typical features (such as a happy, even divinely inspired ending) are reversed. In modern novels, romance is evoked as an absence, not a presence: "The characteristic indirection of a nascent modernism, from Kafka to Cortazar, circumscribes the place of the fantastic as a determinate, marked *absence* at the heart of the secular world." The loss of romance magic produces "Stimmung," another version of enchantment, which Jameson defines as a negative epiphany: "So . . . the last unrecognizable avatars of romance . . . draw their magical power from an unsentimental loyalty to those henceforth abandoned clearings across which high and lower worlds once passed" (p. 135). In twentieth-century fiction, the conflicts of romance are

present within the mind, where they resonate precisely with echoes of what has
been lost. Thus, in my view, in twentieth-century works, romance is precisely
constituted as a sense of the absence of reality, of the world as stark and bare,
which produces a kind of enchantment in reverse.

Jameson describes romance as the mode in which "the *worldness* of *world*
reveals itself" (p. 112), alluding to Heidegger's distinction between world and
earth, in which world represents the mixture of human effort with "earth," the
untransformed physical realm.[11] For Jameson the "world" romance makes manifest is "a very peculiar and specialized social and historical phenomenon"
(p. 112), especially the Utopian visions of Marxism. "World" may be defined
rather as a psychological phenomenon conditioned by historical context, the
realm of thought and feeling already projected onto reality which romance
reveals. In my view, romance reveals the margin of reality which is transformed
by consciousness. That consciousness is, of course, historically constructed and
partly determined by ideology. Jameson's historical view is useful, for romance
must be considered diachronically as well as synchronically. But romance need
not represent a single political plot, for it may have conservative as well as
revolutionary aspects.

In reading the use of romance in nineteenth-century fiction, it is important
to retain both a transhistorical sense of the genre and a conception of its link to
historical contexts. Jameson sees romance "interiorized" (p. 133) and psycholo-
gized in nineteenth-century fiction. This description correlates to the use of
"psychological romance" in Hawthorne and James, who preserve romance adventures in consciousness rather than action.

As Jameson's analysis suggests, the role of consciousness in producing
"world" out of "earth" becomes not just the mode but the subject of much
modern fiction. In nineteenth- and twentieth-century novels, as the overt magic
of romance disappears, enchantment is displaced into mental capacities. The
enchantment of romance is now present only within the mind, and there known
only as a memory. Romance transformation becomes highly self-conscious,
internalized as the consciousness of author or character. Such works at once
displace romance's adventures into a mental realm and testify to the inability
of consciousness to rebuild that magical world. Consciousness becomes the
repository of the senses of meaning, mystery, and beauty which romance conveys, even as it testifies to the disappearance of the magical world romance
represents.

James identifies romance with the artistic faculty itself, which he sees
finally as one of observation as much as creation. For him, romance is the
capacity to observe and absorb physical details: "the kind of reflection the things
we know best and see oftenest may make in our minds."[12] James's adaptation
of romance reflects his ever-growing appreciation of the power of art to "make
life," but in his last novels he increasingly creates the sense of the "modern

fantastic," as Jameson defines it, in which a world of spiritual significance is known only by its absence. The novels of James's Major Phase, despite their fullness of detail, when read through the lens of romance reveal a desacralized world in which objects have lost their meanings and even the most powerful consciousness cannot restore them. The "Stimmung" to which Jameson refers as indicative of a peculiarly modern temperament may be seen in an incident in *The Golden Bowl*, James's last novel of the Major Phase, when the dissolution of a country-house party reduces the setting to the long blank wall at Matcham, which resonates with uncanny emptiness.

The transformation of romance to "interiorized" action in the nineteenth- and twentieth-century novel suggests that we must re-evaluate what we define as the "real." The sense of reality as limited to consciousness, which in modern works often appears as a tragedy, may be seen differently. The philosopher-critic Yves Bonnefoy has suggested that reality is not external to representation but an effect created by representation.[13] For Bonnefoy, this effect is possible because language already acknowledges the fact of absence. Language thus becomes not the source of absence but a possible way to heal it. The real is evoked in language precisely insofar as it evades direct depiction. For the real is an essence we cannot touch: "What seems to remain most worthy of being called real is this mass of words, ceaselessly changing their meanings and often their form, a mass which rolls down through the ages like a huge river across languages and cultures." Reality is constituted not by things but by the words which represent them, at once continuous and constantly changing. Representations may be more permanent than their subjects: "This world which cuts itself off from the world seems to the person who creates it not only more satisfying than the first but also more real."

The sense of full incarnation is achieved precisely by turning away from such embodiment, whether from reality into representation or from mirroring to imagistic language: "This impression of a reality, at last fully incarnate, which comes to us, paradoxically, through words which have turned away from incarnation, I shall call image." For we cannot know reality fully, or rather the impression of reality is gained only through imagination. Nonetheless, "the image is certainly a lie, however sincere the maker of the image." Thus the reality of the image no longer exists objectively, only subjectively. This sense of reality as achieved not through mirroring but through internalization, not "incarnation" but images, leads us to view romance's projective imagination and imagistic representation as convincing in creating a sense of reality. James's works especially manifest the turn of language from reality in Bonnefoy's terms, in his highly figurative style and use of impressions. The reality constituted in those gaps where language is distanced from "incarnation" unites inner and outer worlds to achieve a form of permanence.

Recognizing the admixture of romance in realism, then, forces artists and readers to redefine what they understand to be "real." The continuing presence of romance in realism reveals not only the importance of imagination in creating a rich and intense representation, but the possibility that such richness inheres not only in representation but in experience. The influence of Hawthorne on James serves as a case study to prove the interaction of romance and realism, the connections between representation and reality. To place Hawthorne and James in context, I will consider their theories of romance in light of writings on the subject in nineteenth-century English and American periodicals (Chapter One). Chapter Two traces James's criticism of Hawthorne from an early essay of 1872 to the Centenary essay of 1904. James continually redefines romance, from a mode to a "value" to a whole side of life. In Chapter Three, I begin by considering the characteristics of romance narrative as adapted by Hawthorne and James. I then analyze the use and ironizing of romance in some major works by Hawthorne. Chapters Four through Seven trace the adaptation of romance in James's works from *The Portrait of a Lady* (1881) to *The Golden Bowl* (1904). I begin by tracing the network of allusions to Hawthorne prominent in *The Portrait of a lady,* which in later James works becomes increasingly diffused into the novel's entire mode of creation. As his career progresses, James escaped the direct matrix of Hawthorne's images and narrative method to form his own mode, "the romance of reality," in which he discovered the mystery and glamour of romance even on the surface of everyday life. That this mode of representation could be extended beyond fiction to experience is demonstrated in James's late nonfiction, particularly *The American Scene*, the subject of my conclusion.

Hawthorne was not the only influence on James, one of the most widely influenced of major writers. But since Hawthorne was the American writer about whom his successor wrote most, and whom James identified as the one who "proved that one could be an American writer . . . by being American enough,"[14] his example was crucial for James's self-definition as artist and as individual. James originally considered Hawthorne deficient in realism because of his Americanness and his insufficient contact with the European spectacle. But James found in his own contact with Europe that an American perspective deepened and enhanced his realism. He saw Europe not as a stable external world but as a system of signs to be interpreted. That in the process of so treating Europe James posed some troubling questions about the significance of European civilization or even the reality of the physical world only meant that he followed in the steps of Hawthorne, whose romance explored questions about the nature of reality which James himself could never fully resolve.

1

Romance and Novel

Hawthorne's and James's views of romance were part of an ongoing critical debate that raged in periodicals on both sides of the Atlantic throughout the nineteenth century. The nineteenth-century contexts illustrate precisely what was original about Hawthorne's and James's views, and show that the dichotomy between romance and novel was not absolute in the nineteenth century.

Indeed, recent critics have acknowledged the presence of romance in the novel. In *The Realistic Imagination,* George Levine focuses on the aspects of realism which tend not to reproduce reality but to unsettle our sense of its stability.[1] Levine refers to the forces of anarchy and the phantasmagoric which haunt realistic novels as "the monstrous," beginning with the example of *Frankenstein.* The energies subversive to realism which Levine identifies as the "monstrous" are what I call romance. If one sees realism as aiming to reproduce the world as it is, such energies appear disruptive. But the "monstrous" may rather represent the creative energy which must be released to produce any representation. Critics such as Peter Brooks and Donald Stone have shown the continued and even necessary presence of romanticism—including the use of lyrical moments and the adaptation of melodrama—in Victorian fiction.[2] Erich Auerbach demonstrates that mimesis is never simply a direct mirroring of the world but an exercise in formal manipulation and subjectivity.[3] But Auerbach still presumes the transparence of the realistic work, and the presence of a world "out there" to which realism refers. Instead, by acknowledging that realistic novels, like any form of representation, demand the presence of the writer's imagination, it becomes clearer that realistic works in part describe their own creation. Thus the dramatization of the imaginative process found in romance may be incorporated into the novel rather than constitute a threat to it.

Hawthorne's definition of romance as middle ground between fancy and actuality, dream and waking states, has precedents in early nineteenth-century writings. Hawthorne often defines romance as a space or territory, a place where "actual and imaginary" may meet and intermingle. Many English novelists define their works as occupying a similar space, what Barry Qualls has identified as the "mere film of land" where imagination and actuality meet.[4] For George Eliot, realism is the exhibition of "men and things as they have mirrored themselves in my mind."[5] According to Eliot's definition, realism is achieved through the internalization of experience. Eliot does not claim to "hold the mirror up to nature" through an objective reflection of reality. Instead, she admits that what she depicts is necessarily the product of her own perspective and experience, which does not make her portrayals any less truthful. By locating the mirror of mimesis within the mind, Eliot implies that imagination is the power that reflects and provides true pictures. Her emphasis on internalized vision enables romance's treatment of inner, even unconscious states to be included within the novel.

Sir Walter Scott locates his work in a literal border area, the region between England and Scotland. Though in one essay Scott distinguishes between the ancient romance and the "modern psychological novel," his work seems to bridge the two modes.[6] His works often depict times of transition or revolution, as the disappearance of ancient customs becomes his subject. The loss of "ancient romance" and its traditions deeply affects the psychological state of the characters, so that "modern psychology" depends on the "ancient romance" it seems to supersede. The generic displacement of romance by novel reflects a change of manners which disrupts the society and transforms individual psychology.

Psychological verisimilitude, then, may be achieved through the conjunction of novel and romance. For that middle ground, whether perceived imaginatively, as in Eliot, or historically, as in Scott, provides a perspective in which unconscious thoughts may be subjected to consciousness. Abstraction from ordinary experience illuminates the "inner-worldly" aspect of life to which Jameson refers, providing awareness of the influence of inner thoughts and feelings on the physical world. Scott begins by opposing romance and psychology, which is an opposition continued in later critics, including Chase.[7] But romance could convey psychological insight with uncanny precision. Its dramatization of unlikely or bizarre events often represents a narrative controlled by desire rather than the reality principle, one which externalizes unconscious wishes. Frye notes romance's tendency to compose reality and disclose its archetypal patterns: "Romance's tendency . . . [is] to conventionalize content in an idealized direction."[8] Thus its very abstraction and idealization, which Chase initially saw as preventing romance's full portrayal of character and society, may provide a way to analyze the world and depict it rationally.

In the early part of the nineteenth century, romance was frequently attacked for its idealizing and conventionalizing tendencies, as the demand for verisimilitude grew. Critics felt that romance, by showing things not encountered in ordinary existence, would lead to distaste for regular experience as insufficiently exciting. Such an objection was raised even by Scott, despite his own use of romance for psychological portrayal. In a review of Austen's *Emma,* Scott finds romance dangerous because it may alienate us from life by presenting scenes more vivid than reality.[9] Other critics feel that liveliness is found only in scenes resembling life, for as John Wilson notes, the novel's "power lies in its reality." Wilson opposes art to nature, and objects to romance for its deliberately artificial aspect: "Where everything is to be bent and moulded to meet our ideas of proportion, fitness, beauty, and so forth, in a composition, our mind is apt to feel that art and nature are two different things, and that the latter is sacrificed to the former—the stronger to the weaker—that of which we care little, for that of which we care everything."[10] For Wilson, romance's dramatization of imaginative processes precludes the faithful reproduction of nature.

Both these attacks on romance contain some implicit praise of the genre. Wilson, though he praises nature over art, implicitly concedes that romance is the product of careful artistry rather than wild invention. The dramatized power of imagination in romance leads not to a more chaotic but a more ordered reality, characterized by "proportion, fitness, and beauty." As Chase notes that romance, while, in his view, neglecting "home truths," can provide truths of a more abstract nature, here Wilson virtually attributes to romance an eighteenth-century notion of truth.[11] Imagination composes in an almost painterly fashion. It provides not an anarchic force but one that highlights and organizes the world presented in representation.

Even the more extravagant aspects of romance, its lyrical and pictorial elements, are eventually assimilated into the definition of the novel. In a survey of Victorian critics of the novel, Michael Munday notes that the novelists' imaginations "enabled (them) to fuse their materials . . . into an artist-like unity of form and purpose; investing actual events and real persons with the colours of poetry, and blending old things with new so thoroughly as to merit the praise of creation."[12] Munday's definition of the novel adduces to it some of the qualities originally attributed to romance, such as heightened lyrical expression, the "colours of poetry." The very language of blending, which Hawthorne uses to describe his romance (for example, in the preface to *The House of the Seven Gables*), is here used to describe the novel itself. That combination is seen as the very foundation of the novel's success, its "artist-like unity of form and purpose." Imagination's materials need not be entirely fabricated and fantastical, but can be drawn from everyday life. Thus romance, which begins as the "other" within the novel, becomes incorporated within it.

American critics begin the nineteenth century with even greater skepticism towards romance than English critics exhibit. They note that romance is preeminently a genre of the ideal rather than the actual. But by mid-century some writers reconciled the mimetic with the creative aspects of literature. The transcendentalist Orestes Brownson notes that imagination is not only a "faculty of the soul" but a "fact of human life," which implies the "act of representing."[13]

For him, the imaginative perception of the ideal is part of the perception of the actual. For the writer William Gilmore Simms, the material of America demands romantic treatment: *"The Yemassee* is proposed as an *American* romance. It is so styled as much of the material could have been furnished by no other country. Something too much of extravagance—so some may think,—even beyond the usual license of fiction—may enter into certain parts of the narrative."[14] For Simms, America provides a "natural romance," as its material not only demands romantic treatment but in itself constitutes romance.

Thus this survey of American and English views of romance reveals differences between them, but not necessarily the same ones twentieth-century critics have seen. Writers on both sides of the Atlantic sought to overcome the rigid distinction between romance and realism for a mode of writing that incorporated both genres. While romance was defended largely by showing that it could contribute to realism, by the end of the century, in part through James's influence, the demand for referentiality was abandoned and romance was valued as much for its creative as its mimetic capacities.

Hawthorne and James were perhaps most influential in breaking the boundaries between romance and realism. In their criticism, both strongly protest against rigid distinctions in fiction. In addition, they emphasize the middle ground as a way of knowing. For Hawthorne, this enchanted space is an imaginary realm that bridges past and present, dream and actuality. By offering a new perspective on the ordinary world, romance challenges the distinction between real and illusory things. For James, romance is especially a way to understand unconscious desires and those aspects of reality which are hidden. Both Hawthorne and James adapt elements of the nineteenth-century debate in defining romance and realism.

In the course of his prefaces, Hawthorne increasingly sees romance as drawn from actual rather than fantastic materials. By describing romance as a locale or precinct and invoking its "latitude" to enable him to create, Hawthorne seeks to insulate his work from demands of strict correspondence to a world outside itself. But he does not thereby create pure fantasy. Hawthorne initially locates romance in a realm of ghostly reflections; by his last preface, however, romance finds a "local habitation and a name" in Europe.

In the extended preface to *The Scarlet Letter,* "The Custom-House," though he seeks a historical source of his imaginings in the letter and the documents of Surveyor Pue, Hawthorne finds that without imagination's enlivening reflection his creations remain not just sketchy but dead, grotesquely real "corpses" (I, 3).[15] As the reflecting "mirror" of Hawthorne's imagination initially remains "tarnished" by inactivity (I, 34), creativity arises through another romantic image for imagination: moonlight. Romance as a kind of light is more a medium than a genre, a way of seeing. Moonlight displaces its objects from elements in an external realm to entities within the mind: "Thus . . . the

Figure 1.   Charles Osgood, *Portrait of Nathaniel Hawthorne*, 1840
(Courtesy Essex Institute, Salem, Massachusetts.)

floor of our familiar room has become a neutral territory, somewhere between the real world and fairyland, where the Actual and the Imaginary may meet, and each imbue itself with the nature of the other" (I, 38). Though the moonlight "invests" its objects "with a quality of strangeness and remoteness," they are "still almost as vividly present as by daylight." Thus, romance provides an accurate picture of ordinary life, despite its transforming light.

Hawthorne's figure for romance, the moonlit room, shows how reality is represented as an inner rather than outer realm. Along with the coal-fire that is the symbol of romantic imagination, Hawthorne presents the mirror of mimesis. But its effect here is not "to hold the mirror up to nature": "Glancing at the looking glass, we behold—deep within its haunted verge—the smouldering glow of the first extinguished anthracite, the white moonbeams on the floor, and a repetition of all the gleam and shadow of the picture, with one remove farther from the actual and nearer to the imaginative." As reflection within reflection, the mirror presents the ordinary world at a triple remove. The more it reflects "the actual," the more the mirror carries us "nearer to the imaginative" (I, 36). What remains is not so much the picture itself as the margin of its reflection, its luminous "gleam and shadow." That margin (like the inner-worldly image described by Jameson) represents the translation of reality into the artist's consciousness. Hawthorne implies that the artist as individual is almost lost in the process of creation, for he does not see his own reflection in the mirror. Instead, he creates the third-person narrator who narrates the story with some detachment.

Thus, Hawthorne as individual is freed from the physical limits of "The Custom-House" and the bonds of custom generally. He writes his story from the perspective of someone who has escaped the "Custom-House," which "lies like a dream behind me." Hawthorne ends the preface by seeing nineteenth-century Salem as the subject of historical romance, when it fades not from history but only from his memory: "Soon, likewise, my old native town will loom upon me through the haze of memory, a mist brooding over and around it; as if it were no portion of the real earth." As a "citizen of somewhere else," the realm of imagination which is divorced from the ordinary world, Hawthorne writes his romance. While George Eliot located the mirror of mimesis within her own mind, for Hawthorne the reflecting capacity is virtually displaced by the imaginative one. "Men and things" have been not reflected but replaced by the imagination that encounters them, a usurpation that continues in Hawthorne's later prefaces.

Only a year later, Hawthorne returned to precisely the subject of Salem, in *The House of the Seven Gables,* the historical romance he predicted at the end of "The Custom-House." The "mist" is created by the mingling of past and present, which, according to the preface, is the key to the work's coming "under the Romantic definition" (II, 2). While the past has all the attributes of an

imaginary world—mistiness, distance, picturesqueness—it proves more substantial and enduring than "the very Present that is flitting away from us" (II,
2). The lack of present fullness makes representation necessarily romantic. For
there is no possibility of conveying the life immediately around us; instead,
representation must evoke the past to give the present solidity. So here the
atmosphere of romance enables a more accurate depiction of the "truth of the
human heart" (II, 1).

Hawthorne uses the metaphor of the picturesque, a mode containing strong
contrasts, to illustrate the simultaneous presence of good and evil in the past.
The picturesque, in its contrasts of light and shadow, enables moral judgment
by making the past lend significance to the present, so as to "bring out or mellow
the lights and deepen and enrich the shadows" (II, 1). As Angus Fletcher notes,
in its conveyance of opposites, "the picturesque is a vehicle of emotive ambivalence."[16] The atmosphere of romance, rather than dematerializing its objects,
enriches the "humble texture" of contemporary life. One might expect its contrasts to provide stark moral oppositions (which Hawthorne specifically seeks
to avoid). Instead, its shadings complicate moral issues. As Martin Price notes,
the picturesque exploits ambiguity and ambivalence to provide a complexity
akin to that of Jamesian realism: "The picturesque starts from the irregular and
intimate and moves toward the pleasure in texture, the complex presentation of
what we sometimes call 'felt life.'" (James states in the preface to *The Portrait
of a Lady* that "the 'moral' sense of a work of art . . . (is) perfectly dependent
. . . on the amount of felt life concerned in producing it.")[17] So romantic,
picturesque atmosphere lends three-dimensionality to characters and settings.
At the end of the preface, Hawthorne continues to oppose "the clouds overhead"
to "the actual soil of the County of Essex" (I, 3). But romance, rather than a
middle ground between fancy and actuality, becomes a mode in which one may
reflect and realize the other. The imaginative realm and actuality are related to
each other not as opposites but as mutually reflecting entities that enable each
other to be more clearly known. The border area, which in Scott's works is a
particular place, here becomes a territory where the real and the imaginary
interact and even compete.

Hawthorne transforms romance into another kind of territory in the preface
to his next long work, *The Blithedale Romance,* in which he describes romance
as a "theatre," Here Hawthorne discovers romance in his own past experience
at Brook Farm, which was "certainly the most romantic episode of his own
life—essentially a day-dream, and yet a fact—and thus offering an available
foothold between fiction and reality" (III, 25). Brook Farm itself, though unsuc-
cessful from Hawthorne's point of view as Utopian experiment, did provide the
necessary "Fairy Land" for romance—like Spenser's, a realm parallel to actuality but different in nature. Hawthorne implies that the romantic aspects of Brook
Farm were present in its historical circumstances, not a product of his imagina-

tive creation. History itself at Brook Farm has proved fantastic, in strange events and characters. Rather than seeking romance in Syria, the writer Howadji (George Curtis) could turn his "youthful reminiscences of Brook Farm" into the "rich theme" of romance.

In *The Marble Faun,* romance is defined even more concretely as an actual rather than figurative precinct, specifically Italy. Hawthorne complains that the United States offers no materials for romance—"no shadow, no antiquity, no mystery, no picturesque and gloomy wrong"—but finds those materials ready to hand in Rome. In this work, life itself, not art, is seen as uncanny. The romantic picturesqueness Hawthorne seeks is written out in the environment around him. The distance romance requires is achieved by geographical displacement, as he completes the story elsewhere, "on the broad and dreary sands of Redcar." By "writing in a foreign land" (the "somewhere else" of which he envisioned himself as a citizen at the end of "The Custom-House"), Hawthorne finds romance written out in his own experience. At the end of *The Marble Faun,* he expresses the fear of being taken up too much into the realm of romance when it has been located in an actual place. He notes that when people live in a foreign land, "we defer the reality of life . . . until a future moment, when we shall again breathe our native air; but, by and by, there are no future moments." The effect of Hawthorne's romance is to transform history into myth, blurring the line between fact and fiction to remake reality into romance. Whereas John Wilson saw romance as opposed to nature, Hawthorne uses his imaginative capacities to transform the physical world into the image of romance.

For Hawthorne, then, the middle ground of romance becomes a precinct where he can question the actuality of the physical world and establish the reality of an imaginative realm. For James, romance serves primarily as a way of knowing, as it provides access to an invisible world of unconscious feelings and desires. John Wilson noted the abstracting and generalizing aspects of romance. But for James, romance's value lies in its capacity to reveal the most individualistic and irrational aspects of the mind, the workings of the unconscious. Indeed, for James, desire itself becomes a form of knowing, if always an indirect and ultimately an incomplete one.

James develops his view of romance especially in the preface to *The American,* but his use of the term extends to many other prefaces and critical essays, including those on Balzac and George Sand. The relation between romance and novel becomes a central theme even in the essay often considered his manifesto of realism, "The Art of Fiction." Throughout "The Art of Fiction," James seeks to overturn distinctions between various kinds of fiction, which he sees as false and narrowing.[18] In his view, fiction is not the product exclusively of the projecting or reflecting tendencies of creativity but the combination of both. In accommodating the use of projection, as well as emphasizing the role of pictorialism, he translates elements of romance into the form of the novel.

Romance pictorialism was frequently attacked by critics of the early nineteenth century, including John Wilson, as artificial and distorting. But for James, the analogy to the visual arts is the basis of the novel's claim to convey reality and the source of its psychological verisimilitude. In his view, the artist works by receiving impressions, which he describes most frequently as images. As romance's images frequently form symbolic tableau scenes for the reader to try to understand, James sees the world as a series of impressions demanding interpretation, as the visible world becomes the clue to invisible things.

By making the impression the source of representation, he turns all objects of perception—gestures, words—into images, signs which may be subjected to interpretation. Fixed meaning is undone as every aspect of the visible world becomes symbolic, conveying meaning that does not dwell on the surface. While in Hawthorne's writing the symbolic objects of interpretation are often presented as supernatural, such as the scarlet letter in the sky, or the letter that seems to burn Hester's breast, for James the subjects of interpretation may be ordinary, social, even trivial: how a woman puts her hand on a table, for instance. Such an apparently bare incident becomes rich material for a story.

James begins the essay with a concerted defense of the novel as truth: "The only reason for the existence of the novel is that it does attempt to represent life" (p. 378). At the same time, James redefines that truth through an artistic analogy: "As the picture is reality, so the novel is history." The comparison suggests that novels differ from history only in their material, fictive rather than actual events. But the artistic analogy emphasizes the subjectivity and indirectness of representation, while still asserting its convincingness.

While Hawthorne envisions the imaginative transformation of reality as occurring in a realm of magical light, for James that transformation occurs within the artist's mind. The emphasis on subjectivity is extended in James's most famous formulation of the novel, as "a personal, a direct impression of life" (p. 384). Is truth constituted by correspondence to life or fidelity to the novelist's personal vision? James's definition suggests both aspects, as "personal" and "impression" emphasize subjectivity, while "direct" and "of life" emphasize closeness of depiction and correspondence to life. The examples he cites of realistic characters—Mr. Micawber, Don Quixote—prove that a character may be convincing without corresponding to actuality. Though he admires Dickens and Cervantes, he notes of the work of either that "one would hesitate to propose it as a model" (p. 387). The "measure of reality" in fiction is very difficult to fix, for fiction presents a reality always "colored by the artist's vision."

James's emphasis on subjectivity continues as he redefines the material that novels address, the nature of experience. James does not change Besant's dictum to "write from experience" so much as to say "write from imagination" alone. But he defines experience as more subjective than objective, a mental rather than physical pursuit:

> Experience is never limited, and it is never complete; it is an immense sensibility, a kind of huge spider web of the finest silken threads suspended in the chamber of consciousness, and catching every air-borne particle in its tissue. It is the very atmosphere of the mind; and when the mind is imaginative—much more when it happens to be that of a man of genius—it takes to itself the faintest hints of life, it converts the very pulses of the air into revelations. (p. 388)

Not only is experience converted into "revelations" in the chamber of consciousness, but James implies that experience comprises the very "threads" that make up the chamber and compose the "atmosphere" of the mind. Experience is identified with both the "web" and the "particle" it catches, implying that experience is internalized to build on itself. For every movement of the mind constitutes an act: "Impressions *are* experience, just as . . . they are the very air we breathe." This identification of consciousness and experience breaks down the boundaries between inner and outer worlds. For now thought can project onto experience things not directly known. Reality, at least as constituted in representation, becomes a combination of thought and materiality. Hawthorne uses the moonlit room, where mind and world interact, to symbolize the creative process. James, however, relocates experience itself within the mind. Thus the projection of inner views in romance no longer distorts reality, because those inward ideas comprise reality.

James's famous example of this process resembles the revelation scenes of romances, as a spectator is set before a scene to read and interpret it. James describes the way a young woman novelist wrote a book about French Protestant youth based solely on a momentary view of a group of them at dinner: "The glimpse made a picture; it lasted only a moment, but that moment was experience. She had got her direct personal impression, and she turned out her type" (p. 389). Not only does the impression suffice for experience, but the snapshot-like view can be transformed into a picture in the "chamber of consciousness" because certain ideas are already there: "She knew what youth was and what Protestantism; she also had the advantage of having seen what it was to be French." Both the picture her mind forms and the truth that picture conveys are "concrete realities."

Like the spectator in romance viewing a tableau, the novelist is faced with the task of interpretation. As James defines it, the artist is above all someone who can interpret signs, turning the visible world into a legible realm:

Figure 2.   Alvin Langdon Coburn, *Henry James,* 1906
             Frontispiece to *Roderick Hudson* (volume I of the New York Edition).
             (Courtesy International Museum of Photography at George Eastman House.)

The power to guess the unseen from the seen, to trace the implications of things, to judge the whole piece by the pattern, the condition of feeling life in general so completely that you are well on your way to knowing any particular corner of it—this cluster of gifts may almost be said to constitute experience. (p. 389)

Again, experience is redefined as mental faculty as much as physical act.

In this essay, James notes that the "air of reality" is the prime virtue in a novel, a point which has led many critics to see this work as James's manifesto of realism. But the phrase itself is somewhat ambiguous, as the word "air" implies the opposite of "solidity" of specification. As we have seen, James's views of the impression and the sign emphasizes the subjective aspect of narration provided in romance. Near the end of the essay, James attacks the distinction between romance and novel: "I can think of no obligation to which the 'romancer' would not be held equally with the novelist; the standard of execution is equally high for each" (p. 394). The reversals he proposes here help break down that distinction. For in emphasizing inner rather than outer experience, James incorporates romance's fidelity to the logic of inner states rather than external order and causality. Thus, one may find striking truths "hidden in the bosom of common things" (p. 395), through the romantic development of ordinary materials. For James, art achieves its "immense and exquisite correspondence with life" through its capacity to use any material. Art need only exhibit "beauty and truth," and truth in James's sense is not limited to fact. In advising the young artist, James notes that, by delving fully into his own imagination, he will be led not farther from but closer to life.

James provides his own full-length definition of romance only near the end of his career, in the preface to *The American,* which provides a key not only to the book it precedes but to James's work as a whole.[19] This essay helps identify a strain of Jamesian romance which was not abandoned after this early work but continued until the end of his career. The subject of romance in this essay also occasions one of James's most extended inquiries into the nature of artistic creation, defined especially as an interaction between conscious and unconscious impulses.

James begins by seeing the presence of romance in *The American* as a significant flaw, a "hole in its side more than sufficient to have sunk it" (p. 21). But by the end of the essay, romance becomes an asset rather than a defect. James notes that rereading the book "yields me no interest and no reward comparable to the fond perception of this truth" (the fact that it is romantic— p. 25).

The genre of the work, as James sees it, is influenced especially by the circumstances of its creation. This work is pre-eminently the product of the transference of American ideas to a European setting. The book depends on a contrast between the American background (according to James, his story was conceived in the eminently practical setting of an "American horse-car"), where his subject drops into the "deep well of unconscious celebration" (p. 22), and the European environment, where, according to James, his artistic consciousness could operate. Only when James goes to Paris is his subject resurrected into consciousness and given a name—Christopher Newman. James's creativity depends on this geographical displacement. Though Europe is the source of his artistic consciousness, James sees Europe itself as a highly-constructed representation. James's American is victimized by "persons pretending to represent the highest possible civilization" (p. 22). Apart from the particular viciousness of the Europeans in this work, James suggests that Europe presents, at least to Americans, a facade that at the worst may be false and deceptive, and at least needs to be deciphered.

Another discrepancy in James's representation is the gap between his original view of the work when he was writing it in 1877, when he saw it as entirely realistic, and his current view in 1907, when he deems it romance. The relation between romance and realism is indicative of the distance between the writer's critical and creative faculties. For the use of genre, like other elements of creativity, is not the result of a deliberate decision: "It is a question, no doubt, on the painter's part, very much more of perceived effect, effect *after* the fact, than of conscious design" (p. 30). Retrospection is necessary to recover the work's generic definition, though "the determining condition would at any rate seem so latent that one may well doubt if the full artistic consciousness ever reaches it" (p. 31). But defining artistic creation as a combination of conscious and unconscious activities, James incorporates romance into his representation, which typically operates through the projection of unconscious desires. James's fiction must provide a circuit through which consciousness completes unconscious inspiration.

To write in such a mode, James implies, he must combine romance and realism, which are always joined by the great writer, "by the law of some rich passion in him for extremes" (p. 31). When the flights of fancy in romance are anchored by the novel's fullness of detail, the world presented in fiction becomes not so much a realm of dreams fulfilled as one in which dreams and sorrows are both made vivid. Romance and realism are interfused, the "far and strange" mixed with the "near and familiar" in an "extraordinarily rich and mixed current."

James presents the "real" and the "romantic" not just as literary modes but objects of knowledge and, finally, "values." While the real (which "represents . . . the things we cannot possibly not know") is easily accessible to understanding, the romantic can never be known no matter how much experience we gain: "The romantic stands . . . for the things that, with all the facilties in the world, all the wealth and all the courage and all the wit and all the adventure, we never *can* directly know; the things that can reach us only through the beautiful circuit and subterfuge of our thought and our desire" (pp. 31–32). James implies that romance is also a way of knowing, of completing the circuit to provide us with satisfaction of desire. The writer's articulation of the unconscious impulses which fuel creativity enables the reader to find in romance a representation of his or her own hidden desires. Thus we truly have a circuit of writer and reader, thought and desire.

Even romance's most extreme adventures do not evade experience but confront it directly: "The panting pursuit of danger is the pursuit of life itself, in which danger awaits us possibly at every step and faces us at every turn" (p. 32). The search for heightened experience can lead to abandonment of the reality principal: "the dream of an intense experience easily becomes rather some vision of a sublime security like that enjoyed on the flowery plains of heaven, where we may conceive ourselves proceeding in ecstasy from one prodigious phase and form of it to another" (p. 32). But James shows that romance always maintains a tie to the earth, preserving certain limitations so as to maintain a representational function. In a famous metaphor, James compares romance to the "balloon of experience," beneath which "we swing . . . in the more or less commodious car of the imagination" (p. 33). Clearly, imagination and experience are always combined in fiction, related to each other as tenor to vehicle. For the romancer only cuts those ties secretly; to outward appearances the ghostly limits remain. James's notion of romance is not one of entire disconnection, but of limits transcended without being cut. Representation is most convincing when it maintains its ties to "communities"; not just the limits of the "drag . . . of a related state," but the human relations which define reality for James. The combination of romance and realism maintains both freedom and the ties of "the related state."

As the plot of *The American* dramatizes, such ties constitute true freedom. James now sees *The American* as a work in which imagination operated unfettered: writing it represented "the happiest season of surrender to the invoked muse and the projected fable; the season of images so free and confident and ready that they brush questions aside and disport themselves, like the artless schoolboys of Gray's beautiful Ode, in all the ecstasy of the ignorance attending them" (p. 25). The projection of imagination turns images into allegories, as James implies by comparing his work to Gray's "Ode on a Distant Prospect of Eton College," in which the characters are allegorical figures. James is tempted to give his hero, Christopher Newman, unlimited capacities to match the exercise of power, the free play of fancy, which he felt when writing. But in Newman's case, total freedom, severing the cord, leaves the character "shut up" and imprisoned. At the end of the story, cut off from all connections, Newman seems perfectly free, while his beloved is entombed in a Carmelite convent. But Newman is left in "the romantic *tout craché*—the fine flower of Newman's experience blooming in a medium 'cut off' and shut up to itself" (p. 39).

Newman's imprisonment, though, gives the reader the "illusion of the largest liberty" (p. 39) among other things, the freedom to reforge connections by imagining the tale's conclusion.

At the end of the preface, James notes that creating a sense of life does not necessarily require the "reference" of the fictional work to a world outside itself. The emphasis in representation shifts to the production of fine artistic form: "the content and the 'importance' of a work of art are, in fine, wholly dependent on its *being* one: outside of which all prate of is representative character, its meaning and its bearing, its morality and humanity, are an impudent thing" (p. 38). The abandonment of referentiality creates nonetheless a fuller pursuit and explanation of "what I can have made of 'life'" (p. 38).

In this preface, then, while James begins by seeing the romantic as a "hole" in the work he has presented, he ends by embracing the projecting powers of romance as well as its capacity to show "life." This view of romance finally leads James to reject the notion of the "reference" of a literary work. The creative work originated when the author projected its subject or center of consciousness (Newman) from his imagination onto a foreign environment. Finally, the work depends for its convincingness more on the reader's identification with James's consciousness and the hero it projects than with any reflection in his work of a reality outside itself.

While early nineteenth-century writers defended imagination as a necessary co-worker with reality to produce an artistic vision, for James the exercise of imagination is the clearest and closest way to capture life. James sees the products of unconscious desire and fancy not as imaginary but actual. His views on the perfect freedom of the artist and the importance of subjectivity lead him to celebrate even the projections of allegory common in romance. James captures the extremes of art through a combination of romance and realism, which become the opposites that provide richness for his representation.

In the course of the nineteenth century, while "closeness to life" remains the aim, the means to attain that closeness is increasingly displaced from art's mirroring aspects to its picturing, creative functions, which are primary in romance. As James stated in a letter to H. G. Wells late in life, "Art *makes* life."[20] In the late novels *The Wings of the Dove* and *The Golden Bowl*, James discovered that the more elaborate the represented surfaces, the more they could be seen as revelatory of depths, until the very relation of surface and depth collapses. If romance gave James a way of perfecting his novelistic craft, it was in enabling him to combine "the deeper psychology" with "the light of common day." By adapting Hawthorne's romance, James extended the novel's capacities to provide at once greater range and greater intimacy of depiction.

2

Reading Romance: James's *Hawthorne*

In his essays on Hawthorne, James develops his own idea of romance by reacting to Hawthorne, adapting some aspects of his work and rejecting others. As in the cases of several other writers who influenced him deeply, such as Balzac and Turgenev, James wrote several essays on Hawthorne throughout his career.[1] In the course of the four major essays he wrote on Hawthorne, from 1872 to 1904, James's view of his predecessor changes from critical to ambivalent and finally reverent. These transformations are conditioned on his attitude towards romance, which he often ignores or attacks in the early essays, but which becomes the sole subject of his Hawthorne Centenary essay of 1904. The 1904 essay contains almost no direct quotation from Hawthorne's works, as by that time James had fully assimilated romance into his own methods and style. James links the definition of genre to nationality and, in writing about Hawthorne, also writes about his own connection to America. Hawthorne's influence on James thus furnishes not only an interesting example of literary influence but a way to illustrate "the growth of a writer's mind," James's establishment of personal and literary identify.

For James, such aspects of romance as supernaturalism, symbolism, and pictorialism initially seem to conflict with realism. Yet in the process of critiquing Hawthorne, James also starts to adapt these elements for his own use. In *Hawthorne,* James asserts (or at least seems to assert) the opposition of romance and realism. Yet in the very course of his negative criticism, James subtly transforms aspects of Hawthorne's work into his own method or style. The development of James's art depended on the admixture of romance, which actually heightens its realism. As James himself recognized by 1904, romance has aspects of verisimilitude; romance corresponds to a "side of life." Each critical essay on Hawthorne reflects James's own achievement in his creative work to that point, and in turn influences the novels and short stories which succeed it. James's appropriation and reinterpretation of Hawthorne's mode of representation begins with the 1879 *Hawthorne,* in which, despite his overt critique of romance, James's most powerful, almost unconscious responses are to aspects of Hawthorne's work identified with romance.

At first, the opposition between romance and novel seems to be perpetuated in *Hawthorne*.[2] According to James, it is impossible to write a novel about America because, in his famous formulation, it has "no sovereign, no court, no personal loyalty, no aristocracy ... no Oxford, nor Eton, nor Harrow; no literature, no novels, no museums, no pictures, no political society, no sporting class—no Epsom nor Ascot!" (p. 34). Paradoxically, James's statement is indebted to Hawthorne's list of the elements absent from American life in the preface to *The Marble Faun*. In Hawthorne's view, the absence of "antiquity" and "anything but a commonplace prosperity" makes it impossible to write a romance about America; one must seek the elements of ruin, on which romance grows, in Europe.[3] The relation between the two statements illuminates James's conversion of romance into novel in *Hawthorne*. In this work, written for the English Men of Letters series, James assumes an English perspective in reaction to his American background, with which Hawthorne was associated. But his responses to Hawthorne, both positive and negative, help James discover his own voice in a tone which transcends nationality.

James admitted that he used criticism to rewrite others' works and so formulate his own craft: "I can only read critically, constructively, reconstructively, writing the thing over (if I can swallow it at all) my way, and looking at it, so to speak, from within."[4] In Harold Bloom's analysis of the anxiety of influence, writers misinterpret their predecessors in order to write them anew.[5] Though James rejects Hawthorne's use of the symbolic and supernatural in *Hawthorne*, these elements return in transformed guise in *The Portrait of a Lady*, published two years later. James uses the supernatural especially in the ghostly tales of the 1890s, including *The Turn of the Screw* and "The Altar of the Dead." In the 1897 essay on Hawthorne, he reconciles himself to Hawthorne's symbolism, which he used more extensively in the novels of the Major Phase immediately afterward. The fusion of romance and realism in these works is encapsulated in the 1904 Hawthorne Centenary essay, published in the same year as *The Golden Bowl*.

James's first extended commentary on Hawthorne was an 1872 review of the posthumously published *French and Italian Journals*.[6] He defines Europe as the "fact" (p. 6) which Hawthorne can't confront, setting up the critique in *Hawthorne* in which he charges that Hawthorne's "thin" American subject makes him incapable of realism. James here ignores the realistic aspects of Hawthorne's international romance, *The Marble Faun*, which he drew on extensively from the early *Roderick Hudson* to the late *The Wings of the Dove*. But in James's view, in Europe Hawthorne works not by engagement with but progressive detachment from the world around him: "the fascination of seeing so potent a sovereign in his own fair kingdom of fantasy so busily writing himself simple, during such a succession of months, as to the dense realities of the world." While Hawthorne defined romance as an integration of imagination and reality, James only sees their opposition here.

In the 1879 *Hawthorne,* James sees Hawthorne as insufficient because he is not a realist. James provides a rather narrow definition of realism as truth to fact and even biographical experience. Hawthorne's impoverished surroundings in New England necessarily made his work "something cold, and light, and thin." Nonetheless, James does find in Hawthorne's writing a convincing portrayal of his environment: "He virtually offers the most vivid reflection of New England life that has found its way into literature" (p. 4). Hawthorne's New England milieu was, of course, that in which James grew up. Thus separating himself from Hawthorne also means, for James, severing his connections to his American past.

In *Hawthorne,* James largely ignores or attacks the term romance, so much so that William Dean Howells complained that his misuse of the term could not be accidental: "No one better than Mr. James knows the radical difference between a romance and a novel, but he speaks now of Hawthorne's novels, and now of his romances, throughout, as if the terms were convertible."[7] James violates Hawthorne's prefatory strictures for reading his works as romances, as he refers to Hawthorne's three long works set in America as "The Three American Novels." He quarrels especially with Hawthorne's multiple speculations and symbolism, part of the creation of romance atmosphere, dismissing them as stylistic quirks: "his extreme predilection for a small number of vague ideas which are represented by such terms as 'sphere' and 'sympathies.'" James nonetheless focuses on aspects of Hawthorne's work that I have identified with romance, namely: (1) the use of "fancy"; (2) symbolism; and (3) pictorialism and tableau scenes. Through his critical reading in *Hawthorne,* James attempts to capture the "deeper psychology" of Hawthorne's works without their symbolism or supernaturalism. In effect, James seeks to capture the psychological effects of romance without some of its more fantastic mechanisms. Finally, the interchange of the terms romance and novel to which Howells objected may indicate that here James combines the two.

James begins his critique of Hawthorne's romance with an attack on his "fancy." Though he praises Hawthorne for diffusing Puritan moralism into the aesthetic sense, James implies that in the process he evaded moral issues entirely, escaping the Puritan "sense of sin" through the "little postern door of fancy" (p. 46). James recognizes that Hawthorne is not a *"romancier pessimiste,"* that his attitudes differ from those of such characters as Chillingworth. But by viewing Hawthorne's imagination as purely playful, he separates it from any representational function, seeing Hawthorne's speculations as fanciful conjectures elaborated for their own sake.

This critique is an attack on romance as Hawthorne defines it. For as described in his prefaces, Hawthorne uses the moonlight of romance, which displaces his objects from ordinary reality, to realize them in a different way. James treats the method of romance as a stylistic excrescence. He continually refers to Hawthorne's creative faculty as "fancy," invoking Coleridge's distinctions among primary and secondary imagination and fancy, which make fancy the deadened, devalued category. Hawthorne, however, seeks a Coleridgean synthesis of imagination, which "dissolves, diffuses, dissipates, in order to recreate."[8] James charges Hawthorne with etherealizing moral issues, transforming sin into a mere "pigment." Hawthorne shows, however, in a sketch like "The Haunted Mind," that the creative imagination solicits rather than evades moral complexity.

James's harshest critique is leveled at Hawthorne's use of symbolism and allegory. In James's view, allegory will "spoil . . . a story and a moral, a meaning and a form" (p. 50). James criticizes especially Hawthorne's use of symbolism and the supernatural in the central scaffold scene in *The Scarlet Letter,* the chapter "The Minister's Vigil." Though James disapproves of the appearance of the supernatural "A" in this scene, he finds its depiction of the "electric chain" of intimacy between Dimmesdale, Hester, and Pearl interesting and illuminating.

In some ways, James naturalizes this scene in the direction of his own emphasis on human relationships, especially those of sexual intimacy. In his view, the "A" transforms the scene from high tragedy to low comedy. In fact, the human connection is made visible only through this sign, for the symbol manifests the intimacy of the three characters as well as its repression, as its appearance seems invoked by their intense emotion. Only when the scarlet "A" in the sky "seemed to give another moral interpretation to the things of this world" does the "electric chain" of human connection stand revealed (p. 94). By praising Hawthorne's exhibition of the "deeper psychology" but rejecting the means by which he attains it, James in effect severs the object of depiction, intimacy, from the means to convey it—symbolism.

Despite his explicit critique of Hawthorne, James shows a continuing fascination with the very aspects he most attacks, as shown by his extended treatment of this highly symbolic scene in *The Scarlet Letter.* James exhibits an almost unconscious fascination with Hawthorne, as evinced by his first encounter with a portrait of Hester and Pearl at age seven, when he is enchanted by the image as Hawthorne hopes his readers will be by the romance.

James rejects allegory in *Hawthorne* on the basis of his statement that allegory means telling a story "as if it were another and a very different story" (p. 49). He assumes a one-to-one correspondence between figurative and literal levels. But Hawthorne's writing in particular does not fit this definition. Charles Feidelson, in *Symbolism and American Literature,* distinguishes allegory from symbolism and associates Hawthorne with the latter, which he considers more

multiple in significance.[9] Angus Fletcher has shown the multivalence of allegory itself, in which the literal level often includes complex plots and characters. More recent critics view allegory not as a two-tiered form of narration but
one which continually oscillates between literal and figurative levels of significance, challenging our sense of how things signify.[10] Thus what James sees as
a stylistic excrescence floating above an excessively bare story is in fact a
method by which Hawthorne provides a rich depiction of reality. Hawthorne's
scarlet letter signifies the web of moral intrigue in which his characters are
enmeshed. Contrary to James's view of the opposition of "story and moral" in
allegory, in *The Scarlet Letter* the symbol becomes the site where these two
aspects of the work coalesce.

By the end of *Hawthorne,* James adapts Hawthorne's symbolism to a mode
he finds more congenial by translating figurative and literal into fact and image:
"Hawthorne is perpetually looking for images . . . which shall place themselves
in picturesque correspondence with the spiritual facts with which he is concerned, and of course the search is of the very essence of poetry" (p. 94). James
can accept Hawthorne's symbolism by comparing it to poetry; his conversion
of symbols into images here anticipates *The Portrait of a Lady,* in which he
adapts Hawthornian symbols such as the garden into images. Nonetheless,
James still feels that Hawthorne's taste for the "picturesque" creates lifeless
characters. Hawthorne was interested in gloomy subjects not for moral and
spiritual reasons; rather, "what pleased him in such subjects was their picturesqueness, their rich duskiness of colour, their chiaroscuro" (p. 47), as James
invokes Ruskin's distinction between the "heartless" and the "moral" picturesque. Hawthorne's characters become not dramatized individuals but "aspects
of a single mind picturesquely arranged."

Hawthorne himself suggests the reflection of the author in his characters,
as when he portrays himself in terms that echo those he uses for his characters,
in "The Custom-House." But these connections between Hawthorne and his
characters only make the drama of the story more direct. James's severing of
Hawthorne's style from his substance, manner from method, seemed necessary
for James to develop his own style. As Richard Poirier notes, in this work James
exerts power over Hawthorne stylistically.[11] He rewrites Hawthorne's romance
into a Jamesian mode of depiction by converting symbol into image, tableau
scene into impression, variety of perspective ("various aspects of his mind")
into dramatic action as conveyed through the center of consciousness. These
would become crucial aspects of James's representation, especially in *The Portrait of a Lady,* written shortly after *Hawthorne.* James's later essays on Hawthorne reflect his creative works in the intervening years, and illuminate his use
of Hawthornian romance in *The Portrait of a Lady* (1881), *The Bostonians*
(1886), and the ghostly tales of the 1890s.

In the 1897 essay, James changes his view of symbolism, which he now sees as adding to the story's density of description.[12] By seeing more than literal significance in everything, Hawthorne "ended by living in a world of things symbolic and allegoric, a presentation of objects casting, in every case, far behind them a shadow more curious and more amusing than the apparent figure. Any figure therefore easily became with him an emblem, any story a parable, any appearance a cover. . . ." Here, for James, symbolism makes objects three-dimensional, adding to their meaning rather than etherealizing them.

By contrast to his view in 1879, in 1897 James saw New England as complex precisely because its inner life was far richer than its outward appearances. The "secret play of the Puritan faith" constitutes the "latent romance of New England," especially in the internalization of Puritanism into conscience and neurosis. Hawthorne's speculative and symbolic imagination necessarily developed not to evade but precisely to confront moral issues. James now sees Hawthorne's fancy—here called "imagination"—as the faculty of penetration which sees beneath the surface:

> The direct and ostensible, face to face with common tasks and small conditions . . . , arrived at forms of which the tender imagination could make little. It could make a great deal, on the other hand, of the spiritual contortions, the darkened outlook, of the ingrained sense of sin, of evil, and of responsibility. (pp. 12–13)

Fidelity to the surfaces of existence would falsify New England life. Hawthorne's romance rather endowed ordinary things with "a mystery and a glamour where there were otherwise none very ready to its hand." Fancy now becomes, in James's view, not Hawthorne's way of evading moral issues but evidence of his artistry which authenticates his creations, "the odd little stamp or sign that gives them their value for the collector" (14).

James begins to integrate imagination and reality in this essay. He abandons his demand for referentiality when he speaks of *The Scarlet Letter:* the book "has hung an ineffaceable image in the portrait gallery, the reserved inner cabinet, of literature. Hester Prynne is not one of those characters of fiction whom we use as a term of comparison for a character of fact" (15). In the process, though, he transforms Hawthorne's work into an aesthetic object in the "inner cabinet" of James's mind. By the end of the essay, Hawthorne is seen as an aesthete, his imaginative faculties again contrasted with deep moral analysis: "His beautiful light imagination . . . is a faculty that gives him much more a terrible sense of human abysses than a desire rashly to sound them . . . his habit of diving . . . into the moral world without being in the least a moralist" (p. 23).

James overcomes the oppositions between artistic treatment and subject, imagination and reality, in his essay for the Hawthorne Centenary of 1904. Here James finally sees romance as capable of verisimilitude. He meditates on the creative impulse, the relation of a writer's mind to his surroundings. While in 1879 James criticized Hawthorne because of his environment, here he sees imagination as controlling its surroundings.

Writing from England to the Centenary observation in Salem, he claims that he can recognize Hawthorne's genius by "that spirit of sympathy that makes light of distance."[13] James reconnects himself to the United States, but only by projection. Here, James notes the difficulty of distinguishing between the place which inspired the artist and the artist's creative response to it. At Salem, visiting the sites about which Hawthorne wrote, "one can scarce distinguish . . . between the loan of enthusiasm and the gift, between the sound that starts the echo and the echo that comes back from the sound" (p. 25). Hawthorne's depiction so affects one's view of his subjects that it seems as if the fiction created its subjects rather than the other way around.

James finally sees that Hawthorne, in his romances, combines free exercise of imagination with precise description of things as they are. James now finds in Hawthorne's writings the familiar and extraordinary, the exotic and intimate, joined, an apt description of his own Major Phase novels. Indeed, it is difficult to distinguish the language of this essay from that of James's late novels, as it employs the images of the wings from *The Wings of the Dove* and that of golden air from *The Golden Bowl*. For James, romance is now not only an imaginative creation but an aspect of reality: it represents "man's relation to his environment seen on the side that we call, for our best convenience, the romantic side" (p. 26). Those who write romances about foreign settings and ancient times follow only "the mechanical, at best the pedantic view, of the list of romantic properties," as the fabulous elements of romance are seen as extrinsic to the genre (p. 27). Romance reveals the mystery and intensity of everyday life, discovered not by penetrating the surface of daily existence but finding drama even in ordinary events.

Certainly medieval romances or fairy tales continue to fascinate us because they appeal to universal desires, though disguised in exotic characters and settings. James discerns the meaning beneath the machinery, the often primitive or unconscious desires that romance expresses. According to James, Hawthorne's work maintains the intrinsic nature of romance while appareling it in the form of everyday occurrences. Thus the distinction between inner meanings and outer appearances is elided. While Hawthorne manages to express a hidden significance in the world, in his works surface and depth are fused: "He saw the quaintness or the weirdness, the interest *behind* the interest . . . as continuous with the very life we are leading . . . saw it as something deeply within us, not as something infinitely disconnected from us" (p. 27). The deeper desires which we tend to project into displaced forms, as in the often exaggerated fantasies of romance, are expressed equally in daily events, which desire and imagination continually shape and affect. The "latent romance of New England" is no longer hidden. Romance is now constituted not by a hidden and tortured spiritual life but by the inner experience with which our ordinary existence is continually bound up and which endows it with meaning.

At this point James no longer views Hawthorne as a symbolist, replacing the imagery of surface and depth with the figure of sound and echo. Hawthorne's romance presents us with the things we know imbued with a significance apparent only in representation. His romance thus becomes the artistic faculty, the act of representation, as seeing or reflecting itself transforms its objects: "the very application of the spectator's, the poet's mood, in the kind of reflection the things we know best and see oftenest may make in our minds" (p. 2). By showing "the things we know best" rather than foreign or bizarre settings or events, Hawthorne produces "the real as distinguished from the artificial romantic note," the sense of meaning and mystery in everyday experience, of which fiction can make us aware. The "real romantic note" combines the strange and familiar, appealing both to imagination and recognition of what we know: "Here 'the light that never was on land or sea' keeps all the intimacy and yet adds all the wonder" (p. 28). James's allusion here is to Wordsworth's "Elegiac Stanzas." Identifying romance with the transforming light of romantic vision, James suggests (as does Wordsworth) that the light is not so much a faculty of creative perception as an element already existing outside the mind which creative imagination reveals. When romance is identified as a kind of light, it can transform any scene; the light James describes resembles the light which bathes the quintessentially European scene of Gardencourt at the opening of *The Portrait of a Lady.* So in Hawthorne, romance can be applied to the most mundane scene without distorting it: "This very freedom of the spell remains all the while truth to the objects observed—truth to the very Salem in which the vision was born." James here sees imagination as a faculty not only of invention but representation. Romance enchantment is not fabricated, but an aspect of the world we know. In his view, romance becomes a "side of life" that exists in reality, not only in the writer's imagination.

James began his criticism of Hawthorne by objecting to Hawthorne's way of linking imagination and reality. But by 1904 he defines romance as a way of seeing which can be applied virtually to any object. In some ways James assimilates Hawthorne's symbolic method to a more transparent medium. But James adapts from Hawthorne's romance the "inner-worldliness" Jameson describes, the presence of creativity in perception of the physical world. For James in 1904, even representation and reality begin to coalesce; the distance between the creative mind and what it represents becomes minimal, or rather the two become virtually interchangeable. For James, romance presents a reality that is otherwise unknown, not the same as the visible world but the truth at its heart. Hawthorne's work presents a reality defined as a philosophical ideal, an essence in the mind: "The book *(The House of the Seven Gables)* takes up the parti-colored, angular, audible, traceable Real, the New England earnest, aspiring, reforming Real . . . and so invests and colors it, makes it rich and strange . . . that its characters and images remain for us curious winged creatures preserved in the purest amber of the imagination" (28–29). James's essays on Hawthorne help us see that romance constitutes the inner meaning of the world we know, a reality which Hawthorne's romance retains as its inner, almost ungraspable truth.

One way of seeing James's adaptation of Hawthorne is to say that James "realizes" Hawthorne's romance. But by adapting romance, James redefined the nature of novelistic representation and of the "reality" the novel represents. Romance provides intensity and vividness through its symbolism and use of extremes. At the same time, it creates a sense of mystery and enchantment. Hawthorne and James adapt the psychological acuity of romance to representations in contemporary settings. Nonetheless, both base their representations on distance or displacement from the familiar; thus they preserve the enchantment of romance, which James identifies with the workings of creativity itself.

3

Hawthorne and the Mirror of Imagination

James, in the early part of his career, claimed that Hawthorne's work was "cold and light and thin." But close analysis of those elements in Hawthorne which James attacks—specifically the use of allegory and the supernatural—reveals that these aspects of romance do not forestall but heighten depiction of character and social conditions. The fact that Hawthorne uses the devices of romance self-consciously and often ironically allows him to employ their intensity while questioning their mystical quality.[1] Instead, Hawthorne attempts to convey the reality within romance, the mystery at its heart, in a largely inarticulate drama conveyed by gestures and symbols. Though romance gives access to the hidden feelings revealed by gestures in a drama of intimacy, that reality cannot yet be fully articulated by Hawthorne. This reality within romance becomes James's explicit subject.

Reading Hawthorne in the light of James's commentary, despite James's sometimes negative assessments, reveals an incipient Jamesian drama of intimacy. Hawthorne invokes romance's conventions, such as the supernatural, to uncover the subtle psychological drama which they represent. He internalizes the drama of romance by shifting its action from public spectacle to private reverie and meditation. At the same time, in *The Scarlet Letter,* by setting the story in a recognizable historical context, Hawthorne implies that romance may correspond to actual experience.[2]

The psychological verisimilitude and moral acuity which James sought in Hawthorne's works, and which is frequently conveyed by the very romance devices James criticized, may be discerned as well in earlier works of romance. Indeed, the novelistic element of romance is apparent long before the nineteenth century. Here I will use Spenser, as a writer who deeply influenced Hawthorne, to provide a model of romance narration which can then be discerned in displaced form in the works of Hawthorne and James.[3] Three distinctive features of romance mentioned in James's book on Hawthorne are central to Spenser's *The Faerie Queene,* and adapted by Hawthorne and James. These aspects are: (1) action determined not by cause and effect but by the logic of the unconscious; (2) the use of epiphanic tableau scenes, in which the accumulated meaning of the story is gathered up in an emblem to be read and interpreted; and (3) ecphrasis, the use of works of art to mirror the story's action. In each of these cases, romance is not so much false to fact as true to a different order of determination, that of the imagination and the unconscious.

A. C. Hamilton describes in Renaissance prose romances an effect similar to that we have been tracing in the novel, in which the creative imagination strengthens the illusion of reality. Though the exercise of imagination in romance does not mime the existing order of things, by releasing emotion in the reader or spectator it enables a more intense engagement with the world. The reader's role is not fulfilled until he or she symbolically enters the story, a participation often invoked in the endings of dramatic romances when the characters become spectators of an artistic performance (as in *The Winter's Tale*): "Especially at the end, they may join the observers astonished at the events." According to Hamilton, the reader of romance must make a leap of faith to succumb to its enchantment. Therefore, in his view, romance deviates from realistic depiction and moral teaching. Release from the constraints of ordinary reality enables us to be "caught up in wonder from which there is no release but only greater intensification until the climax."[4] This definition, however, shows that romance leads to deeper involvement with experience, by heightening the reader's engagement in the action. Romance spectatorship may provide a rehearsal for active engagement in life.

Romance dramatizes the role of imagination as the composing faculty, especially in its use of pictorialism and scenes of revelation. As John Bender notes of Spenser, "not completeness but intensity and vividness, not quantity but form and context determine pictorial effect."[5] Imagination composes in an almost painterly fashion. Even the fabulous elements of romance may contribute to our sense of reality. Thus romance's unlikely plots may provide engagement with, rather than detachment from, life by releasing unconscious desires in the reader as well as the characters.

The noncausal nature of romance plotting is apparent from the opening of *The Faerie Queene*.[6] In book I, canto vii, the hero, the Redcrosse Knight, newly released from the House of Pride, encounters "an hideous Geant horrible and hye." This appearance succeeds Redcrosse's satiation of desire with the enchantress Duessa. Redcrosse feels very self-satisfied at this moment, "till at the last he heard a dreadful sownd." Orgoglio represents that satisfaction, misbegotten by duplicity on loose desire. The giant seems to come out of nowhere; as child of Aeolus, god of winds, and Earth, he is literally nothing, a mere bag of wind. But the allegory shows that Orgoglio's entrance is anticipated, as a projection of Redcrosse's untamed Pride. The action occurs almost behind the narrative (which is interrupted in vii, 9 by a genealogy and in vii, 13 by a simile), but the stanzas convey the sequence of emotional states—from illusion and duplicity to passivity and excess to pride. Narrative can seem merely a decorative surface, an aspect of romance which culminates when action is stilled into a pictorial tableau.

A striking tableau is found at the opening of book 2, when Guyon, Knight of Temperance, stumbles on an appalling scene, a particularly distorted family romance: a baby with its hands imbrued in blood from its mother's bosom. The scene is described as a "portrait," picturesque in the contrast between the woman's "white alabaster brest" and the "deepe sanguine" of blood. The picture represents the dangers of living wholly for love, like Amavia, or inflicting pain on others, like Mordant, as their names imply. The story then unfolds in Amavia's narration. Nothing illustrates Guyon's lack of temperance more than his reaction to the scene and the vow of vengeance he imposes on it as a motto: "Such and such evil God on Guyon reare, / And worse and worse yong Orphane be thy paine, / If I or thou dew vengeance doe forbeare, / Till guiltie bloud her guerdon doe obtaine" (II, i, 61). Guyon has not yet attained the virtue of temperance, which he can only achieve inwardly through harsh experience of extremes. Because Guyon cannot yet interpret the scene properly, the portrait remains motionless, frozen outside the book it precedes.

In another, more overt example of pictorialism, the tableau viewed by the hero does influence the ongoing action: Britomart's confrontation with the tapestries at Busyrane's palace in book 3. Here Spenser uses pictures which later unfold into allegorical action when the tapestries of the palace are succeeded by the mask of Cupid, a procession in which psychological feelings take on form and substance as characters. Britomart's willingness to subject herself to the meaning the tableau represents, to experience the pain and emotion she has repressed in herself, results in the emergence of the allegorical procession and the reassimilation of these alienated feelings to herself. In the procession, the narrative shifts from the sequential to the paratactic; each story is described in a sequence of brief sentences until the effect is that of reading a series of images, all of which are "figures" for love's trials. After Britomart has expressed her fears, the fire at the door blocking her path disappears. The passage shows that the obstacles faced by romance heroes represent inner rather than outer barriers—in this case, the fire may stand for Britomart's unacknowledged desire.

The use of figures and symbols, especially pictorial ones, to express the inexpressible gives romance its cathartic effect; when language cannot evoke another world, pictures, at least as an alternative to language, can. Romance does not so much mime action through continuous narration as represent the workings of the mind through various imaging procedures. There are many examples of these three aspects of romance—noncausal logic, scenes of revelation, and ecphrasis—in Hawthorne.[7] Though James attacks them in *Hawthorne,* he eventually finds ways to adapt all of them for his own fiction.

The Scarlet Letter features many moments in which an unconscious logic rather than ordinary cause and effect seems to govern the course of events, as when Mistress Hibbins appears at both the scaffold and the Governor's house. Revelation scenes are particularly central to Hawthorne's art. In dramatic moments in *The Scarlet Letter,* action progresses not on the public stage of the scaffold but on the inner stage of the characters' minds. Finally, the use of ecphrasis as in *The Faerie Queene,* book 3, occurs in the middle of *The Scarlet Letter.* Tapestry provides silent commentary on the larger action in the description of Dimmesdale's chamber: "the tapestry, said to be from the Gobelin looms . . . representing the Scriptural story of David and Bathsheba, and Nathan the Prophet, in colors . . . which made the fair woman of the scene almost as grimly picturesque as the woe-denouncing seer." As in Spenser, the tapestry presents an earlier, symbolic version of the story transpiring in the foreground.

These elements are central to James's work as well. An event which seems not to be governed by logic of narrative sequence (except in retrospect) is the sudden appearance of Madame Merle, originally glimpsed from behind, at the time of Daniel Touchett's death in *The Portrait of a Lady.* Tableau scenes become revelations of intimacy to hidden spectators—Isabel's glimpse of Madame Merle and Gilbert Osmond, Hyacinth's view of Captain Sholto and Millicent in *The Princess Casamassima,* and the famous view of Chad and Madame Vionnet by Strether in *The Ambassadors.* James continually employs ecphrasis through allusions to paintings; when Isabel, on her final visit to Gardencourt, spends a long time perusing a "small Bonington," the painting symbolizes the feelings she cannot otherwise articulate. As, in the Mask of Cupid in book 3 of *The Faerie Queene,* narrative is replaced by images, James's incorporation of "picture" (tableau, visual impression) transforms narrative from literal to figurative.

Spenserian narration served as an important model for Hawthorne's use of romance. In Hawthorne's hands, the psychological truths often registered only subconsciously in the reader's mind in Spenser are more continuously acted out. Indeed, dramatizing the allegory of romance became a crucial task for Hawthorne, for Hawthorne struggled throughout his career to balance or reconcile the observing with the projecting faculties of his imagination. As James notes in his 1872 review of Hawthorne's *French and Italian Notebooks,* Hawthorne's journals alternate between excessively practical facts and overtly abstract symbols, as when he deliberates about the proper way to embody egotism, beginning with the pure idea and eventually arriving at the symbol of the serpent.[8] If these two faculties may be associated with the realistic and romantic aspects of Hawthorne's imagination, Hawthorne gradually fuses the two into the "real romantic note" which James acknowledges. Hawthorne increasingly developed the psychological aspect of allegory to provide a more detailed and penetrating analysis of character. Despite the claims of Chase and other critics that allegory precludes close analysis of character and social issues, Hawthorne uses allegory precisely to accomplish such ends.

As Hawthorne suggests in the early sketch "The Haunted Mind," allegory provides not only a model for mental operations, but a way to dramatize the deepest emotions.[9] In this work, Hawthorne's description of his own creative processes yields to a detailed unfolding of his emotions. "The Haunted Mind" begins in what Poe calls the "hypnagogic" state, halfway between walking and dreaming, where creativity can occur as the conscious mind becomes aware of the unconscious. The narrator's thought processes reproduce the narrative pattern of romance, with its sudden transitions and transformations.

The sketch becomes highly self-reflexive as Hawthorne portrays the thoughts passing through his mind as allegorical figures. These figures are at once personal and universal: sorrow with a "sable robe," hope with "dust among her golden hair" (306–7). Passion and the other feelings are sufficiently individuated to become embryonic fictional characters, as Fatality is an apt forerunner of Chillingworth in *The Scarlet Letter*.

The thoughts of the unconscious are projected upwards by the imagination, which acts as a "mirror, imparting vividness to all ideas, without the power of selecting or controlling them." The mirror of imagination, unlike that of mimesis, rather projects inner thoughts than reflects outer objects.[10] Hawthorne's mirror differs from George Eliot's in the kind of material it reflects—not "men and things" but the thoughts, often unconscious, of his own mind.

Yet, as the mirror image implies, such projection does not prevent accurate representation. Indeed, the projections of imagination may connect inner and outer worlds. After these meditations, visions enter from outside the narrator's room as well as from within his mind. Suddenly, he is able to project himself into various scenes, as if time and space had been eliminated: "You stand in the sunny rain of a summer shower, and wander among the sunny trees of an autumnal world, and look upward at the brightest of all rainbows, overarching the unbroken sheet of snow, on the American side of Niagara." Now wonder is attached to an actual scene rather than an imaginative one. The pageant of human life is seen as a theatrical spectacle, like the dramatic presentations of romance. The reader's role as spectator is literalized when you "find yourself in the brilliant circle of a crowded theatre, as the curtain falls over a light and airy scene" (308–9). Participation in romance, Hawthorne implies, can lead to deeper engagement with life, as the dramatization of inner conflicts makes possible greater emotional involvement.

The slight distance or estrangement created by a romantic perspective leads one closer to what was originally familiar—an inner, more permanent reality at once more shadowy and more lasting than that of the visible world: "Your spirit has departed and strays like a free citizen, among the people of a shadowy world, beholding strange sights, yet without wonder or dismay" (p. 309). Thus romance implies another reality beyond that of the visible world.

Hawthorne addresses the question of reflection again in "The Old Manse," the preface to *Mosses from an Old Manse*.[11] Here Hawthorne realigns the opposition of substance and shadow to that of immortality versus mortality, ideality versus reality, to find substance in the nonmaterial and in romance. Hawthorne sees influence as the result of things from without flowing into the mind, not of the mind's thoughts being imposed on the physical world, as in Emerson.[12]

Hawthorne presents the house from the outset as a setting of romance, divorced from the material world "the glimmering shadows . . . were a kind of spiritual medium, seen through which the edifice had not quite the aspect of belonging to the real world" (p. 3). He hopes that, like all Gothic mansions, the house will contain a buried secret. The wealth Hawthorne seeks here is not financial but intellectual "treasure," the rich heritage of the Puritan divines. By contrast with the weighty works of the divines, Hawthorne's own work seems to him insubstantial or even immoral. To live up to their precedent, he "resolved at least to achieve a novel" (p. 5). Yet by the end of the essay, Hawthorne is able to repudiate their example, so that finally his predecessors do not appear to be tutelary deities but "looked strangely like bad angels" (p. 5).

When he looks at the river running near the house (the Concord, for Emerson the "type of all influence"), Hawthorne notes that reflections of objects are more appealing than the actuality: "Each tree and rock, and every blade of grass, is distinctly imaged, and however unsightly in reality, assumes ideal beauty in the reflection" (p. 7). Hawthorne here shows that the simple act of reflection translates the physical world into an ideal realm, as if to say that even the most direct mimesis has the idealizing qualities of romance. Rather than seeing "ideality" as a sign of the power and beauty of the human mind, as Emerson does, Hawthorne notes that such transformative reflection is simply a capacity of Nature.

While questioning Emerson's certainties about Nature, Hawthorne also attacks the positivism of historical fact. He undermines its authority by disregarding the official history of Concord Bridge. Instead, he seeks the story within history. He finds the inner meaning of the Revolution in a legend related to him by the poet Lowell, which "comes home to me like truth," rather than in any official history. Lowell's story, about the murder of a British soldier by a young boy, reveals the psychological truth of the Revolution, the outbreak of violence in an Oedipal rebellion by one previously considered "innocent." The sense of guilt engendered by the Revolution is revealed by Lowell's tale and seems uncanny to Hawthorne because it strikes a chord within him, echoing universal feelings.

By seeing meaning in inner feelings rather than facts, Hawthorne can now question the substantiality of the works of the Puritan divines. He is both disillusioned and elated to realize that their works of "substance" are also transitory, for "the works of man's intellect decay like those of his hands." Instead, paradoxically, the past is best preserved by such transitory documents as newspapers, "bits of magic looking-glass" reflecting the reality of their times (pp. 20–21). Hawthorne adjures literature of "substance" to find in romance another mode of truth.

When Hawthorne ventures out to the natural world one last time, now freed of the burden of influence and the "substance" of written tomes, he finds his true subject. He goes to the Assabeth River with Ellery Channing, a brilliant though largely unpublished poet. In traveling on the river, Hawthorne seems to journey inward rather than outward; the Assabeth is described as if it were a region within the poet's mind, like the river Alph in Coleridge's "Kubla Khan," which seems "to lave the interior regions of a poet's imagination" (p. 22). Hawthorne questions whether reality lies in the original or the reflection:

> Of all this scene, the slumbering river had a dream picture in its bosom. Which, after all, was the most real—the picture, or the original?—the objects palpable to our grosser senses, or their apotheosis in the stream beneath? Surely the disembodied images stand in closer relation to the soul. (p. 22)

Here mental visions become the reality of which the visible world is the shadow.

Finally, actuality is less vivid than the mind's conceptions: "I could have fancied that this river had strayed forth out of the rich scenery of my companion's inner world; only the vegetation along its banks should then have had an Oriental character" (p. 22). Hawthorne's recovery of an authentic relation to Nature enables him to overthrow all external authority, as he remarks on "the freedom which we thereby won from all custom and conventionalism and fettering influences of man on man. We were so free today that it as impossible to be slaves again to-morrow" (p. 25).

For Hawthorne, then, the Old Manse, site of writing and the past, becomes a desired destination. When Hawthorne and Channing return to the Old Manse, the gates of Eden are rebuilt: "It had been a home for many years, in spite of all" (p. 25). The Old Manse appears to promise an ultimate home for the soul. Yet this final certainty, too, is soon lost, as Hawthorne and his wife are forced to uproot themselves again "like wandering Arabs."

Hawthorne's inability to "achieve a novel" at the Old Manse is not a failure, as he soon realizes. Rather, the notion that literary ancestors could bequeath a legacy of thought proves as illusory as the hope of discovering buried treasure: "The treasure of intellectual good . . . had never come light." Hawthorne did not "achieve a novel" because "no novel" was to be found (p. 34). The revised notion of romance as substantial is strengthened by Hawthorne's view of his "mosses," the stories which this essay introduces. For his "mosses" recapture the "charm" of the surroundings of the Manse. If his meditation has led Hawthorne to glimpses of ultimate being "far inward," and insights into our "deep hearts" (p. 27), his mosses "blossomed out like flowers in the calm summer of my heart and mind," originating from the same place. Though they have "so little of external life about them" (p. 34), Hawthorne's "flowers of romantic art" gain substance by being penetrated by the influences of the river, the sunlight, the manse, through which, Hawthorne implies, are expressed the higher influences of immortality, the premonition of Paradise.

In "The Custom-House" and *The Scarlet Letter,* Hawthorne strives to link his imaginative projections with facts, to find a historical embodiment for romance.[13] He translates the action of romance into the mental processes of his characters, which tend to follow such narrative patterns as tableau scenes, moments of revelation, and processions familiar from Spenser and other Renaissance writers. Hawthorne uses these inner narratives to subvert the meanings imposed by the Puritans, who often use the representational conventions of romance, as their use of typology resembles romance's symbolism. But while the Puritans seek to impose symbolic roles on individuals to uphold the public sphere and limit individuality, Hawthorne translates romance from the governors' public spectacles into individuals' private meditations. By transforming romance into a mode of thought rather than a physical adventure, Hawthorne destabilizes the metaphysical status of the genre.

In "The Custom-House," Hawthorne feels compelled to write fiction based on the contemporary world around him: "A better book than I shall ever write was there; leaf after leaf presenting itself to me, just as it was written out by the reality of the flitting hour." Yet the book Hawthorne writes from within the Custom-House is not the novel of the Custom-House but the romance of *The Scarlet Letter,* which is considerably more vivid than the material on "The Custom-House" presented in the preface.

By his own account, Hawthorne went to the Custom-House in search of reality, "after my fellowship of toil and impractical schemes, with the dreamy brethren of Brook Farm." But in "The Custom-House," he discovers that reality is largely absent. Instead, the Custom-House seems material eminently suitable for romance. It is a border territory which lies on the edge of the town, surrounded by "a border of unthrifty grass" (p. 5). The Custom-House has long since ceased to have any practical function, for it "exhibits few or no symptoms of commercial life." The old men who sit in front of it resemble the ruins which, according to the preface to *The Marble Faun,* are the necessary materials for romance.

Hawthorne realizes that excessive practicality may lead to loss of reality, a problem demonstrated especially by the Inspector: "a rare phenomenon; so perfect in one point of view; so shallow, so delusive, so impalpable, such an absolute nonentity, in every other." The Inspector's lack of spiritual qualities makes him nearly an animal: "My conclusion was that he had no soul, no heart, no mind, nothing . . . but instincts" (pp. 17–18). Hawthorne, who has also come to the Custom-House driven by instinct, his "home-feeling with the past," realizes that a purely instinctual life is narrowing and degrading.

Nonetheless, Hawthorne must revive some of his instincts to release his creativity, which has become stifled in "The Custom-House." This reawakening begins when he recognizes that, despite his longing to escape the dominion of his ancestors, "the past was not dead." What he presents as a discovery—the scarlet letter, the representation of history—actually represents a return to himself of his creativity. "The past" here refers at once to the historical past represented by the documents among which the scarlet letter is discovered and to Hawthorne's own earlier habits and abilities.

The main impetus to creation here is not Hester's but Hawthorne's affair with language and sexuality, suggested by the burning heat manifested when he places the letter on his breast. The intensity of feeling here implies that Hawthorne recollects something previously repressed, either creative or sexual feelings. By repressing the literal meaning of the letter ("*A* for adultery"), Hawthorne confines passion to symbolic expression throughout *The Scarlet Letter*. The letter is allegedly discovered wrapped around a manuscript which contains a narrative, a "reasonably complete explanation of the whole affair." But both the letter and the manuscript are, of course, Hawthorne's inventions. Hawthorne guarantees his tale's authenticity not in its "facts" (which he says may or may not be fabricated) but in the outline or narrative structure of the story, which is a projection of his creativity: "I have allowed myself, as to such points, nearly or altogether as much license as if the facts had been entirely of my own invention. What I contend for is the authenticity of the outline" (pp. 32–33). The truth of the story is guaranteed not by its reflective but its projective aspect, which corresponds to the mode of romance.[14]

But Hawthorne's imagination must unite itself with some actual background before the story can unfold and his characters be enlivened. The link is not forged until Hawthorne leaves the Custom-House for home, to a "study" in which the implements of work are mingled with clear evidence of the presence of a wife and children: "a child's shoe; the doll, seated in her little wicker carriage; the hobby horse;—whatever, in a word, has been used or played with, during the day" (p. 35). These domestic details—the deepest truths of any person's life—represent the inner, emotional reality with which Hawthorne's imagination must be linked. The negative examples of the Custom-House inhabitants make Hawthorne realize the necessity of integrating public and private, official and domestic realms. In the deserted chamber, Hawthorne can transform his thoughts into imaginary scenes, though what he sees here are primarily the signs of absent people. Hawthorne views not an external world but a simulacrum of it, transformed by the moonlight to become "invested with a quality of strangeness and remoteness" (p. 35). Nevertheless, in the moonlight, all the details are "almost as vividly present as by daylight."[15]

Reflection itself, as moonlight transforms things of "substance" to "things of intellect," brings objects through "repetition . . . one remove farther from the actual, and nearer to the imaginative" (p. 36). In the reflecting "looking-glass," Hawthorne perceives no image of himself, implying that in this work the author will be present only as a ghostly phantasm. At this point, though, the possible conflict between domestic and professional roles is partly resolved when Hawthorne accepts his roles as writer and father, taking up his own "authority" in both literary and domestic realms.

In the last part of the preface, Hawthorne completes the reversal of the conventional view of reality. In his public and political role, Hawthorne becomes a fantastic figure of romance: "careering through the public prints, in my decapitated state, like Irving's Headless Horseman . . . So much for my figurative self" (pp. 42–44). Meanwhile, the practical side of his life is reestablished through the creative activity of writing: "The real human being, all this time, with his head safely on his shoulders . . . had opened his long-disused writing-desk, and was again a literary man" (p. 43).

At the end of "The Custom-House," Hawthorne separates himself from history, Salem, and supposedly life itself. Hawthorne's "posthumous" perspective leads our way into his romance, the world of shadows made real, by showing how, from the perspective of the grave, the physical world seems unreal; it presents "but shadows in my view. . . . Soon . . . my old native town will loom upon me . . . as if it were no portion of the real earth, but an overgrown village in cloud-land. Henceforth, it ceases to be a reality of my life. I am a citizen of somewhere else . . ." (p. 44). As a "citizen of somewhere else," no particular place, Hawthorne writes his tale, with the detachment of a third-person narrator. Hawthorne has released himself from the bond of "custom" which imprisoned him in the Custom-House. The "somewhere else" he inhabits is created by the perspective of imagination, from which the physical world appears slightly unreal.

Traces of Renaissance romance are present in *The Scarlet Letter,* in the use of symbolism and supernaturalism.[16] But Hawthorne tends to subvert the grand meaning of romance's scenes of revelation. In the process, he discovers the subjectivity and desire which romance's symbolism and supernaturalism represent. Hawthorne shows how, to constitute their society, the Puritans attempt to impose on the inhabitants of Boston allegorical roles like those of romances, especially by trying to make private lives conform to public rules and "offices." By dramatizing the gap between office and identity, Hawthorne parodies the

Puritan mode and uses their devices to point to private, not public meanings. Their typology is translated into Hawthorne's multivalent symbolism and pictorialism (as when he compares Hester to a portrait of the Virgin Mary). Their dramatic presentation of the public sphere is displaced by the characters' meditations, which reveal the fictiveness of the state's representations and make private perspectives the locus of narration.[17]

Hawthorne provides a version of romance which reflects individual states of mind. In the process, he translates romance's extravagant and supernatural spectacles into a subtle, almost inarticulate drama conveyed mostly by gestures. Gesture plays an important role in romance; in Shakespeare's *Pericles,* for instance, meaning is conveyed by the actors' placement or their silent gestures, as when Pericles' grief for his wife is conveyed in dumb show (IV, iv). In *The Scarlet Letter,* such gestures convey a truth opposed to that of Puritan authority, the reality within romance which cannot yet be entirely articulated. Such depiction presages James's subtle and delicate dramas in which, as he notes in "The Art of Fiction," the way a woman puts her hand on a table can tell volumes. Romance, but romance ironized through a demonstration of the discrepancy between its conventional forms and the inner states they convey, becomes for Hawthorne the only mode of access to the psychological truth belied by public appearances. Though James criticizes Hawthorne's use of "spheres and sympathies," Hawthorne's use of these terms is already ironic or ambiguous. For Hawthorne, not only Puritan typology but romance symbolism itself must ultimately be discarded, as a form from which meaning must be liberated.

As romance narrative frequently must "deviate" into error to begin (as in *The Faerie Queene* and Sidney's *Arcadia),* Hawthorne's work is simultaneously initiated and disrupted by the entrance of Hester Prynne across the threshold of the prison door. Hester appears in what is meant to be a procession signifying the punishment of "iniquity" in Massachusetts, which she immediately transforms by stepping forward "as if by her own free-will" (p. 52). In the process, as several critics have noted, she changes the allegorical procession into a symbolic one, changing a single intended meaning into multiple possibilities of signification.[18] She translates a public drama (the representation of the "Puritanic code of law") into a personal one.

Though Hester follows the forms of Puritan punishment—she ascends the scaffold, "knowing well her part" (p. 55)—she subverts them even as she enacts them. As Hester stands on the scaffold, Hawthorne replaces the speeches of the Puritan ministers with her thoughts and memories of a European past. As the Collector of "The Custom-House" lived a "more real life within his thoughts" than in the physical world of the Custom-House, Hester's memories supplant her present-day circumstances. The "realities" with which she is confronted dwindle to a mass of "spectral images": "there were intervals when the whole scene, in which she was the most conspicuous object, seemed to vanish from her eyes, or, at least, glimmered indistinctly before them, like a mass of imperfectly shaped and spectral images." Meanwhile, Hawthorne gives reality to the "phantasmagoric forms" of her memories by making them the foreground narrative. The Puritans' imposition of judgment is replaced by Hester's own judgment of her past, which she reviews with mingled pleasure and regret. As Hester's thoughts arise in a series of images, her standpoint on the scaffold affords her a new "point of view" on Puritan society.

Nonetheless, Hawthorne implies that Hester's subjective projections are reliable and indeed shape reality. For just as her meditation concludes, Hester spots in the crowd a man with one shoulder higher than the other. Though his appearance will later be explained as an unlikely coincidence, here it appears that Hester's imaginings have actually been confirmed by reality. For a long time we know this character (Chillingworth) only by this sign, as his identity seems defined by her view of him. Whether or not such projections are accurate, they constitute reality for the individual (as Hawthorne notes that even a dream can change one's world as irrevocably as actual events).

Hawthorne subverts not only Puritan ceremonies but language itself, for language carries the burden of both private and public meanings. When Dimmesdale, as one of the Puritan judges, speaks to Hester as she stands on the scaffold, he suffers an irresolvable conflict between professional and personal roles, public and private duty. In this situation, he is forced to act as judge and criminal at once. As a result, his language enters a state of symbolic expression from which it will never emerge throughout the book. His speech is perfectly ambiguous, as he urges Hester in one sense to reveal the secret and in another to conceal it: "If thou feelest it to be for thy soul's peace, and that thy earthly punishment will thereby be made more effectual to salvation, I charge thee to speak out the name of thy fellow-sinner and fellow-sufferer."

Despite the ambiguity of his language, Dimmesdale's emotion is conveyed clearly through such nonlinguistic signs as his tone of voice (which is "tremulously sweet, rich, deep, and broken") and his gestures. Pearl responds to his nonverbal, almost unconscious message by reaching out her arms to him. At the end of the scene, as Hester refuses to reveal the name of the father, Dimmesdale is affixed with a gesture which will become habitual to him: "Mr. Dimmesdale . . . leaning over the balcony with his hand upon his heart, had awaited the result of his appeal. He now drew back, with a long respiration" (p. 68). Such gestures convey emotion symbolically. They also represent a realm of feeling which language can depict only indirectly, suggesting Hawthorne's desire to convey passion less ambiguously, by leaving behind romance's symbolic conventions for the truths of intimacy which they represent.

In this first scaffold scene, Hawthorne drives the action inward through reflection and retrospection, making subjective views the only reality that can be known. Finally, the forms of romance themselves, such as symbolism and projection, become only "offices" which must be discarded. The action expected in the great scenes of revelation, the three scaffold scenes, either does not occur or is highly subject to doubt. Instead, action transpires in the minds of the characters, who construct a drama beyond the reach of the Puritans' public ceremonies. In some ways, the characters enact in more private ways the very actions which the Puritans attempt to enforce, such as punishment and confession. But as a result the public sphere is virtually dissolved, revealed as a construct or representation which no longer expresses the desires of the people, the "truth of the human heart."

The dissolution of the public sphere can be seen especially in the description of the governor's house.[19] Here Hester's perspective, or even that of the narrator, turns the heart of the government into a mere house in the clouds. Studded with mirrored glass, the mansion appears to Hester and Pearl like "Aladdin's palace" (p. 103). The artifacts of public enterprise, such as the governor's suit of armor, are quickly overshadowed by the private sphere represented by the mother and child, Hester and Pearl. Hester's reflection in the suit of armor greatly magnifies her scarlet "A." For some critics, this makes her even more subject to the criticism of the magistrates, who see in Hester nothing but the symbol of her "sin," but I would say Hester's concerns rather overpower the governor's. In the course of the scene, the public discourse of the magistrates is continually displaced to a private realm. Pearl insists that her place of origin is the rose bush outside the prison, as she replaces the orthodoxy of the "black flower" with the undisciplined passion of the "red flower." When Hester pleads with Dimmesdale to speak to the child, she seeks to conceal their intimacy by her very publicity. Nonetheless, other signs of it remain for those acute enough to read them—Hester's unusual tone of voice, Dimmesdale's gentleness with Pearl. While Hester attempts to communicate with Dimmesdale, these unconscious gestures are noted by Chillingworth, as throughout *The Scarlet Letter* knowledge of intimacy is attained by an onlooker or third-person observer (p. 115).

At the end of the scene, the public sphere is translated entirely into fantasy when Hawthorne introduces the Governor's sister, Mistress Hibbins, supposedly a witch. The presence of this apparently supernatural being at the home of the governor undercuts his authority. When Hester refuses Mistress Hibbins's invitation to meet her at a witches' gathering, Hawthorne remarks: "Here, if we suppose this interview betwixt Mistress Hibbins and Hester to be authentic, and not a parable—was already an illustration of the young minister's argument against sundering the relation of a fallen mother to the offspring of her frailty. Even thus early had the child saved her from Satan's snare." Though Hawthorne doubts the authenticity of the story, he can evoke the intensity of the supernatural without confirming its truth.

Thus Hawthorne shows how the public sphere has ceased to be the realm of reality, because it has so fully denied private feeling. For Dimmesdale, the emptiness of the public sphere is intensified by his attempt to use it to express private feeling. His attempts at confession from the pulpit only deprive Dimmesdale of his identity, as role and self become entirely confused. Constant denial of his feelings and especially of the inner, imaginative truth of love has rearranged reality for Dimmesdale, so that he lives solely in his thoughts and "the whole universe is false,—it is impalpable,—it shrinks to nothing within his grasp" (p. 145). Dimmesdale's insistence on maintaining the "mask" of sanctity even as he judges himself a sinner results in an intolerable paradox, which leads to his self-inflicted punishment.[20] Dimmesdale now assumes the dual role of judge and sinner in which he was cast in the first scaffold scene.

In Dimmesdale, Hawthorne explores the negative possibilities of the insistent projection and imaginative enterprise which can lead to alienation from reality. While in "The Custom-House," Hawthorne finds in romance a mode of resolving conflicts, mingling inner thoughts and outer objects, private and professional realms. In Dimmesdale's case, however, romance becomes a mode of separation from reality rather than more intense engagement with it. The confinement of Dimmesdale's feelings to symbolic expression undoes rather than creates his "truth of the human heart," depriving him of humanity and almost of existence itself.

In Hawthorne's case in "The Custom-House," through the symbol of the letter, repression is transformed into creative expression. But in the case of Dimmesdale, repression becomes a wasting disease, the letter a self-imposed trauma or wound. Dimmesdale's moonlit vigils are a parodic version of Hawthorne's creative reveries in "The Custom-House." While Hawthorne's vision integrates fancy and actuality in moonlight, Dimmesdale's vision splits the light into the opposites of "utter darkness" and the "most powerful light" (p. 145). Hawthorne looks in the mirror to see the outer scene reflected, but Dimmesdale sees in it only his own face, subjecting all objects to his merciless "introspection." For Dimmesdale, Hester has become yet another character on the stage of his mind rather than an actual individual. Subjectivity, a "point of view" entirely self-contained, becomes the foreground of the narrative here, until both the reader and Dimmesdale are left "in the shadow of a dream." In this underside of reality, the projective aspect of romance takes over the narration, so that it becomes impossible to judge what is real and what isn't—and the narrator offers us no clues.

The unconscious inner life of Dimmesdale's private realm is entirely confused with his professional role when he walks out in the middle of a reverie "attiring himself with as much care as if it had been for public worship, and precisely in the same manner" (p. 146). Role and identity have become one. Dimmesdale can no longer differentiate between his imaginings and actual events; as he stands on the scaffold in this second and climactic scaffold scene, he does not know whether he has actually shouted or only imagined that he did. Indeed, the reader too cannot tell, since the narration is entirely contained within Dimmesdale's point of view. Hawthorne suggests at one point that Dimmesdale may not even be present at the scaffold, that the whole sequence may be a dream, for an observer "would have discerned no face above the platform, nor hardly the outline of a human shape, in the dark gray of the midnight" (p. 147). Yet even as the glimmering light makes everything in the scene seem to occur within Dimmesdale's imagination, it illuminates every detail precisely: "The great vault brightened, like the dome of an immense lamp. . . . The wooden houses . . .—all were visible, but with a singularity of aspect that seemed to give another moral interpretation to the things of this world" (p. 154). Here Hawthorne affirms that, however fanciful or imaginative romance's projections, it nonetheless illuminates reality.

In this scene the revelations of romance seem fully enacted. The mystery of intimacy at the heart of the story is finally dramatized in a symbolic tableau which reveals the bond that links Hester, Pearl, and Dimmesdale. As in the first scaffold scene, action is stilled as the three characters join hands. Their arrangement provides a symbolic tableau of their relationship: "There stood the minister, with his hand over his heart; and Hester Prynne, with the embroidered letter glimmering on her bosom, and little Pearl, herself a symbol, and the connecting link between those two" (p. 154).

The exposure of this bond, as well as the passion that is awakened in Dimmesdale as a result of this embrace, seems to be embodied in the scarlet "A" which appears in the sky at this point. For James, this was the moment that turned the scene from pathetic tragedy to mere comedy. Yet James failed to note that, in fact, the appearance of the "A" precedes and indeed illuminates the symbolic bond of the characters. Only through the supernatural symbol can the intimacy be revealed.[21]

Hawthorne himself raises the same objections as James to an event which seems to provide a supernatural revelation. While evoking the mystery and power of the supernatural, Hawthorne shows that this appearance was probably not supernatural but rather either natural (a meteoric shower) or imagined (a projection of Dimmesdale's own neuroses). Nonetheless, the letter is all the more valuable as a clue to Dimmesdale's inner state. For as Hawthorne explicitly states, the scarlet "A" is as much a "symptom" as a symbol, a projection of Dimmesdale's repressed passion and guilt. At the end of the chapter, Dimmesdale's vision appears to receive external confirmation when one of the Puritans notes that the "A" was seen by everyone in the community and that they associate the "A" with "Angel," to signify the death of John Winthrop, the original governor, that night (p. 158). But their view of the letter does not validate its appearance so much as confirm that Dimmesdale's disease of repression and projection is universal in the Puritan community.

For James, the spectacular presence of the "A" distracted the reader from the depiction of intimacy. But Hawthorne uses the supernatural element to reveal psychological truths. The connection between the supernatural and the intimate is shown when, at the same moment, Dimmesdale sees both the "A" in the sky and Roger Chillingworth, whose animosity becomes clear to him at this moment: "There was a singular circumstance that characterized Mr. Dimmesdale's psychological state, at this moment. All the time that he gazed upward to the zenith, he was, nevertheless, perfectly aware that little Pearl was pointing her finger towards old Roger Chillingworth, who stood at no great distance from the scaffold. The minister appeared to see him, with the same glance that discerned the miraculous letter" (pp. 155–56). The supernatural may be a result of projection, but that does not invalidate it as a means of describing. Rather, it becomes the more valuable as a clue to repressed feelings; "there may be more truth in the ancient rumors than our modern credulity is inclined to admit." Recognition of his own guilt shows Dimmesdale the malevolence of someone who has played on that guilt. Symbolism here enables the externalization of unconscious feelings and so reveals to Dimmesdale the threat to his moral well-being posed by Chillingworth, which is imperceptible to a standard Puritan view.

While Hawthorne may attack the supernatural and the conventions of romance generally, nonetheless he uses them for his own purposes. In Dimmesdale, he presents an image of the romancer as a creature of projection, whose writings do not reveal truth but express his own anxieties. Dimmesdale's attempt to write his inner visions on the "page of the universe" manifests not so much some universal "truth of the human heart" as Dimmesdale's own neuroses. Hawthorne implies his own egotism here, by revealing the "A" to be a projection of neurotic feeling rather than as the physical, historical object which he presented in "The Custom-House."

If Hawthorne used subjectivity initially in *The Scarlet Letter* to reveal the psychological truth belied by public ceremonies (in Hester's opening "point of view" from the scaffold), by the time it takes over the narrative entirely, subjectivity has become a form of self-deception. In the chapter "Another View of Hester," we see that Hester Prynne has in some ways followed the opposite course to that of Dimmesdale. Her public role and private identity have grown entirely disjunct. For, while acting the role of a virtual Sister of Mercy, Hester harbors the "guests" (p. 164) of thoughts which constitute a far greater threat to the Puritan community than her act of adultery. Hester's thoughts connect her to the radical movements of Europe, where revolutions are especially accomplished "within the sphere of theory, which was their most real abode." In some ways, Hester, unlike Dimmesdale, achieves real freedom in her speculations, and Hawthorne implies that this freedom also connects her to the larger history of Europe. Nonetheless, she is led astray by subjectivity as much as

Dimmesdale is. As Hawthorne implies, she is more morally lost than she was before she assumed the scarlet letter: "Hester Prynne, whose heart had lost its regular and healthy throb, wandered without a clew in the dark labyrinth of mind; now turned aside by an insurmountable precipice; now starting back from a deep chasm. There was a wild and ghastly scenery all around her, and a home and comfort nowhere" (p. 166). The figurative landscape of Hester's mind becomes actualized in the forest scene, in which Hawthorne finally seems to venture into the mysteries of intimacy which have been at the outskirts of his narration all along.

Hester and Dimmesdale have grown so immersed in worlds of their own that, in the forest, they recognize each other's ghostly forms only through the symbols attached to them; Dimmesdale acknowledges Hester only after he sees her scarlet letter. For a moment, they seem to escape symbolic representation, as the truth is unveiled simply by the passage of time: "The soul beheld its features in the mirror of the passing moment" (p. 190). The result of their communion after Hester discards the letter, however, is to reduce Pearl to a glimmering phantom across the brook which separates her from her parents. The renewal of their adultery is a denial of Pearl's very being, so Pearl forces her mother to reinstate the letter. Hester's reassumption of the letter becomes a symbol of the way in which "an evil deed invests itself with the character of doom" (p. 211). Hester is driven back into grayness, Dimmesdale even more fully into the painful "revolutions" of his inner world.

In the last part of the book, Hawthorne divests himself of the form of romance, as its revelation and pictorialism grow increasingly disjointed from inner feelings. Hawthorne implies that the symbolism which he has used to reflect neurosis cannot fully convey the more positive "truth of the human heart," the love and intimacy which here can only be expressed silently. In the book's final scenes, his questioning of romance forms grows so pronounced that they become purely ceremonial. The symbol of the scarlet letter loses some of the intensity of emotion attached to it. The mechanisms of romance are identified with the community as a whole, in part because the letter becomes the subject of so many conflicting interpretations that Hawthorne leaves the reader to choose its meaning at the end of the book. Now the scarlet letter must exist in the reader's mind and heart as well as Hawthorne's, where "long meditation has fixed it in very undesirable distinctness" (p. 259). In the last scene, the pageant of the Puritan community is revealed in its status as symbolic representation, one falsely constituted. Hester's estranged perspective illustrates that the community's attempt to embody itself in the form of romances is clearly fictive; the forms no longer represent the reality. So, too, Hawthorne suggests that he must divest himself of the form of romance.

As Hester watches the procession of the community, her feeling of isolation from Dimmesdale reflects the extent to which he has been absorbed into his professional role. Hester's already established irreverence towards the signs of these roles, such as the "clerical band" (p. 199), shows the falseness of such representations. In effect, every symbolic vestment by which the community seeks to display and create itself is subverted. By contrast to the formal representation of the community in the procession, we see the rough, novelistic description of wrestlers on the scaffold. For a moment, the exposure of the fictions of romance enables Hawthorne to escape the matrix of that mode of writing for a more direct and less fanciful kind of fiction.

The reality within romance cannot be directly conveyed, though Hester catches intimations of it. While, in Dimmesdale's Election Day sermon, the rest of the community hears the letter of the speech, its actual words, Hester hears only the spirit—the low undertone which is the voice of instinct itself, as yet incapable of full articulation. The dream of a language that could express instinct, the voice of "a tongue native to the human heart, wherever educated" (p. 243), remains unfulfilled.[22] Hester and Dimmesdale now inhabit two different realms, as the link between them exists only imaginatively: "The sainted minister in the church! The woman of the scarlet letter in the market-place! What imagination would have been irreverent enough to surmise that the same scorching stigma was on them both?" (p. 247). The "irreverent imagination," of course, is that of Hawthorne, who invites the reader to join in his subversive point of view. The intimacy of Hester and Dimmesdale, then, can exist only as an imaginative leap of faith on the part of the reader, as all intimacy to some extent depends on such a leap of faith. In the final scenes, Hawthorne transfers the scene of emotions from the physical world, which he increasingly portrays only from the outside, to the mind of the reader, where intimacy must be imaginatively constructed or reconstructed.

Romances like *The Winter's Tale* often end with a scene which re-establishes family bonds and associates such restoration with divine or supernatural revelation. All of these features are present at the end of *The Scarlet Letter:* a divine revelation in the manifestation of the scarlet letter on Dimmesdale's breast, its link to larger harmonies in Dimmesdale's vision of a reconciliation after death, and a family reunion in the acknowledgment of Pearl not only by Dimmesdale but also by Chillingworth.

But Hawthorne casts doubt on the authenticity of these events, especially as they are perceived by a group of spectators who cannot agree on their meaning or even on whether they occurred. Is there or is there not a letter on Dimmesdale's breast? If so, what does it mean? Did he acknowledge Pearl or didn't he? Dimmesdale's language is never released from its encasement in symbolism in his opening speech; he cannot escape the shadowy realm he has inhabited throughout the book and so dies out of this world. There is no confession, for even Dimmesdale's attempted revelation is only a gesture, pointing to a symbol (not "I sinned" but "behold a . . . witness" or a symbol—p. 255). Hawthorne destabilizes the meaning of the final tableau. Whereas most romances include an interpreter to clarify the meaning of the final revelation (like the historian Gower, who utters the concluding moral in Shakespeare's *Pericles*), at the end of *The Scarlet Letter*, though all the spectators assert that they have seen a visual tableau, they cannot agree on its meaning. Some say Dimmesdale arranged it to represent something like "Sin and Goodness in the World" ("how utterly nugatory is the choicest of man's own righteousness"— p. 259). Others would read it, like the opening tableau of *The Faerie Queene*, book 2, as a representation of a disordered reality.

As for the meaning of Dimmesdale's revelation, what it signifies and whether it occurs, about such things "the reader may choose" (p. 259). As a result, the reader is placed in the position of the spectator in the final scene of romances, with his or her mind vibrating between fancy and actuality. Just as the scarlet letter has imprinted itself on Hawthorne, it will engrave itself on the minds of others (an effect to which James, for one, testifies): "We have thrown all the light we could acquire upon the portent, and would gladly, now that it has done its office, erase its deep print out of our own brain; where long meditation has fixed it in very undesirable distinctness" (p. 259).

In displacing the tale from symbolic representation to what the symbols stand for—intimacy and love—Hawthorne translates romance representation into an inner narrative of interpretation that occurs first within his mind (in "The Custom-House"), then within the minds of his characters, and finally in the mind of the reader. In the last chapter, by leaving the reader to choose, he makes the reader in part the narrator of *The Scarlet Letter*, writer as well as reader.

The last chapter of *The Scarlet Letter* sounds more like a novel than a romance, in its distribution of people and things in an eminently practical manner.[23] The chapter moves forward from the seventeenth to the nineteenth century. Hawthorne relates the bequest of Chillingworth to Pearl in an exceedingly pragmatic tone, as a "matter of business to communicate to the reader" (p. 261). At the end of the work, Hester Prynne still exists in the realm between reality and imagination which she previously inhabited. But she also emerges into historical reality. Despite her ghostly appearance, there is "more real life" (p. 262) for Hester Prynne in New England, site of her past deeds and misdeeds, than anywhere else.

Emphasizing throughout that he uses romance as suggestion or illusion, Hawthorne employs the conventions of romance to illustrate truths of character (such as Dimmesdale's egotism and Chillingworth's fatalism) and to focus the unconscious intentions manifested by gestures but not yet susceptible to articulation in language. This level of perception constitutes the allegory of the book—

what Hawthorne calls the "typical illusion."[24] The phrase is used in two senses—the "type" or symbol of allegory, and the "illusion" of inner perceptions that may or may not correspond to reality.

At the end of *The Scarlet Letter,* romance subsides into no more than a visual mode of representation. The meanings are finally not on the page but in the reader's mind, where they vibrate long after the symbols or images used to embody them have relapsed into decorative signs, like the emblem with which *The Scarlet Letter* concludes. The letter itself, in its final form, becomes "the semblance of an engraved escutcheon. It bore a device, a herald's wording of which might serve for a motto and brief description of our now concluded legend; so sombre is it, and relieved only by one ever-glowing point of light gloomier than the shadow: 'On a field, sable, the letter A, gules'" (p. 264). If romance's symbols, especially that of the scarlet letter, originally served as vehicles for conveying the "truth of the human heart," by the end of the work that truth has been liberated from its embodiment in such representations. Though it cannot be fully articulated in language (as Dimmesdale's final speech remains unheard, his last words ambiguous), the "truth of the human heart" has been transmitted into the mind and heart of the reader, leaving behind as mere visual markers on the page the scarlet letter and even the letters and words with which Hawthorne created it.

4

From Picture to Portrait:
The Scarlet Letter and *The Portrait of a Lady*

Though Hawthorne's presence is strong throughout James's early works, only in the novel published soon after *Hawthorne, The Portrait of a Lady* (1881), does James translate Hawthornian romance into his own distinctive mode of narration and, in the process, revolutionize the form of the novel. In this work, he transforms what he sees as Hawthorne's static pictorialism into a more dramatic narrative, changing picture into portrait. In fact, as James ultimately acknowledges, Hawthorne's use of picture adds intensity to his plot. In addition, Hawthorne's pioneering use of subjectivity becomes, in James, the development of a center of consciousness. Hawthorne translates romance's spectacular action into inner reverie. James internalizes romance, with its melodramatic moral oppositions, projections, and symbolizing tendencies, to reach reality. By translating romance's symbolism and pictorialism into mental processes, James can represent the hidden desires of his heroine, Isabel Archer. Isabel's conscious awareness of those desires finally enables her to "touch the earth" and to become connected to life.

Leo Bersani and Peter Brooks have described what Bersani identifies as the "unlimited power of desire" and Brooks the "melodrama of consciousness" in *The Portrait of a Lady*.[1] In my view, James locates the melodramatic extremes of romance within consciousness not in order to make consciousness autonomous but to connect it with a reality fully knowable only through desire. By making a character's reverie the substance of the story, James internalizes narration. Harold Bloom has described "the internalization of quest-romance" in the writings of romantic poets, in which quests of adventure become strivings of intellect.[2] In James the drama is that of thinking itself. In this work, he begins by emphasizing the inadequacies of an unreflective romantic imagination, as personified by Isabel. But he eventually indicates that only with a perspective informed by romance can one fully comprehend the experience of Europe. While Isabel's imagination begins, like Hawthorne's in the 1879 *Hawthorne*, as excessively innocent and isolated from reality, it eventually becomes the vehicle for conveying reality, as James viewed Hawthorne's imagination in 1904.

According to Laurence Holland, *The Portrait of a Lady* begins where *The Scarlet Letter* ends, as James inherits from Hawthorne the incipient International Theme sketched in the final description of Pearl, who apparently marries a European nobleman. Holland's comment that *The Scarlet Letter* constitutes "the very matrix of James's fabulation" may be applied to the form as well as the substance of James's narrative.[3] In *The Portrait of a Lady,* aspects of Hawthorne's narration which James originally considered pictorial or static—imagery, interpretation—become the very source of James's drama. James preserves the intensity and economy of Hawthornian symbolism and pictorialism while transforming them into a more mobile form of narration to enrich his story.

James's view of Hawthorne's writing as pictorial begins with his earliest understanding of Hawthorne's work. One of the most striking passages in *Hawthorne* is James's recollection of his initial encounter with *The Scarlet Letter.* Since at his age when the work was published (seven years), James was prohibited from reading the book (ostensibly because of its sexual subject), he first gains access to Hawthorne's work by viewing a picture of Hester and Pearl at an art exhibition. He describes this moment of revelation in a way which recalls Hawthorne's own discovery of the scarlet letter in "The Custom-House." James remembers the book as an object of particular interest because it seemingly represents the mystery of sexuality, alluring yet "sinful":

> The writer of these lines, who was a child at the time, remembers dimly the sensation the book produced . . . as if a peculiar horror were mixed with its attraction . . . The mystery was at last partly dispelled by his being taken to see a collection of pictures . . . where he encountered a representation of a pale, handsome woman . . . holding between her knees an elfish-looking little girl . . . Embroidered on the woman's breast was a great crimson A, over which the child's fingers, as she glanced strangely out of the picture, were maliciously playing. I was told that this was Hester Prynne and little Pearl, and that when I grew older I might read their interesting history. But the picture remained vividly imprinted on my mind; I had been vaguely frightened and made uneasy by it, and when, years afterwards, I first read the novel, I seemed to myself to have read it before, and to be familiar with its two strange heroines.[4]

The literary work has become a portrait, not of mother and child but of "two strange heroines." Like the original red "A" in "The Custom-House," Hawthorne's book has become "most worthy of interpretation," as mysterious as the symbol it was designed to explain. The work undergoes several transformations (at the beginning of the passage James describes it as a letter received in the mail), from book to portrait to internal picture and back to book. James's increasing involvement with Hawthorne's creation is shown by the shift in the above passage from third to first person.

As James describes it, Hawthorne's work is already being transformed into a Jamesian mode of representation. His emphasis is on the imagistic rather than symbolic elements of the portrait—the color of the scarlet letter, not its significance. An emblematic center of consciousness emerges in the figure of Pearl, here perhaps a forerunner of Isabel, who glances "strangely out of the picture," giving her privileged contact with the spectator. The translation of Hawthorne's mother and child into "two strange heroines" anticipates James's use of the paired cases of Isabel and Pansy, eventually described not as stepmother and child but "sisters." For Hawthorne, discovering the "A" means assuming the authority to create. James uses an image of Hawthorne's work to claim his own literary authority.

The picture here, in which a child-like spectator views a scene of intimacy, is echoed in a central scene in *The Portrait of a Lady,* when Isabel glimpses Madame Merle and Gilbert Osmond "grouped unconsciously and familiarly." In both *The Scarlet Letter* and *The Portrait of a Lady,* the plot is pre-determined by an act of adultery which occurred long before the events actually depicted. In the last part of James's work, the adultery is revealed as Isabel discovers the "plot, nefarious name" of Osmond and Merle. When the resemblances to the story of *The Scarlet Letter* become evident, echoes of Hawthorne proliferate.

This view of *The Scarlet Letter* as a portrait separates the "characters of Hester Prynne and little Pearl" from "their interesting history," their incarnation in story. In later essays James continues to see picture and action in *The Scarlet Letter* as separate, for he feels that Hester and Pearl are not part of the plot: "strangely enough, this pair are almost wholly outside the action: yet they preserve and vivify the work." Nonetheless, the strength of his initial impression leads James to find the power of Hawthorne's work in its nonnarrative, pictorial aspect: *"The Scarlet Letter* lives . . . by something noble and truthful in the image of the branded mother and the beautiful child."[5]

Thus the static quality of Hawthorne's work is not necessarily a defect. James feels that by focusing his tale, in effect, on the period after the major action (the adultery), Hawthorne eschewed the vulgar interest in plot or the sentimental aspects of a love story for moral and psychological concerns: "what appealed to him was the idea of their moral situation in the long years that were to follow." Hawthorne's subjects are the inner reactions to earlier acts—guilt, shame, repentance. Despite its retrospective nature, *The Scarlet Letter,* in James's view, does develop, not sequentially but through alternating perspectives. The same event is regarded again and again from different points of view, giving the story "little progression but a certain stable variation."[6]

As so described, the narration of *The Scarlet Letter* resembles that of *The Portrait of a Lady.* J. A. Ward has identified as a typical mode of Jamesian narration the progression of the story not by unfolding new events but by discovering and understanding those long past.[7] Though *The Portrait of a Lady* begins with possibilities of freedom and exploration, the book becomes increasingly retrospective, as Isabel's own first acts in the novel become "historical." Isabel's movement to "affront her destiny" is modified by James's need to portray her in the round. By mustering several points of view—those of Ralph, Lord Warburton, Ned Rosier, and others—to depict Isabel, James also gives his work a "certain stable variation" around a "single character" (Hawthorne's "A," James's Isabel). Thus James's book shows the apparently free sequence of events at the beginning to be somewhat illusory. Hawthorne's story progresses through a series of symbols unfolding into interpretations. James's portraiture throughout *The Portrait of a Lady* also condenses meaning into charged images, which infuse narrative with richer significance.

In *Portrait of a Lady,* James tries to make a pictorial mode into a dramatic one. In the prefaces, he characteristically defines "picture" as description or subjective interpretation which alternates with "scene," the dramatic mode of presentation.[8] James can convert picture into action because of his view of picture as subjectively perceived. In the acts of the mind, James finds the drama of the "exciting inward life." In the preface to *The Portrait of a Lady,* as Robert Caserio has noted, James "ends by transsubstantiating picture" into the other modes of depiction in his works—"plot, drama, and 'even story.' "[9]

James cites as an example of this "mystic conversion" Isabel's meditation in chapter 42. In this chapter, the most extensive depiction of a "drama of consciousness" in the novel, James adapts Hawthorne's method of narration through multiple interpretations. According to James, he made consciousness into drama in *The Portrait of a Lady* by internalizing romance. For he made the workings of consciousness an adventure, with all the intensity and excitement of the "far and strange" in romance. James describes the interest generated by Isabel's reverie in chapter 41 (the "best thing in the book" and also "the most typical") in the same terms with which he defines romance: "It was . . . an attempt withal to make the mere still lucidity of her act as 'interesting' as the surprise of a caravan or the identification of a pirate."[10] In the preface to *The American,* James identifies as typical subjects of romance "caravans . . . or forgers . . . or pistols and knives."[11] Isabel's adventures, "mild" on "the side of their independence of the moving accident," become dramatic to the extent that they are converted into consciousness, her "sense for them." Only when mirrored in Isabel's consciousness does the plot become an ethically significant action, "drama and even story."

The predominant action of this inner life is "seeing," and chapter 42 is an "attempt to make (seeing itself) interesting." In Hawthorne's "The Custom-House," the process of viewing and interpreting symbols becomes the story of the book. So here James's subject is the exercise of critical faculties, the "vigil of searching criticism." Isabel's meditation is "retrospective," the attempt to understand her situation by looking back at a traumatic incident. Paradoxically, retrospection most advances the tale's progression: "It throws the action further forward than twenty 'incidents' might have done." Narration progresses internally, though from outward appearances this chapter is the stillest moment in the book, as Isabel sits before a fire. For James, pictures provide intensity, and the use of pictures as incidents in themselves adds both compression and fullness: "the maximum of intensity" with "all the vivacity of incident and all the economy of picture." Isabel's vigil is a "series of shocking recognitions," its action "simply of her motionlessly seeing." The vigil infuses the action, the movement of consciousness, with the motionless but intense concentration of picture: "the still lucidity of her act" (pp. 56–57). James's phrasing here implies that picture and drama are one.

Isabel's meditation, with its frequent reversals of vision—from dark conjecture to sudden enlightenment, from images of elevation to those of depression, memories to intimations of the future—recapitulates the sudden transformations and apparent lack of causal sequence of romance. By converting events into consciousness, releasing the unconscious desires manifested by romance adventures, Isabel achieves a deeply "felt life." Chapter 42 is an example of the unfolding of picture into narrative action, and James calls the chapter typical rather than extraordinary, a "supreme illustration of the general plan" (p. 57).

According to Peter Brooks, James creates a "melodrama of consciousness" in which every gesture and aspect of social behavlior becomes the sign of an intense inner drama. For Brooks, the use of melodrama finally makes "surface realities" a matter of indifference.[12] What Brooks calls melodrama, I would identify as a "romance of consciousness." In my view, the moral polarities associated with romance must be linked to surface appearances, or romance will be the "romantic *tout craché,*" leading to isolation. Through the understanding yielded by her adventures of consciousness, Isabel achieves knowledge of her own experience and her relations to others, the connections which constitute reality in James's view.

Despite James's statement, in *Hawthorne,* that Hawthorne is incapable of describing a rich social milieu, in *The Portrait of a Lady* James initiates his character into the European world by means of Hawthornian romance. Though Isabel begins with a naive imagination rather like that of Hawthorne as James describes him in *Hawthorne,* by the end of the novel she has internalized her experience by means of romance, and so finally touches the reality which long eluded her. James suggests that this internalization of romance is the only way an American character can confront the reality of Europe. An American perspective on Europe reveals its codes and manners as just that, sign systems rather than absolute forms. In Hawthorne's International work, *The Marble Faun,* he cautions his readers against looking at "the wrong side of the tapestry" by demanding too detailed an explanation of events. In *The Portrait of a Lady,* James shows us the wrong side of the tapestry of European civilization, as he exposes beneath its beautiful appearance a world of sordid but dramatic intrigue, through the use of an American, romantic perspective.[13] Ultimately, that flawed world must be confronted so that the romantic American spirit may embrace the reality it appears to resist but ultimately seeks.

The opening scenes of *The Scarlet Letter* and *The Portrait of a Lady* are characteristic of the techniques of the two books: Hawthorne's highly symbolic scene before the prison door, James's perfectly composed "picture" of Gardencourt.[14] (See figure 3.) In both, the elaboration of the initial scene tends to forestall the progression of narrative. Hawthorne's first chapter remains before the "threshold of our narrative," leaving us with a symbol, a "sweet moral blossom," which, after various transformations, reappears as the emblem with which the work concludes. James's opening description is also set apart, in a scene and time so remote from ordinary cares that it seems "a little eternity; . . . an eternity of pleasure."[15] Yet the scene is not, as Hawthorne's seems to be, outside of temporal progression; even as its perfection is described, the "shadows" are lengthening on the lawn.

In its opening description of a "peculiarly English picture" (p. 194), *The Portrait of a Lady* seems to provide a particularly detailed setting. James, however, presents an impression of a scene rather than an actual one. He describes not so much a particular place as a mood and even a kind of light. In the 1904 Hawthorne essay, James saw in Hawthorne's romance the "light that never was on land or sea" transformed into the "light of common day." Here that illumination takes a European scene into a realm halfway between the fanciful and the actual. The accumulation of detail serves to de-realize rather than realize it, as Gardencourt is placed in a never-never land: "the perfect middle of a splendid summer afternoon" (p. 193). Gardencourt is an earthly paradise which includes the accoutrements of civilized society. It appears not as an object but a picture, so "perfect" that it becomes an emblem of England itself. But the social signs of which the initial picture is composed cannot be reliably interpreted. The tea ceremony is not being observed by the sex to which it is usually assigned, women, and the house in this "peculiarly English picture" (p. 194) is the property of an American banker. The scene is shifting and subject to multiple interpretations.

Isabel Archer seems to free the novel from picture into narrative when she enters across the threshold of Gardencourt, just as the entrance of Hester Prynne in *The Scarlet Letter* appears to initiate the narration of that work. In stepping across a portal, Isabel implicitly emerges from the "house of fiction" in the preface into life as a character in the novel. Laurence Holland compares Isabel to Pearl as the heroine of the International Theme adumbrated in Pearl's journey to the Old World.[16] Yet even in her first appearance, Isabel corresponds more closely to Hester than to Pearl, as James originally described *The Scarlet Letter*

Figure 3.   Alvin Langdon Coburn, *The English Home*, 1907
Frontispiece to *The Portrait of a Lady* (volume III of the New York Edition).
(Courtesy International Museum of Photography at George Eastman House.)

as an earlier portrait of a lady. James's title recalls Hawthorne's introduction of his heroine:

> She was lady-like, too, after the manner of the feminine gentility of those days; characterized by a certain state and dignity, rather than by the delicate, evanescent, and indescribable grace, which is now recognized as its indicator. And never had Hester Prynne appeared more lady-like, in the antique interpretation of the term, than as she issued from the prison. (p. 53)

As Hester appears most a lady when she emerges from the prison, James commences his portrait of a lady by showing Isabel in a doorway; the details of the portrait will be added and completed as she stands in other doorways.

In Hester's entrance, her freedom exists only hypothetically, "as if": "She . . . stepped into the open air, as if by her own free-will" (p. 52). In fact, she leaves the jail under compulsion to approach the scene of greater punishment, the scaffold. Isabel, by contrast, seems truly to have "free will." Hawthorne's description of his heroine is detailed: "The young woman was tall, with a figure of perfect elegance, on a large scale. She had dark and abundant hair . . . and a face which . . . had the impressiveness belonging to a marked brow and deep black eyes" (p. 53). Isabel, as viewed by Ralph, is merely a "tall girl in a black dress, who at first sight looked pretty" (p. 204). Both are bareheaded; in the case of Isabel, this is a sign of freedom from convention, while in Hester's case it signifies subjection to exposure. Though her free stride seems to release the story into action, Hester herself is being turned into a static symbol ("the figure, the body, the reality of sin") by all who regard her. Isabel, however, emerges initially into the freest realm of action she will know. The threshold dramatizes the transformation of James's "disponible" figure from the preface into life as a particular character with a name and an identity. As, in *The Scarlet Letter,* Hester hesitated on the "threshold of narrative," Isabel "lingered . . . in the doorway"(p. 206) as if to delay her involvement in the "tangle, to which we look for . . . the impress that constitutes an identity." With each crossing of a threshold, Isabel seems to solidify her identity as she enters another realm of experience.

In her initial encounter with Europe, Isabel seeks not so much reality as romance—the kind of romance James sees as "artificial," not real. For she insistently projects her preconceived ideas onto the reality of Europe. As Ralph warns her, "there is no romance here but what you may have brought with you" (p. 237), but Isabel has brought a great deal. But her initial projections impose on Europe preconceived notions that do not fit the reality. By viewing European people and places as "specimens" (p. 256), Isabel seeks to match them to her preexisting literary impressions. Thus she is blind to the real romance of certain situations: when Lord Warburton proposes to her, she can only perceive that the situation resembles something in a story, without realizing that its glamour and mystery are now within her own experience: "Her situation was one which a few weeks ago she would have deemed deeply romantic. . . . But if she were now the heroine of the situation, she succeeded scarcely the less in looking at it from the outside" (p. 298). Her most passionate involvement with Europe occurs when she tours the picture gallery at Gardencourt in near darkness.[17]

The imagination which leads Isabel on a search for "romance" in Europe was founded in her musings in her grandmother's house in Albany (which also seems "romantic" to her). In his first description of Isabel's imagination, James shows how its exercise depends at once on wide speculation and certain exclusions. In some ways, Isabel's imagination is too restricted, making her incapable of using it to understand reality. In "The Lesson of Balzac," James praised Balzac's ability to grasp the meaning of life by "smashing the window pane of the real"; Isabel wants the barriers between her imagination and the outer world to remain. As James implies in the preface, without "the need of the individual vision and the pressure of the individual will," the front of the House of Fiction remains merely a "dead wall." In Isabel's grandmother's house, the barred entrance is in fact a "hinged door opening straight upon life." But Isabel wishes to leave the door closed so that she can recreate the world as a projection of her imagination: "She had no wish to look out, for this would have interfered with her theory that there was a strange, unseen place on the other side—a place which became, to the child's imagination, according to its different moods, a region of delight or of terror." When Isabel refuses access to the world around her, the "door opening straight upon life" becomes a "silent, motionless portal" (p. 214).

Perhaps the most important limit of Isabel's imagination is her inability to reflect on her own experience, despite her seeming self-absorption. As James suggests in an early image of her introspection, Isabel has mistaken her mental realm for a place of its own. The image foreshadows his description of her imagination in another preface as "the deepest depth of her imbroglio."[18] Indeed, the imagination which in some ways entraps her finally must become the site where she achieves freedom. Isabel's desire to avoid experience is apparent in her view of her imagination as a garden, so rich and self-enclosed that its fragrance becomes overpowering:

> Her nature had, for her own imagination, a certain garden-like quality, a suggestion of perfume and murmuring boughs, of shady bowers and lengthening vistas, which made her feel that introspection was, after all, an exercise in the open air. . . . But she was often reminded . . . that there were . . . a great many places that were not gardens at all—only dusky pestiferous tracts, planted thick with ugliness and misery. (p. 244)

Here Isabel confuses inner and outer realms, taking self-cultivation as the equivalent of experience. The elaborate language and sensual imagery of the passage recall the garden of Hawthorne's "Rappaccini's Daughter." For James, such images provide the best way to symbolize Isabel's inner realm. The sublime scenery of Hester's "moral wilderness," with its "chasms" and "abysses" (chapter 13 of *The Scarlet Letter*), is much wilder than Isabel's relatively tame garden. Yet in this Rappaccini-garden, Isabel is equally endangered and susceptible to a fall. The closing echo of Hawthorne, which recalls both the prison in *The Scarlet Letter* and the analogy between Chillingworth and such poisonous growths, suggests that Isabel's downfall will come at the hands of a Chillingworth-like character.

As Henrietta Stackpole suggests, living solely in one's imagination insures that romantic imaginings will be enacted in a deadly way, through continual confinement to illusion:

> You live too much in the world of your own dreams—you are not enough in contact with reality. . . . You are too fastidious; you have too many graceful illusions. Whatever life you lead, you must put your soul into it—to make any sort of success of it; and from the moment you do that it ceases to be romance, I assure you; it becomes reality! (p. 413)

Henrietta's statement recalls Hawthorne's description of how Pearl is finally humanized when her father acknowledges her: "As her tears fell . . . , they were the pledge that she would grow up amid human joy and sorrow, nor for ever do battle with the world, but be a woman it it" (p. 256, *The Scarlet Letter*). For Henrietta, undergoing the transition from romance to reality means becoming human, subject to the world but capable of action in it. Pearl begins as wild and demonic; when her heart is touched, she abandons battle with the world. For Isabel, who sets herself above life's strife and suffering, humanization rather means descent into the battlefield of adult action and moral conflict. Only then can Isabel, rather than projecting her illusions, recapture within consciousness the conflict and suffering of her own experience. Charles Feidelson claims that Isabel must "turn away from . . . the 'romantic' imagination . . . and embrace the perilous freedom of an embattled consciousness."[19] But such a transformation must be achieved precisely by internalizing romance, capturing the passionate intensity of its battles and adventures within consciousness.[20] Though Henrietta tells Isabel that she must give up romance for reality, Isabel's penetration to reality is precipitated by and through the romantic. Only when one invests oneself in experience is romance realized so as to enhance, not limit life, and the "disponible" spirit made capable of significant action. Rather than confining one to illusion, romance may realize the concept of the "soul" and so enable precisely the kind of spiritual engagement with life which Henrietta advocates.

In other ways, Henrietta's predictions prove all too accurate. According to Henrietta, Isabel's "graceful illusions" will lead her astray: "Your newly-acquired thousands will shut you up more and more to the society of a few selfish and heartless people, who will be interested in keeping up those illusions" (p. 413). The premonition is fulfilled with ironic precision two chapters later, when we see the "few selfish and heartless people" of Osmond's menage, with whom Isabel will be almost literally "shut up." Isabel's infatuation with her first image of Osmond precipitates her downfall. Her gradual awakening from illusion proceeds through her growing ability to interpret pictures. In the course of the section of the book set in Italy, picture progresses from deceptive image to significant symbol to the deepest vehicle of moral meaning. Every picture Isabel sees tells a story, as pictures cease to be artificial images of life and are translated into human lifelikeness and activity. Finally, pictures do not impede but enrich the flow of narrative, as James diffuses their condensed or symbolic meaning across a sequence of action. Thus James transforms what he saw as static in Hawthorne's writing into the very impetus of action in his work. He retains from Hawthorne the use of the symbolic properties of pictures, which he adapts into charged images.

The description of the first scene in Italy (which initially appears to Isabel as a "land of dreams," like the equally deceptive vision of the world as beautiful in Matthew Arnold's "Dover Beach") echoes that of Gardencourt in some ways: in both places, the apparent entrance to the house is not the real one. But whereas, at Gardencourt, this discrepancy was the product of desire for privacy, here, at Gilbert Osmond's villa, it is the result of purposeful deception: "It was the mask of the house; it was not its face" (p. 423). The picture is conveyed by the narrator: Gilbert's family is a "picturesque little group" (p. 423).[21] While, at Gardencourt, the signs have become unmoored from fixed meaning, leading to multiple possibilities of action, at Osmond's villa life has been perfectly arranged into representation.

Isabel perceives a discrepancy between surface and depth, appearance and reality, at Osmond's house on her first visit: "the place, the occasion, the combination of people, signified more than lay on the surface; she would try to understand" (p. 453). But instead of interpreting that discrepancy and seeing the possibly symbolic aspects of the situation, Isabel focuses on the surface of the visual image. She interprets the scene incorrectly, taking Gilbert's created "mask" as his face. She composes the rest of the scene for herself, reducing it to a landscape or perspective study, a pleasing arrangement of color and line:

> She had carried away an image . . . which happened to take her fancy particularly . . . —the image of a quiet, clever, sensitive, distinguished man, strolling on a moss-grown terrace . . . and holding by the hand a little girl whose sympathetic docility gave a new aspect to childhood. The picture was not brilliant, but she liked its lowness of tone, and the atmosphere of summer twilight that pervaded it. (p. 476)

To Isabel, the picture "seemed to tell a story" (p. 476), and as she has harmonized its incongruities, it appears to foretell a lifetime of harmony.[22] The picture does indeed generate "histories within histories," though it unfolds more according to the narrator's perceptions than Isabel's, for the narrator's view reveals Osmond's capacity to deceive and his desire for "careful arrangement." The scene has a past and a future, not the quiet timelessness projected by Isabel's ideal image. Isabel believes that by marrying Osmond she will be initiated into a more complex experience. In fact, by mistaking the surface for the depth, she is led away from life to an existence arranged as representation. She will later realize of Osmond that "she had not read him correctly." Her vision of life with him as a series of artistic tableaux is ironically fulfilled in their life together.

While, in her relation to Gilbert, Isabel reduces life to a picture, in her visit to Rome, works of art insistently come to life. As Ralph Touchett notes, "Rome testified to the psychological moment." In her encounter with Lord Warburton, Isabel's aesthetic contemplation yields to emotional confrontation in the gallery of the Capitol. The relevance of the sculptures to the human situation is inescapable: Lord Warburton, at the time Isabel's "attributive victim," is discovered in front of the "Dying Gladiator" (p. 499). The scene contains explicit allusions to Hawthorne, as it is set in the same gallery as the opening scene of *The Marble Faun*. The other figures Hawthorne mentions are also relevant to Isabel's situation—the "human Soul assaulted by Evil" in the form of a snake is enacted in subsequent images of Gilbert as a serpent and Isabel's trouble as the imperilment of a soul. In a sense, this room contains Isabel's entire story conveyed symbolically in works of art.

In the New York Edition, James strengthens the allusion to Hawthorne by mentioning the statues of the Faun and Antinous. James's allusions to *The Marble Faun* here imply that he, like Hawthorne, will use works of art to convey moral knowledge symbolically. But while Hawthorne develops the symbolic traits of the human characters, James sees a human presence in the works of art themselves. Isabel awakens to the past by viewing the statues as presences, turning "eternal silence" itself into something which can be listened to (p. 500). (In the New York Edition, she imagines "to what . . . their absent eyes were open" and "how . . . their alien lips would sound.") Isabel sees the parallel between art and life by recognizing the statues as "more perfectly human," seeing "life between their gazing eyelids" (p. 500). Now her contemplation provides access to something apart from the self, to what is most human in the other, which redoubles her aesthetic appreciation: "she had seen them all before, but her enjoyment repeated itself, and it was all the greater because she was glad, for the time, to be alone" (p. 500). In this scene, by contrast to her initial contemplations in her grandmother's house, Isabel's meditations connect her to a realm outside herself. In the process she also begins reflecting on her own actions, perhaps feeling sympathy for Lord Warburton for the first time.

Isabel's view of the statues shows that fixing human beings into works of art alienates personality. Another way of turning people into art is pursued by Gilbert Osmond, who at this point sees Isabel as, because of her rejection of Lord Warburton, a "young lady who had qualified herself to figure in his collection of choice objects" (p. 501). While Isabel's sympathetic view seems to reawaken the life within works of art, in transforming her into an artwork Osmond tries to reduce her from human being to object.

Osmond's attempt at portraiture is an ironic version of James's use of portraiture to give his characters life. Osmond's portrait of Isabel comes closest to fulfilling the title of the novel: "framed in the gilded doorway, she struck our young man as the picture of a gracious lady" (p. 570). (See figure 4.) While, in her first appearance at a threshold, Isabel emerged into life as a character from James's imagination in the preface, here the doorway fixes her in a frame, turning her from fictive life back into representation. This description is probably the most highly-contrived "picture" in the book, a portrait framed and positioned for appreciation by the connoisseur (the perspective is that of the collector Ned Rosier). The dangers of portraiture are evident: by being transformed into a painting, Isabel has lost freedom and life. James's echoes of his own enterprise in Osmond's here indicate his awareness of the possible deadliness of all framing of characters in representation, and the necessity of finding a mobile form of portraiture.

Despite the apparent fixity of this image, however, it becomes a point of revelation and a pivot for the plot. Unlike the aesthete Ned Rosier, we see its ironies because our attitude to Isabel has become like James's own: as James says of Balzac's creation of characters, "it was by loving them he knew them." So the reader's sympathy for Isabel is continually solicited by the narrator from the beginning of the work. The picture serves James's purposes as well as Osmond's. The portrait of Isabel gilded and framed indicates that she no longer acts for herself but plays a role and even illustrates an idea. As Ralph perceives, by being forced to wear the mask of aristocracy and convention, Isabel becomes a mere representation. He recognizes the figurative nature of the "picture of a gracious lady" as the "fine lady who was supposed to represent something" (p. 597). As Hester was "transfigured" by the scarlet letter to become a symbol herself—the "figure, the body, the reality of sin"—Isabel is transformed from an individual to a figure, the visible sign of Osmond's taste. The addition to her light step of a "mass of drapery" and a "majesty of ornament" (p. 597) restricts her movement rather than increasing her substance, making her more fully a screen for displaying Osmond. Thus the picture reveals Osmond's manipulativeness to those who can read it correctly.

The use of picture as a vehicle of moral revelation culminates in the famous meditation of chapter 42, provoked by a "picture" discovered two chapters earlier. The retrospection is set in motion by Isabel's unexpected glimpse of

Figure 4.   John Singer Sargent, *Madame X,* 1884
"... Framed in the gilded doorway, she struck our young
man as the picture of a gracious lady"—*The Portrait of
a Lady,* p. 570.

Madame Merle and Gilbert Osmond "grouped unconsciously and familiarly" (p. 639): "The thing made an image, lasting only a moment, like a sudden flicker of light. Their relative position, their absorbed mutual gaze, struck her as something detected" (p. 612). Like the artist in "The Art of Fiction," she must interpret the impression by "guessing the unseen from the seen" to "convert the very pulses of the air . . . into revelations."[23] In "The Art of Fiction," James says that "impressions *are* experience." So Isabel's vision marks an epoch in her development: "she felt it as something new." As in the portrait of Hester and Pearl, James provides a revelation even in the relative position of the two characters, as Gilbert Osmond sits while Madame Merle stands; that breach of manners becomes the clue to their intimacy.

Chapter 42 begins by awakening a sequence of images in Isabel's mind, provoked by that initial, jarring impression. In "The Haunted Mind," Hawthorne constructs an allegorical narrative through the emergence of pictures over the threshold from the unconscious to the conscious mind. So Isabel's "soul was haunted with terrors which crowded to the foreground of thought" (p. 628), as they rise up from the unconscious. Isabel's reverie commences with an image, the view of her relation with Warburton which Osmond had "put . . . before" her (p. 627), and the shock of the initial impression animates the series of pictures into "livelier motion" (p. 628), as picture turns into revelation.

In its use of sudden transformations, its apparently illogical sequence of reflections, and its treatment of extreme goodness and evil, chapter 42 follows the structure of romance narration.[24] The "transformation scenes" which Jameson identifies with romance are enacted as categories turn into their opposites—expansion becomes restriction, exaltation depression: "she had suddenly found the infinite vista of a multiplied life to be a dark, narrow alley, with a dead wall at the end" (p. 629). In chapter 42, the architecture of the novel becomes archetypal, including locales like the fortress and labyrinth, which shows that Isabel is imprisoned by evil. The images of the dungeon and the prison later appear as actual places: the Palazzo Roccanera is no longer an old Roman palace but a dungeon, Pansy's convent no convent but a "well-appointed prison." Isabel's freedom has been conveyed in images of elevation, like the balloon of imagination in the preface to *The American*. But in marriage to Osmond she finds herself not above, but in or even below the earth: "Her life led rather downward and earthward, into realms of restriction and depression" (p. 629) until she feels "shut up with an odour of mould and decay" (pp. 635–36). The images show that Isabel has not only endured repression and restriction, but is threatened with spiritual death.

For James, the "infallible sign" of romance is its dramatization of the battle of good and evil: "the power of bad people that good get into, or vice versa."[25] In recognizing that her conflict with her husband is an opposition in which "the vital principle of one was deadly to the other," Isabel sees her own marriage as a version of this battle. Allusions to Hawthorne in images such as the garden become more explicit in this chapter. Gilbert's egotism is revealed when he is identified with Hawthorne's "bosom serpent": "Under all his culture . . . his egotism lay hidden like a serpent in a bank of flowers" (p. 634). Isabel's view of her imagination as a garden is ironically fulfilled in Gilbert's desire to make her mind "attached to his own like a small garden-plot to a deer-park" (p. 636), a possible echo of "Rappaccini's Daughter." The resurgence of these images in the overt allusions to Hawthorne here suggest that, for James, the moral aspects of the characters and story can best be conveyed through symbolism.

In his extensive use of Hawthorne in chapter 42, James gives the events of his book, previously considered in aesthetic terms, a moral import.[26] The symbolic and melodramatic patterns of this chapter, while they may not correspond to Isabel's actual existence, reveal her unconscious feelings. Isabel can achieve understanding only retrospectively, in the aftermath of suffering. In this respect, she resembles Hester Prynne in *The Scarlet Letter*. The most melodramatic part of chapter 42 provides a sequence of almost direct quotations from Hawthorne, especially chapter 15 of *The Scarlet Letter,* which, in its use of retrospection, is a model for James's use of the center of consciousness in this chapter. Only through reflection of her experience into consciousness can Isabel be initiated into reality.

Chapter 15 of *The Scarlet Letter* also represents a woman's reflections on her marriage in retrospect. Here Hester quite literally takes the backward view, looking back at Chillingworth as he departs after they have spoken. Though Chillingworth has gradually degenerated from a gentle scholar into jealousy personified, in Hester's view he assumes the appearance of a Gothic villain, not a man but a devil. Hester's view of Chillingworth is phrased as a series of rhetorical questions or conjectures ("Would not . . . would he not"—p. 175). When the same images appear in Isabel's meditation, they are not hypothetical but figuratively true. In this chapter, for the first time, Hester reflects passionately on her life with Chillingworth: "She marveled how such scenes could have been! She marveled how she could have been wrought upon to marry him!" (p. 176). So Isabel muses about the extreme unlikelihood of her falling in love with Gilbert Osmond, concluding that their marriage occurred through mutual deception.

The closest parallels between Hawthorne's and James's chapters occur in the descriptions of Chillingworth and Osmond. Hester gazes to see "whether the tender grass . . . would not be blighted beneath him (Chillingworth)," and Isabel reflects on Gilbert's "faculty for making everything wither that he touched" (p. 628). Hester wonders whether Chillingworth would be swallowed up by the "earth, quickened to an evil purpose by the sympathy of his eye. . . . Or might it suffice him, that every wholesome growth should be converted into something deleterious and malignant at his touch?"[27] Osmond shares this magical power of negative transformation: "It was as if he had the evil eye; as if his presence were a blight and his favour a misfortune" (pp. 628–29). Here James tempers the fanciful assertion through simile, to match the uncertainty of Hawthornesque conjecture ("It might be . . ."). But while Hester questions her own perception ("Was there . . . a circle of ominous shadow?"), Isabel is sure that the shadow of evil created by Gilbert is not her projection. Rather, "the shadows . . . were a part of her husband's very presence" (p. 630). Hester's speculations become Isabel's metaphorical realities. Hester only conjectures "would he not suddenly sink into the earth, leaving a barren and blasted spot" (p. 175), while Isabel, after speaking to Osmond, with his manner that is "dry as a burned-out fire" (p. 637), knows that she cannot escape the narrowed sphere of her existence, "the blasted circle round which she walked." The view of Osmond as a kind of devil is more than just a projection of Isabel's subjectivity.

After chapter 42, the air of the Palazzo Roccanera almost literally turns into revelations, as Isabel progresses from darkness to recognition. In one of the final chapters, Isabel "seemed . . . to be living in a world illuminated by lurid flashes" (p. 766). To operate in the world to which her eyes have suddenly been opened, Isabel must, as the Countess Gemini advises, become more "simple." Isabel recognizes that such absolute categories as good and evil exist and must be applied, so that she can judge Madame Merle not as merely manipulative but "wicked" (p. 725). In a world where evil is so powerful, simple optimism or good nature (like that of Mr. Bantling) becomes "kindness" (p. 771) itself. The descent into romance enables Isabel to emerge onto the plain of adult moral experience.

In the last part of the novel, James reveals the concealed plot which subverts yet directs his work, the adultery of Merle and Osmond. This is the "plot, nefarious name" which resembles that of *The Scarlet Letter,* the hidden adultery which moved James in the portrait of Hester and Pearl. Isabel understands that in her manipulation by Merle and Osmond "there had been intention" and the "intention had not been good" (p. 720). She becomes imprisoned, as it were, by the form of the novel itself, which James has so carefully constructed around her: "The truth of things, their mutual relations, their meaning, and for the most part their horror, rose before her with a kind of architectural vastness" (p. 760). Indeed, in James's own creation and emplotment one may question, as he implicitly does in the preface, whether the intention was good; certainly there has been "intention," the governing hand of the author over the acts of his character. James must redeem his own tendency to frame his characters by reconciling aesthetic creation with morality. He notes in the preface that the moral quality of a work "is dependent on the amount of 'felt life' concerned in producing it." By using romance as internalized by Isabel's consciousness and enacted in subsequent scenes of revelation, James makes the story a vehicle for moral illumination. Isabel achieves a deeply "felt life" through the awakening of her emotions in romance.

In chapter 42, Isabel finally crosses the barrier between imagination and reality. As James predicted, it is a barren and dangerous passage: "a dusky, uncertain tract which looked ambiguous and even slightly treacherous, like a moorland seen in the winter twilight." The image is a version of Gilbert's sterile nature or of the barrenness of their marriage. Isabel's descent into romance may leave her stranded in a wasteland. To return to life, Isabel must abandon the image of herself as a prisoner in a dungeon or a labyrinth.

In the final chapters of the book, having attained the intensity and moral pitch of romance, James proceeds to qualify its absolutism to bring romance into accord with ongoing life. He accomplishes this aim partly through several allusions to scenes from *The Scarlet Letter.* The first is a transformed version of the moment of greatest beauty and freedom in *The Scarlet Letter,* Hester and Dimmesdale's reunion in the forest. James reenacts this scene in the claustrophobic setting of Madame Merle's drawing room, in the colloquy of Merle and Osmond, another consultation between lovers about their "common crime" (p. 728).

Here a debate about the soul's fate occurs in a highly civilized setting replete with details of social ceremonies, like the slightly cracked teacup which becomes a symbol of Madame Merle herself. Though Merle attempts to play the scene as romance, claiming to Osmond that "you have dried up my soul," Gilbert denies that a soul can be "ruined," perhaps as an excuse for further tampering with it: "Don't you know the soul is an immortal principle? How can it suffer alteration?" (p. 728). Osmond warns Madame Merle, "You always see too much in everything; you overdo it; you lose sight of the real. I am much simpler than you think." In some ways, Osmond is right; one can "lose sight" of the real through a romantic view. Instead, one must realize romance by reconnecting it to civilized society and to history.

The last part of the book is almost entirely retrospective, as Isabel makes connections to her own past experience and to history generally. In the final chapters, some of her early romantic illusions are realized in unexpected ways. The ghost of Gardencourt finally appears to Isabel in a form she could not have foreseen. She abandons the tourist's taste for the picturesque to see the historical and moral import of the European landscape. Isabel learns sympathy, which enables her to understand first the "ache of antiquity" most deeply felt in Rome, and finally her own history as defined by the book's events.

Isabel's inner realm of consciousness and the external, pictorial scene are finally linked when she sees the continuum between inner suffering and outer ruin. As a result, her romantic subjectivity becomes a classical sense of tragedy, and therefore "objective": "In a world of ruins the ruin of her happiness seemed a less unnatural catastrophe. . . . She had grown to think of it chiefly as the place where people had suffered." For Isabel, the features of the landscape do not any longer simply form a pattern of "far gradations and soft confusions of colour" but reveal the suffering of the shepherd who is an element of the pastoral picture and the elegiac import of the picture itself, "the splendid sadness of the scene" (p. 724).[28]

When Isabel sees the ghost of Gardencourt, it is no "castle-spectre," as she had expected, but the departing spirit of Ralph. The ghost affirms another sort of continuity, guaranteeing that the spirit exists and persists after death. The vision appears to guarantee the survival of the souls of Isabel and Pansy. As Ralph foretold, for Isabel suffering brings greater awareness, for to see the ghost "you must have suffered first, have suffered greatly, have gained some miserable knowledge."

Isabel's spiritual imprisonment threatens to leave her permanently isolated from life, as her future seems cut off behind a "grey curtain" (p. 770). In her final trip to Gardencourt, Isabel appears to contemplate suicide. Nonetheless, she is convinced that "it couldn't be she was to live only to suffer" (p. 769), and yet she has "lived to suffer enough." While, at the end of *The American,* the hero Christopher Newman is separated from life into the "romantic *tout craché,"* here James reconnects romance to ordinary experience to initiate his heroine into "felt life." Isabel must learn to embrace her history as what has made her, to recognize the meaning of an unfolding narrative that cannot be confined to a single picture. Isabel now sees the truth as "subjective facts," imaginative visions which are confirmed by experience. Now her imagination provides a means of access to truth rather than illusion, even when that truth is unpleasant, as when she intuits the evil of Madame Merle: "Isabel heard a cold, mocking voice proceed from she knew not where, in the dim void that surrounded her, and declare that this bright, strong, definite, worldly woman . . . was a powerful agent in her destiny" (p. 720). Her freedom at the book's end is not the immunity of a character in romance from the ordinary conditions of life; rather, Isabel's independence is determined by her own actions and enmeshed in the "related state" of actual existence.

In the book's final scene, Isabel returns to a bench which seems to her "historic," the site of her first proposal. Here Isabel's search for life is given a possibly romantic ending as Caspar renews his proposal. His plea echoes the second half of the forest scene in *The Scarlet Letter*. As Hester urges Dimmesdale to "Write! Act! Do anything, save to lie down and die" (p. 198), Caspar urges Isabel to dramatic action, provoking a crisis that nearly ends the book. Isabel's series of "lurid flashes" culminate in the kiss which affects her like a "flash of lightning." Caspar's exhortation that "the world's all before us" echoes Hester's admonition to "begin all anew." But Isabel, who repeated those words (from the ending of *Paradise Lost*) about midway through the book, just before her marriage, has learned that the world is not a realm of infinite expansion. For James, being on the side of life means abandoning romantic possibilities of an unlimited existence. At the end, he projects his characters into continued life, though it is not directly represented. The book does not conclude with the crisis Caspar provokes, as its ending remains open in the depiction both of Isabel and the possible shape of her future experience.

At the end of *The Scarlet Letter,* Hester seeks "more real life" (p. 262) by returning to the site of her punishment and suffering. Hester's return to New England implies that the shame and suffering of her past represent "more real life" than any break from the past could bring. Once again, Hester seems to enter into punishment "by her own free will." As she began by crossing the threshold of the prison, from isolation into open air, she ends by crossing the threshold of her hut to live again in solitude. The narrative action which commences with Hester subsides with her return, as the heroine and her tale are absorbed into the artistic symbol which gave rise to the story as narrative. The scarlet letter becomes, in the conclusion, a "device" on an "escutcheon" (p. 264), an emblem divorced from action.

While the action of Hester's story is absorbed back into a static emblem, Isabel is never fully resolved into the frame of her portrait, evading the grasp of the reader as she does that of Caspar.[29] Isabel's final acts in the novel resemble Hester's; she finds escape to a new land (Pearl's Europe, Caspar's America) illusory as a means of engaging with life. Suffering directs her to embrace her past and take up the experience into which pain both circumscribes and initiates her. Isabel seeks duty not as renunciation but as the only "path" which can give her emotions the "real life" of moral significance. The last sight of Isabel recalls Hester's return to her cottage:

> In an extraordinary short time—for the distance was considerable—she had moved through the darkness (for she saw nothing) and reached the door. Here only she paused. She looked all about her; she listened a little; then she put her hand on the latch. She had not known where to turn; but she knew now. There was a very straight path. (*The Portrait of a Lady*, p. 799)

> They beheld a tall woman, in a gray robe, approach the cottage-door. In all those years it had never once been opened; but either she unlocked it . . . , or she glided shadow-like through these impediments,—and, at all events, went in.
>   On the threshold she paused,—turned partly round,—for, perchance, the idea of entering, all alone, and all so changed, the home of so intense a former life, was more dreary and desolate than even she could bear. But her hesitation was only for an instant. . . . (*The Scarlet Letter*, p. 262)

Isabel's exit is full of premonitions of an uncertain future—darkness, blind forward movement, a sudden turn. Hester seems drawn back to New England by necessity, the "home-feeling with the past," as the passage emphasizes the still overwhelming power of her earlier history—"the home of so intense a former life." While Hawthorne concludes by resolving his character back into the symbol of her suffering, for James, Isabel's real existence begins by taking up the burden of suffering, with which she can cross the doorway to experience. While the ending of *The Scarlet Letter* refers back to the rest of the story, that of *The Portrait of a Lady* is almost literally unimaginable, the positing of a future that would be a turn away from the life Isabel knew before.

In disappearing across the same threshold from which she entered the book, Isabel does not withdraw into her original state as a figure isolated from relations but is finally fully "placed." At the moment of completion of the portrait as a literary creation, the portrait serves its larger purpose. It has become so complete a conveyance of character that it releases its subject from the literary structure, as the frame of the portrait dissolves to open onto the gray expanse of real life.

In the context of his often excessive rejection or denial of romance in *Hawthorne,* it is not surprising that James begins *The Portrait of a Lady* with some attacks on Isabel's romantic imagination. Indeed, his description of Isabel at the outset in some ways resembles his description of Hawthorne as naive American. But when James depicts his heroine's initiation into European experience, he can best embody her moral and emotional passage through romance. In the process, he transforms the more static aspects of Hawthorne's narration, such as the use of pictorialism, into the most dramatic elements of his own. The mode James criticized in 1879 as incapable of providing moral depth and depicting a complex society becomes, in his novel of 1881, the most effective way to achieve those ends. James finds that he cannot write a novel which portrays the American experience in Europe realistically without employing romance.

5

The Romance of Politics, the Politics of Romance: *The Blithedale Romance* and *The Bostonians*

James's next major novel after *The Portrait of a Lady, The Bostonians* (1886), has often been classified as a naturalist novel. James himself mentions Daudet's *L'Evangeliste* as a source for the work. It has also been seen as exemplifying James's tenets in "The Art of Fiction" about how to practice the "realism" which was the dominant literary mode of the 1880s. But the influence of Hawthorne's *The Blithedale Romance* on this work is inescapable. Not only does *The Bostonians* take up the same theme of New England reform, though in a later generation, but it even uses occasional verbal echoes: Olive asks Verena, "Will you be my friend of friends?", the same question that Hollingsworth poses to Coverdale in *The Blithedale Romance*.[1] James emphasized the role of the book as an analysis of American society; it is his effort here "to write a very American tale, to prove that I *can* do so."[2] But the influence of Hawthorne on this work by James has been underplayed, in part because of James's omission of any mention of it, as critics tend to contrast the two works by viewing *The Blithedale Romance* as a romance and *The Bostonians* as a realist work.[3] These statements initially seem supported by some of James's commentary on *The Blithedale Romance,* which at one point he sees as a particularly dream-like creation of Hawthorne's.

In fact, though, *The Blithedale Romance* and *The Bostonians* can better be understood as two halves of a diptych portraying nineteenth-century American life which dramatizes the discrepancy between utopian ideals and individual passions. In both cases the apparent, idealistic structure of the community is undermined by the individualistic desires of its members. For James, this meant that *The Blithedale Romance* presented two forms of romance—that of Utopian idealism and that of desires gone astray in a web of conflicting passions. The interest of the work lies in the interaction between the two. These two levels are retained and even fused in James's work, where the love story becomes the political one, a plot of power as well as passion. Hawthorne's work is present in James's not just in specific verbal allusions but in the presence of numerous recollections of the earlier era of the 1840s. Such references turn the historical past itself into romance, as Hawthorne's presence provides a romantic under-layer in James's work.

Thus, rather than viewing Hawthorne's work as romance, James's as realis-tic, we can see in both the ironic juxtaposition of a Utopian romance with a far more realistic realm. Hawthorne's *The Blithedale Romance* is already highly satiric about romance and Utopian possibilities. In *The Bostonians,* though, an ever harsher satire of the contemporary characters makes James recall Haw-thorne's era with nostalgia as a time of higher ideals. *The Blithedale Romance* provides the most ironic version of romance of any of Hawthorne's works, especially in the use of the narrator, Coverdale. While realism undoes romantic idealism in Hawthorne, James uses romance to enrich his realism by including awareness of lost Utopian visions. Even as they satirize political reformers, in the very form of their representations Hawthorne and James seek to explore some of the reforms suggested—in arrangements of community in *The Blithedale Romance,* in relations between men and women in *The Bostonians.* Thus romance, despite its apparent distance from contemporary reality, becomes in its very form a means of commenting on politics.

As James suggests in his commentary on *The Blithedale Romance,* despite Hawthorne's disavowal of any political subject or purpose in the preface to that work, romance is the best mode for portraying Utopian reformers, because it dramatizes an ideal realm. The danger Hawthorne faces is that his mode may recapitulate the mistaken aspirations and ultimate failure of Blithedale by pro-jecting a false ideal. As James describes it, Hawthorne's subject in *The Blithe-dale Romance* is the discrepancy between ideal and reality: "the unconscious way in which the search for the common good may cover a hundred interested impulses and personal motives; the suggestion that such a company could only be bound together more by its delusions, its mutual suspicions and frictions, than by any successful surrender of self."[4] The distance from ordinary life achieved by romance enchantment resembles the separation from society en-forced by the reformers. Romance's supernaturalism was invoked by Hawthorne to convey the characters' manipulations of each other, especially through mes-merism. What Hawthorne and James consider the political aspect of Utopian experiments is precisely the failure of communal enterprises, while the intricate web of manipulations and betrayals among their participants constitutes a differ-ent form of political activity, a maneuvering for power. A romance of idealized action is replaced by a drama of passionate manipulation, a romance of another sort.

While, in his *Notebooks,* the terms in which James sets out to write *The Bostonians* imply a Zolaesque social analysis ("I asked myself what was the most salient and peculiar point in our social life. The answer was: the situation of women . . . the agitation on their behalf"), James's way of treating politics is more indebted to Hawthorne's romance than to sources in naturalism. In *The Blithedale Romance,* Hawthorne shows that politics includes not only public movements but the internalized presence of history and ideology in the minds and acts of individuals. James continues this kind of analysis in *The Bostonians* when he addresses the subject of feminist reform by dramatizing the power struggles in love relationships. As James realized, by concentrating on personal relationships, Hawthorne did not abandon but refocussed the political issues of reform.

As James says in several essays on Hawthorne, the real life of New England transpires not in public politics but in the underlying spiritual conflicts between and within individuals. In his 1897 essay on Hawthorne, James notes that the "latent romance of New England" exists in the discrepancy between its surface life and the "secret play of the Puritan faith":

> the direct and ostensible . . . arrived at forms of which the tender imagination could make little. It could make a great deal, on the other hand, of the spiritual contortions, the darkened outlook, of the ingrained sense of sin, of evil, and of responsibility.

James here attributes to Hawthorne the "penetrating imagination" which reveals the life below the surface. In the preface to *The Princess Casamassima* (written shortly after *The Bostonians*), he sees politics itself as a kind of underworld, as "what 'goes on' irreconcilably, subversively, beneath the vast smug surface."[5] Here the penetrating imagination reveals not only the "sinister anarchic underworld" of political activity, but that of mysterious human motives generally; one who has it can apprehend "mysteries abysmal." The penetrating imagination seems to be identified with the realist's or naturalist's faculty of analysis. But, as James says, what it uncovers is a "latent romance," a realm of mystery and spirituality.

Whereas many critics claim that a novel that swerves from historical facts misses the political realities of a situation, in fact, as James notes, Hawthorne makes that swerve precisely to confront the politics of his reformers, which have become internal rather than external. In *The Bostonians,* James is less concerned with the movement of feminist reform, the "agitation on their behalf," than with "the decline of the sentiment of sex." The "sentiment of sex" may refer to chivalry or more generally to love relationships between the sexes, which are necessarily transformed by changes in the relative power of women. Finally, for James, the political issue of feminism must be resolved in the private, not the public, realm. James internalizes political issues even more than Hawthorne by showing them ultimately as conflicts not between but within individuals, as in the case of Olive Chancellor, who virtually embodies the "Puritan conscience" which finally leads only to desire for martyrdom.

James notes that the action of *The Blithedale Romance* transpires to a great extent in the minds of the characters, who imagine a more romantic realm than that which actually exists. Zenobia, especially, is seen as "looking, with her fine imagination, for adventures that were hardly, under the circumstances, to be met."[6] In *The Bostonians,* romance exists solely in the characters' imaginings, while it is entirely absent from their actual surroundings. By emphasizing the discrepancy between their imaginings and reality, James uses romance to heighten realism, emphasizing the bleakness of the world he depicts. James's characters have a romance with politics in two senses. First, they consider it the field of mythic and heroic activity, despite the shabbiness to which the New England reform movement was debased by the late nineteenth century. Secondly, the language of ideology becomes a means of seduction in this work. The Southerner Basil Ransom courts Verena Terrant by making political observations; Verena's public lectures sound (to his ears at least) like pleas for romantic love. Whereas in *The Blithedale Romance* love subverts the political enterprise, in *The Bostonians* love becomes the arena of political conflict. In Hawthorne, not just the Utopian enterprise but mesmerism and the "tender passion" seem to promise the means to fulfillment of desire. The fact that all lead only to further frustration, or even destruction, is what makes Hawthorne's title ironic. In James, love itself becomes a political act, a constant maneuvering for power, which implies that the fulfillment of romantic desire in this realm is impossible.

Both writers, then, reveal beneath the abstractions of Utopian reform a dangerous, even deadly drama of human passion. Hawthorne shows the power play in the creation of romance, which distances reality to control chaotic situations. The apparent detachment of Coverdale's voyeuristic enterprise is in fact invasive, violating his own individuality as well as that of others. While many critics have charged James with aestheticizing politics, he shows the political aspect of representation itself, which also involves the author's projection of power over his subject. James recognizes that in his use of the penetrating imagination, he may be recapitulating his characters' invasions of each other's privacy.

In *The Blithedale Romance* and *The Bostonians,* the search for the spirit ends not by incarnating but destroying it. In both books, the spirit is seen as embodied in a young girl (Priscilla, Verena) when more abstract versions of its embodiment in reforming communities fail. To maintain the girl's innocence, both communities turn away from the larger society, in *The Bostonians* through abjuration of social contact, in *The Blithedale Romance* through isolation form not only the city but the more brutal aspects of nature. The initial rejection of these larger realms becomes a pervasive repression or abjuration of experience. Yet the repressed aspects eventually reappear, in the city scenes of *The Blithedale Romance* and the final crowd scene of *The Bostonians,* as the authors reproduce the forces which the characters try to deny.

While the romance of Utopia quickly fails, romance enchantment is translated into a kind of personal mesmerism. A complicated series of bondages enchains almost all of the characters of *The Blithedale Romance* to each other, until, as Coverdale notes, "our souls are not our own." When Priscilla is rescued form her role as Veiled Lady by Hollingsworth, Hawthorne implies that release from the domination of another in mesmerism can be achieved through heterosexual love: "The true heart-throb of a man's affection was too powerful for the jugglery that had hitherto environed her."[7]

In *The Bostonians,* love or sexuality has become yet another form of domination. Here the influence of one person over another is almost exclusively sexual, as desire becomes a form of mesmerism. Mrs. Terrant acquiesces to her husband Selah's deceptions only because of his "magnetism," and is ashamed of her susceptibility to him: "She hated her husband for having magnetized her so that she consented to certain things."[8] Attraction and domination are conflated, as the chief effect of sexual desirability seems to be the ability to make others obey you.

In *The Blithedale Romance,* magnetism retains some of its original meaning. Coverdale sees each individual as possessing a sphere of influence, almost a magnetic field of force. Coverdale, who considers his susceptibility to influence great but his ability to dominate others infinitesimal, places Zenobia, Hollingsworth, and Priscilla in a kind of aristocracy of deeply influential spirits: "the intentness of their feelings gave them the exclusive property of the soil and atmosphere" (p. 214). The use of mesmerism gives a magical element to *The Bostonians* and even more to *The Blithedale Romance.* Yet Hawthorne shows in *The Blithedale Romance* that despite, or because of, this seemingly supernatural force, the characters' relationships and betrayals of each other have real and disastrous effects.

While James frequently criticizes Hawthorne for being insufficiently satirical of the Transcendentalists, James's own memory of the Brook Farm reformers (whom he met through his father) is reverent: "They seemed excellently good."[9] One character in *The Bostonians,* Miss Birdseye, was widely recognized (by William James, among others) as a portrait of Hawthorne's sister-in-law, Elizabeth Peabody, providing a historical link to Hawthorne. Though James vigorously denied the resemblance, claiming that Miss Birdseye, "like every other character I've invented, came from my own imagination," clearly she was based on a historical figure.[10] As Daniel Heaton has shown, the portrait of Miss Birdseye, which begins as rather satirical, ends as beatifying.[11] The example of Miss Birdseye condemns the contemporary characters for their lack of "the old high-thinking, . . . the old sanctity, the old sense of sanctity."[12]

For James, *The Blithedale Romance* imbued its readers with a "consciousness of history." In *The Bostonians,* continual references to the past, especially to Hawthorne's generation, provide a counterpoint to the relentlessly modern world. James's insight into Hawthorne's mode of penetration enabled his own analysis of the "latent romance of New England," the personal conflicts and internalization of Puritan conscience which constituted New England political life in the late nineteenth century. Political conflicts tend to repeat themselves, as the failure of Utopian reform in *The Bostonians* in some ways recapitulates the action of *The Blithedale Romance,* indicating that "progress" has only led to continuing dissolution of the "New England spirit."

The link between memory and romance is stated in Hawthorne's preface to *The Blithedale Romance,* which is based on his own experience. In the preface, Hawthorne transforms Brook Farm from an historical place to his fictional Blithedale, a "theater removed" from ordinary reality which still contains many of its features. While Brook Farm was already "the most romantic episode of his own life," Hawthorne dislocates his "old home" from the sphere of received to created experience through the distancing perspective of memory. Using Spenser's image for allegory, the veil, Hawthorne implies that the figures of Blithedale are allegorical creations rather than "likenesses": the "self-concentrated Philanthropist; the high-spirited Woman . . . the weakly Maiden of sibylline attributes" (p. 28). Blithedale constitutes a figurative version of actual experience, as Hawthorne suggests that romance may capture an experience in which, at the time, "the real Me was never there."

Indeed, his "atmosphere of strange enchantment" may reveal the truth more than would the works of Brook Farm's rightful "historians." Hawthorne notes that those who were more closely involved in founding Brook Farm— "Ripley, with whom rests the honorable paternity of the institution, Dana, Dwight" and others—might be expected to produce more historical works containing "both the outward narrative and the inner truth and spirit of the whole affair." But Hawthorne notes that these individuals are, if anything, even more self-concealing than he is. They "veil themselves from the public eye," as if they too were allegorical figures. George William Curtis, who now writes melodramatic romances under the name Howadji, could find his theme close at hand in "his youthful reminiscences of Brook Farm," which might produce as bizarre a story as "those which he has since made so distant a pilgrimage to seek, in Syria, and along the current of the Nile." The very facts of Brook Farm would constitute an exotic romance.

Hawthorne's work may violate the probability of an "outward narrative" of historical fact precisely to capture the "inner truth and spirit" of the enterprise. Yet Hawthorne fears that in the process he may violate the "spirit" he seeks to evoke. In search of a spirit which continually eludes him, Coverdale loses himself in the defensive activity of narration. Hawthorne exhibits in this character his anxieties abut his own creation. Romance, as Hawthorns defines it in the preface, depends on both retrospection and a personal point of view, and both of these works about progressive reformers have a retrospective or elegiac orientation. Their generic expectations, then, seem opposed to the Utopian aims of the reformers they depict.[13] For both Hawthorne and James, the Utopian romance of their reformers is undone in part through its representation.

Hawthorne continues to seek in romance a middle realm, like that between the fanciful and actual which he discovered in "The Custom-House." But in *The Blithedale Romance,* the opposites Hawthorne seeks to reconcile tend rather to negate each other. A realm which combines material and spiritual worlds is also sought by the Utopian reformers of Brook Farm, who seek to imbue daily life with spiritual meaning, to leaven material labor with expansion of consciousness. Ripley's manifesto for Brook Farm envisioned overcoming various antinomies: between the individual and the community, spiritual and mental labor. The mesmerist employs the same language of matter and spirit as reformer and romancer, claiming, by using the body as the medium for a foreign spirit, to approach "the Absolute." Yet his pursuit becomes a dangerous parody of the romantic quest. By literalizing the oppositions of romance, and reducing spirit to a material essence, mesmerism physicalizes the spiritual and so not only inverts but undoes the poetic synthesis of romance. Thus the three major activities at Blithedale—the pursuit of spiritual life in the reforming community, the search for the absolute manifestation of spirit of mesmerism, and the attempt to imbue material facts with spiritual meaning of the writer—are all versions of romance.[14] Although they mirror each other, they cannot coexist. While mesmerism seems to violate the human spirit most, by reducing it to a physical essence, the personal manipulations of the Blithedalers prove even more deadly to their souls.

As Leo Levy notes, *The Blithedale Romance* begins with a conflict between past and present methods of mesmeric performance.[15] In the first chapter, mesmerism is described in the same terms as those which Hawthorne uses to define romance. Hawthorne shows in both activities a capacity to blend or join disparate realms, as well as a form of dramatic presentation. The spectacle of the Veiled Lady conjoins "all the arts of picturesque disposition," an eighteenth-century aesthetic concern, with the "simplicity and openness of scientific experiment," a modern, nineteenth-century development (pp. 5–6). The book begins with both revelation and mystery: the Veiled Lady's prophecy about the fate of Blithedale and Coverdale's unanswered question to Moodie. Its double plot indicates the presence of oppositions which control the work throughout. Mesmerism and romance are both seen as forms of alternate veiling and unveiling. While mesmerism claims to provide ultimate knowledge, the partial revelations of romance may finally be truer to the human spirit. The Veiled Lady is the symbol of the narrative itself. Her silvery veil, like the veil of fictive representation in romance, isolates its subject from the material bounds of time and place:

"It was white, with somewhat of a subdued silvery sheen . . . and, falling over the wearer form head to foot, was supposed to insulate her from the material world, from time and space, and to endow her with many of the privileges of a disembodied spirit" (p. 6). The Veiled Lady is the personification of the "inner truth and spirit" Hawthorne seeks. Throughout *The Blithedale Romance,* radical reformers seek to lift the veil which exists not only between the Veiled Lady and the earthly world but between past and future, individual and community, body and spirit.

Coverdale, first presented at a performance of the Veiled Lady, may seek a revelation of nature, of art, of personality, or even, in his habitual debasement of view, of Zenobia unclothed. Widespread anticipation of a time when truth will be more fully revealed to men and women leads the Blithedalers to create their Utopian experiment as an exercise in human perfectibility. Having discarded the "old system," the Blithedale reformers seek to remake themselves into spiritually "new men," like redeemed Christians. This spiritual vision, however, is quickly translated into a merely physical one. Coverdale sees his rather superficial conversion by illness as part of the forward progress of the race: "I had a lively sense of the exultation with which the spirit will enter on the next stage of its eternal progress, after leaving the heavy burthen of its mortality in an earthly grave" (p. 61).

Despite Coverdale's anticipation of future progress, he shows little sympathy for Utopian visions. His view of the philosophers on whose writings Brook Farm was based is very literalistic, as he reduces Fourier's complex ideas to the infamous notion of turning the sea into lemonade. He sees Emerson and Fourier as leading their followers towards greater isolation rather than closer community, for the future seems to lie "considerably further into the waste of chaos than the shattered ruins of the past" (p. 52). In this view of human history as moving away from rather than towards order, Blithedale becomes not a dreamlike "theater removed" from the age but the very focus of its tumult; "Everything in nature and human existence was fluid . . . and . . . we ourselves were in the critical vortex" (p. 140). The Blithedale experiment becomes a stormy Melvillean whirlpool on which chaotic pressures threaten to converge.

According to Coverdale, by establishing society and especially labor on a new basis, the Blithedalers hope "to produce an effect upon the material world and its climate" (p. 61). Spiritualization of human life will be implemented, paradoxically, through manual labor, as the Blithedalers attempt to put into practice Emerson's claim in "Nature" that "natural facts are symbols of particular spiritual facts." The Blithedalers seem to harvest symbols rather than crops, seeking "to uncover some aromatic root of wisdom" (p. 65). Labor is their mode of communion with the divine, "our form of prayer and ceremonial of worship." But the sought-for "glimpses into the far-off soul of truth" are not attained: rather, as Hawthorne noted in letters to his future wife Sophia Peabody from Brook Farm, man's soul could be buried under a dung heap. Instead of making nature share the progress of the human spirit, man suffers reverse evolution: "The clods of earth . . . were never etherealized into thoughts. Our thoughts, on the contrary, were fast becoming cloddish. Our labor symbolized nothing, and it left us mentally sluggish in the dusk of the evening" (p. 66). Labor provides the poet with neither leisure nor inspiring material; again, the spiritualization of physical material to poetic expression fails.

While the community exerts itself unsuccessfully to elevate matter into spirit, a figure arrives in the community who personifies the spirit in a different sense. Zenobia says of Priscilla that "as she has hardly any physique, a poet, like Mr. Miles Coverdale, may be allowed to think her spiritual" (p. 3). Though she gradually becomes "more a creature of this world," Priscilla retains uncanny contact with an invisible realm, hearing mysterious voices. She is partly able to attain the Blithedalers' aim, extending the realm of the spirit by projecting herself imaginatively into unseen worlds, She attains uncanny knowledge of the sins of others. Unlike another Hawthorne character with that ability, Young Goodman Brown, Priscilla views others with sympathy rather then condemnation: "She sometimes talked of distant places and splendid rooms, as if she had just left them. Hidden things were visible to her and silence was audible. And in all the world there was nothing so difficult to be endured, by those who had any dark secret to conceal, than the glance of Priscilla's timid and melancholy eyes" (p. 187). Though Priscilla's spirituality seems supernatural, her capacities are the result of sympathy, love for an unknown sister. Rather than seeking to penetrate an otherworldly realm, Priscilla exercises her uncanny "spiritualism" through thwarted longing for her sister and the fashionable world which she inhabits.

Coverdale thinks that he, like Priscilla, can project his spirit by penetrating other lives. By identifying with the spiritual lives of others, Coverdale proposes to know them better than they know themselves: "to live in other lives—by generous sympathies, by delicate intuitions, by taking note of things too slight for record, and by bringing one's human spirit into manifold accordance with the companions whom God assigned—to learn the secret which was hidden even from themselves" (p. 160). Imitation or projection becomes invasion, as Coverdale conflates intimacy and analysis. The nature of friendship, though, according to Emerson, is to forestall analysis: "We are associated . . . with some friend . . . who . . . we lack power to put at such focal distance from us, that we can mend or even analyze them. We cannot choose but love them. . . . When he has . . . become an object of thought . . . his office is closing."[16] Coverdale's attempt to penetrate the lives of others distances him from those he seeks to know best. His "sympathy" becomes a pretext for the Unpardonable Sin, the violation of the human heart by the attempt to learn its deepest secrets. In trying to become clairvoyant, Coverdale has transformed himself into an Ethan Brand, managed to "unhumanize [his] heart" (p. 154). Thus, as Hawthorne implies in that story, the very romantic quest for the spirit is what destroys it.

The search for the spirit in the reform movement is degraded through its literalistic application in mesmerism. While the Blithedalers tend to invade one another's spiritual realms, only when they leave the community for the mesmerist's show is the spirit actually violated, sold for material gain (supposedly to benefit the community). The reformers Zenobia (the sister for whom Priscilla longed) and Hollingsworth betray Priscilla back into servitude as the mesmeric medium, the Veiled Lady. In the hands of the mesmerist, the extension of spirit is degraded into physical sharing of animal spirits: "Nor would it have surprised me had he pretended to hold up . . . the universally pervasive fluid . . . in a glass phial" (p. 200). Mesmerism claims to expand human connections to the rapport of the living and dead, but actually dissolves this world's emotional bonds. Through mesmerism, human emotions are degraded into merely physical substances: "settled grief was but a shadow beneath the influence of a man possessing this potency, and the strong love of years melted away like a vapor" (p. 198). Mesmerism upsets spiritual bonds by releasing one from consciousness of time, the principle of memory on which human relations are based.[17] As an extreme form of the romantic quest, it seeks quite literally to penetrate the veil of mortality, showing the coercive nature of any search for perfect revelation. As an extreme version of the Utopian ideals of the community, mesmerism illustrates the ultimately selfish and illusory nature of any such attempt to remake reality. Yet in its wholesale degradation of ideals, it makes the community's goals seem laudable, if optimistic, by contrast.

Emerson acknowledged that "mesmerism broke into the inmost shrines," but for him this was a valiant revolutionary effort: mesmerism "was human, it was genial, it affirmed unity and connection between remote points."[18] For Hawthorne, by contrast, mesmerism penetrated the "inmost shrine" of the heart. He viewed his fiancée Sophia Peabody's mesmeric treatment as virtually a sexual act: "The sacredness of an individual is violated by it; there would be an intrusion into thy holy of holies—and the intruder would not be thy husband." The devil's bargain of mesmerism sacrifices the highest human aspirations for immediate, doubtful revelation: "What so miserable as to lose the soul's true, though hidden, knowledge and consciousness of heaven, in the midst of an earth-born vision?"[19] By contrast, Hawthorne views the imagination as holy.

Mesmerism seems the inverse of the Blithedalers' hopes for the spiritual evolution of man. The growth of spirit is replaced by a vision of reverse evolution, regression rather than progression, as the course of the human spirit: "We are pursuing a downward course in the eternal march, and thus bring ourselves into the same range with beings whom death, in requital of their gross, evil lives, has degraded below humanity" (p. 199). Mesmerism poses as the price for contact with other spirits the loss of one's individuality, in an absurd parody of the communal ideal: "If these things were to be believed, the individual soul was virtually annihilated . . . and immortality rendered at once impossible and not worth acceptance" (p. 198). Mesmerism imbues the spirit with the mortal odor of death, so that immortality becomes a dreaded fate rather than a desired consummation.

The Utopia proves no Arcadia but a vortex, drawing to it the ceaseless flux of the age. Mesmerism is the most dangerous of the chaotic movements of the time, for it irresponsibly liberates the soul from the body. This "release" leads, on the one hand, to negative evolution into bodies devoid of spirit, and on the other to death, foreshadowing Blithedale's final configuration with the death of Zenobia and the apparent spiritual deaths of Hollingsworth and Coverdale. The inhabitants of Blithedale eventually share only a spiritual purgatory. Finally their spirits can be known only by the death of their bodies, and even then the evidence of their existence is the hated material being rather than the immortal soul.

The conflict between matter and spirit is enacted not only in the plot but the book's mode of representation, in which the status of the community as a version of romance is continually raised. Romance, Hawthorne suggests, may represent a liberating ideal or a false, artificial construction. Images of Blithedale as Eden vie with views of the community as the cruelest sort of "mock-life," with deadly consequences for those who penetrate the artifice.[20] Like the frozen landscape with which the book opens, Blithedale seems to present a "lifeless copy of the world in marble" (p. 38). Coverdale's premonition that this landscape offers a "dim shadow of its [the tale's] catastrophe" is borne out by the pairing of this image with the final vision of Zenobia as the "marble-image of a death-agony" (p. 235). In the death of Zenobia, Arcadian affectation becomes not merely chilling but killing.

Beside the initially vibrant presence of Zenobia, Blithedale "showed like an illusion, a masquerade, a pastoral, a counterfeit Arcadia, in which we grown-up men and women are making a play-day of the years that were given us to live in" (p. 21). The Biblical cadence of the closing phrase alludes to one side of the Blithedale enterprise—the heroic effort to reconsecrate labor, what might be termed its georgic aspect. The "playday" is that of the holiday Arcadia which Blithedale, composed of dreamers and poets, more closely resembles.

The preciousness and artificiality of pastoral in this book is occasionally broken by direct contact with and observation of Nature. Nature, rather than the city, is the realm not accounted for by the Blithedalers' pastoral schemes. Only when he dedicates both body and spirit to physical labor is Coverdale granted a revelation of Nature, though it is partial, transitory, and unexpectedly simple:

> It is very true that, sometimes, gazing casually around me, out of the midst of my toil, I used to discern a richer picturesqueness in the visible scene of earth and sky. There was, at such moments, a novelty, an unwonted aspect, on the face of Nature, as if she had been taken by surprise . . . with no opportunity to put off her real look, and assume the mask with which she mysteriously hides herself from mortals. But this was all. (p. 66)

Coverdale (who is, like Theodore, granted a peek beneath the veil) misses the revelation's meaning by failing to recognize in Nature another being capable of love:

> that peculiar picturesqueness of the scene where capes and headlands put themselves bodily forth upon the perfect level of the meadow . . . the sultry heat-vapor, which rose everywhere like incense, and in which my soul delighted, as indicating so rich a fervor in the passionate day, and in the earth that was burning with its love. (p. 84)

This revelation eschews pastoral for a direct understanding of Nature, the reality that underlies it. The passage shows that the juxtaposition of opposites in the picturesque is a product of passionate feeling which binds man to the earth by an irresistible tie. Here, for a moment, Coverdale seems to see the very origins of the book's creation, as he glimpses the reality behind the romantic convention of the picturesque. Hawthorne suggests that all such conventions are based on a living reality, and that romance at its core is based on sexual desire which is natural and universal. In the nature of representation, that reality can be revealed only sporadically and incompletely.

On his final journey to Blithedale, Coverdale no longer sees the landscape in symbolic terms. Rather, he observes Nature directly, a practice antithetical to the pastoral mode: "My mental eye can even now discern the September grass, bordering the pleasant roadside with a brighter verdure than while the summer heats were scorching it. . . . I see the tufted barberry-bushes, with their small cluster of scarlet fruit; the toadstools, likewise" (p. 205). Yet Coverdale's real revelation of Nature is not the humanized landscape of the picturesque but a glimpse into the river, the heart of darkness in Nature: "a broad, black, inscrutable depth, keeping its own secrets from the eye of man" (p. 237).

By the end of the book, the Blithedale Arcadia is unmasked. The final act of "Arcadian affectation," Zenobia's suicide, shows even Zenobia's subjection to the indignities of Nature after death, as her corpse is found frozen in a humiliating posture. Coverdale has long envisioned the final triumph of the Blithedale community, the fullest extension of spirit over the material world, in the conquest of death: "the final scene shall lose its terrors" (p. 130). Yet the ending of *The Blithedale Romance* illustrates instead man's subjection to death in all its horror: "perhaps the skeleton . . . lay beneath the inscrutable depth . . . with the gripe of its old despair" (p. 208). Zenobia dies in the fear of mortality rather than the hope of eternal life. In life, Zenobia was the most vital member of the community, the only one who could have infused it with "human nature." In death, she exhibits its rigidity and coldness, becoming the "marble image" used earlier to describe Blithedale.

By the end of *The Blithedale Romance,* the attempts of romancer, reformer, and mesmerist to unite the spiritual and material have resulted in the separation of those realms. The "one true system" of human labor gives way to the "system" of Nature, which converts Zenobia into a "crop of weeds." When the Blithedalers, through pride and impetuousness, fail to attain the spiritual development for which they are destined by Nature, Nature quietly claims them for herself. Hawthorne and Coverdale can only testify to the continued ineffability of the spirit which Coverdale has lost more than gained: "It is because the spirit is inestimable that the lifeless body is so little valued." Hawthorne's "mock-world" is overturned by Nature, which tears the veil of romance to show a bleak reality.

Only twelve years after the event can Coverdale bear to recollect his life at Blithedale and attempt to interpret it. With the death of Zenobia, the possibility for further experience in the book fades. Hollingsworth grows weak and submissive, Coverdale incapable of activity. Blithedale has robbed Coverdale of further capacity for experience as well as of the limited abilities he had when he went there—poetic talent and willingness to work. Coverdale's narration is a way of trying to break the stranglehold of the past on the present, the unendurable way in which "a past mode of life prolongs itself into a succeeding one" (p. 154). In his retrospective narration, Coverdale attempts to conquer "real life" by rearranging it into the artificial form of romance.[21]

The interlude at Blithedale has deprived Coverdale of future satisfaction as surely as it has Hollingsworth, who remains haunted by Zenobia. The characters are reconstructed to become creations of Coverdale's "haunted mind." The opening image of the glowing coal (p. 9), a metaphor for romantic imagination, which becomes the glowing fire of Blithedale, implies that the scene is set within Coverdale's mind. The transformation of Zenobia, Hollingsworth, and Priscilla into figures in Coverdale's imagination enables him to "turn the affair into a ballad" (p. 33). The diminution of characters accomplished in this process is revealed in Hawthorne's preface, in which Zenobia, Hollingsworth, and Priscilla become two-dimensional, miniaturized figures in order to fit his "fancy-sketch."

Though James recognized in *The Blithedale Romance* the presence of the "vulgar, many-coloured world of actuality" which pervades his *The Bostonians,* he increasingly viewed the action of *Blithedale* as imaginary and abstract, getting more and more "out of reality" as the story progresses. For James, *The Blithedale Romance* presented life as seen in a mental mirror, "the kind of reflection the things we know best and see oftenest may make in our minds."[22] The view of *The Blithedale Romance*'s actions as projections from Coverdale's mental realm is shown especially by his dreams. In his view they often fore-shadow later events, for, like the opening prediction of the Veiled Lady, they provide a riddle "one of whose interpretations has certainly accorded with the event" (p. 6). The dreams are a static and symbolic version of the situations which are eventually spun out into narrative. The "fixed idea" of Coverdale's first night's dreams, if recorded, he feels "would have anticipated several of the chief incidents of this narrative, including a dim Shadow of its catastrophe" (p. 38). Coverdale believes that his dreams foreshadow future events, like ro-mance's allegorical "shadowings" of reality, though this seems to be his self-centered view.

The use of dream or reverie as the foundation of imaginative creation does not imply that the visions so produced are shadowy or vague. Rather, in an image which shows artistic creativity stemming directly from unconscious sources, Coverdale describes Silas Foster's wife, knitting while asleep, "abso-lutely footing a stocking out of the texture of a dream. And a very substantial stocking it seemed to be" (p. 32). But Coverdale's attempts to understand or solve the problems raised at Blithedale through his narration remain unsuccess-ful. According to Coverdale, Blithedale was "but a dream-work and an enchant-ment" (p. 207). The retreat to Blithedale was intended to "work out" the prob-lems of daily life. But Coverdale's subsequent inability to engage in experience may indicate either that the purgation was incomplete, or that dreamlike Blithe-dale became a real, traumatic experience.

The composition of romance is the final dream-work, Coverdale's way of trying to overcome a disturbing experience. As Hawthorne shows, however, Coverdale's romance has only kept him imprisoned in an empty reality. Blithe-dale has indeed become a "fixed idea" with Coverdale, as if its characters had become a permanent part of his mental furniture. His efforts to interpret the situation, even at a distance of twelve years, fail: "I tried to analyze this impres-sion, but not with much success" (p. 21). The riddles and puzzles which pervade *The Blithedale Romance* remain enigmatic. Their symbolic solution is found not in analysis but dreams, the vital source of romance, which remain resistant to explanation. The veil of romance narrative finally conceals as much as it reveals; Hawthorne dramatizes the distorting qualities of representation to es-cape being enchanted by romance into the spiritual paralysis of Coverdale.

The desolate, demystified atmosphere in which *The Blithedale Romance* concludes is that of *The Bostonians* from the outset. Many critics of the two books see James as expanding Hawthorne's characters and situations. James himself lends credence to this view when he says of Zenobia (whom he consid-ered Hawthorne's fullest creation as a character) that "we fill out the figure and even lend to the vision something more than Hawthorne intended."[23] Yet James fills out his work in part by using figurative or symbolic aspects. James's extensive descriptions of settings provide not so much a social background as a theatrical backdrop for his characters. As he says, in giving a detailed picture of New York's Second Avenue when Basil Ransom moves there, "A figure is nothing without a setting." While James attempts to link his story more fully than Hawthorne's to actual time and place, setting scenes in Boston, New York, and Cape Cod, each of those scenes is somewhat romanticized (Cape Cod becomes a New England Arcadia, the "Italy of Massachusetts"). James also makes several allusions to themes of Hawthorne associated with the enchantments of romance. Mesmerism is translated into the charlatanic ministrations of Selah Tarrant to his daughter (he is described in the same terms as Hawthorne's mesmerist, Westervelt). Without evoking the mysticism of Hawthorne's mesmerism, James reveals the sexual manipulation mesmerism implies. The silvery veil Zenobia flings over Priscilla becomes the ordinary cloak with which Olive enwraps Verena, but the elements of coercion and evil remain.

In *The Blithedale Romance,* Coverdale tries to recoup his experience by transforming the characters he remembers into figures in his own mind. In *The Bostonians,* James also treats the distortions of point of view, as his characters seem largely impenetrable to each other. Yet in James's work retrospection is clarifying rather than distorting. Memory is a source of revelation in *The Bostonians,* and when it occasionally appears, the whole landscape is ennobled. In *The Bostonians,* "the atmosphere of strange enchantment" of Hawthorne's preface to *The Blithedale Romance* is largely absent, though characters try to evoke this atmosphere, especially in their views of landscapes. The inescapably prosaic modern world makes characters try to romanticize it. When Verena looks at the urban landscape revealed in Olive's view over the Back Bay, she sees in it an instance of the sublime:

> The western windows of Olive's drawing room, looking over the water, took in the red sunsets of winter; . . . the casual patches of ice and snow; . . . the extrusion . . . of a few chimneys and steeples, straight, sordid tubes of factories and engine-shops. . . . There was something inexorable in the poverty of he scene, shameful in the meanness of its details, which gave a collective impression of boards and tin and frozen earth, sheds and rotting piles, . . . and bare wooden backs of places. Verena thought such a view lovely, and she was by no means without excuse when, as the afternoon closed, the ugly picture was tinted with a clear, cold rosiness. . . . There were pink flushes on snow . . . lonely outlines of distant dusky undulations against the fading glow. (p. 963)

Verena's back view over the Back Bay reveals a realm of romance which is not entirely an illusion; James seems to affirm her view not only by direct statement but in the lyricism of the closing line of this passage. Here a romantic perspective is provided on a present-day scene to create the urban sublime. But James usually provides romantic associations through a "backward view" in another sense, the retrospective and elegiac bias of the book. From the romantic heritage of the defeated South to the Arcadian imagery associated with Verena, *The*

Bostonians affords glimpses of an older world underlying the relentlessly modern 1870s. While Hawthorne, in his preface to *The Blithedale Romance,* contrasts romance with history, James turns historical events themselves into romance.

As James implies in *Hawthorne,* for him Hawthorne represents the pre-Civil War past of America and his own youth. By means of the scene in Memorial Hall, when the war is explicitly recalled, James reaches across the barrier between them. Though the nation may have lost its spiritual values after the war, the war itself seems their finest expression. Memorial Hall, which Basil and Verena visit in a climactic scene, is represented as a temple to memory. The image of union, whose sundering has resulted in the desolate world of *The Bostonians,* is reconstructed in this memorial to the Union dead. Basil's willingness to visit such a monument implicitly evokes for both him and Verena the possibility of their future union. The Civil War, whose effects are elsewhere subliminally evident, is presented in the scene in Memorial Hall as a host of values treasured by memory, almost as the restorative and ennobling force of memory itself. The narrative shifts into present tense as James recreates a scene familiar to him: "It stands there for duty and honor, it speaks of sacrifice and example, seems a kind of temple to youth, manhood, generosity." The place is testimony to the real existence of the past and of moral values. Memorial Hall is the only true symbol of union in the book: "It arched over friends as well as enemies, the victims of defeat as well as the sons of triumph." It serves as a center of value by releasing the emotions which elsewhere in *The Bostonians* seem impossible to attain: the "lifting of the heart" in the presence of nobility, "the sentiment of beauty" (pp. 1024–25). James implies that the new generation has lost its moral tone through a collective loss of memory. Only rarely does the past illuminate the present, and then, as in Olive's case, memory may be too painful to bear: "These hours of backward clearness come to all men and women, once at least, when they read the past in the light of the present" (p. 1181).[24]

In *The Blithedale Romance,* memory is the light in which characters are ennobled and idealized, as Cloverdale predicts that after their deaths the Blithedalers will be seen as legendary or epic figures, larger than life: "What legends of Zenobia's beauty, and Priscilla's slender and shadowy grace [will be told]. . . . In due course of ages, we must all figure heroically in an epic poem" (p. 129). That idealization of character is fulfilled in *The Bostonians,* in which the reformers of Hawthorne's era assume heroic stature. James accuses *The Blithedale Romance* of insufficient satire. But James's realistic satire of contemporary reformers depends on romance as embodied by Hawthorne's generation, an alternative world that is now irrecoverable. Hawthorne's contemporaries are the ideal against which James's degenerate reformers are measured.

Political conflict is expressed by the form of representation as well as its subject. In *The Bostonians,* the divisions between the regions and the sexes after the Civil War are expressed partly by the lack of a central consciousness (there is an intrusive narrator), and the separation of sequences by geographical location. James has been widely accused of "aestheticizing" politics in his political novels, *The Bostonians* and *The Princess Casamassima.* But politics is not so much aestheticized as internalized in these works. The conflicting aims of anarchists and society are recapitulated in the consciousness of *The Princess Casamassima*'s hero, Hyacinth Robinson. In addition, as Lionel Trilling has shown that Hyacinth's choice is ultimately between art and tradition on the one hand and revolution on the other, James shows the political dimension of art itself.[25]

In *The Bostonians,* by treating the politics of personal relationships, James does not so much dematerialize political issues as address the principal sphere in which they were constituted in the late nineteenth century, the "latent romance" of New England. The transformation of politics into personality is shown in the figure James uses to describe Olive Chancellor. He notes that her smile "was like a ray of moonlight on a prison wall," recalling the opening of *The Scarlet Letter,* when Hawthorne presents the prison as a symbol of Puritan society and institutions. Now the prison appears within the mind of Olive Chancellor, which has internalized Puritan conscience.

In *The Bostonians,* the Blithedalers' Utopian, reformist enterprise has been reduced to communities which uneasily combine political and social life: the Oneida community, viewed as sexually decadent, or the Wednesday Club of New York, presenting social issues for the enjoyment of aristocrats. James shows how political issues have become personal ones—almost necessarily so in the case of feminism, but generally true in a world where the distinctions between private and public realms have collapsed.

Despite these debased versions of community, the panacea for most of the book's characters seems to be a "union" in one of several senses: the union of women in the feminist movement envisioned by Olive; the union of those in the larger political "movement," which, for Miss Birdseye, overrides personal distinctions; or the union of the "marriage-tie." In the background of all these unions is the Union so recently sundered in the Civil War. The desire to repair this breach is expressed by the first act of the book, Olive's invitation to her Southern cousin to visit her and heal the wounds of war. Though the war is rarely mentioned specifically, its results are apparent in many of the book's phenomena: the wasted and wintry landscape, the fracturing of regions, and the disjunction between the sexes. In the "reconstruction" of union in the pleas of the feminists or the actions of the Southerner turned "carpetbagger-in-reverse," the conflict between the sexes replays, in its imagery, the war between the states, as "war to the knife."[26] Politics is internalized, based largely on the romantic convictions of the reformers that they are engaged in a new war or "revolution."

Olive's conviction that Basil "had admitted that North and South were a single, indivisible political organism" (p. 812) is belied by his acute regionalism and his vast hunger for success, which represents a refusal to admit defeat. Once the idea of reunion has been abandoned, Olive feels "an unreasoned terror of the effect of his [Basil's] presence" (p. 820). From the third chapter on, the rivalry of Olive and Basil is described as a war. Olive departs from the feminist meeting at Miss Birdseye's in a "retreat"; Basil, unexpectedly entering her home, had "stolen a march upon her privacy." Olive finds battle imagery seductive, viewing feminism as war to the death: "This was the great, the just revolution . . . it must exact from the other, the brutal, blood-stained, ravening race, the last particle of expiation" (pp. 834–35). Olive's notion of the oppression of women as an "organized wrong" implies an analogy between the institution of slavery and the institutionalized subjugation of women.[27] By conceiving of feminism itself as a battle, she repeats the strife of war. Olive's romantic imaginings here are melodramatic and apocalyptic, enabling her to play a role she was denied in the Civil War because she is a woman.

In fact, the revolution Olive envisions would in some ways be as conservative as the overtly reactionary schemes of Basil. She seeks to reinfuse the age with "the great feminine element" (p. 918), which in her view will enable her contemporaries to "feel and speak more sharply." Basil seeks, by contrast, to re-establish "the ability to dare and venture, to know and yet not fear reality" which he sees as the province of the "masculine character" (p.1111). Both see the age as demoralized, as does James, but neither of their solutions seems to correspond to traits distinctive to men or women. Though both are out of tune with their time to some extent, their view that the age is devitalized is borne out by many of the phenomena of *The Bostonians*. The stunted landscape, like its inhabitants, seems to long for renewal. In an age of "masculine women and feminine men," new birth requires redefinition and reunion of the sexes. The land cannot achieve a springtime, and if in *The Blithedale Romance* "the world had imposed itself as a hitherto unwedded bride" (p. 128), in *The Bostonians* Nature has become infertile, as desire for union is present on the side neither of Nature nor of man.

The reform movement, to which Olive looks as a source of regeneration, has, as embodied in a figure like Mrs. Tarrant, "blinked and shuffled and . . . grown dreadfully limp" (p. 867). Reformers have become continual performers, with an "air of living always in the gaslight." In all of the reformers who gather at Miss Birdseye's house, public life has effected some distortion. The presumptive savior of the reform movement, as well as the harbinger of sexual reconciliation and renewal, is Verena Tarrant. Verena is seen as a version of the "New England spirit" also represented by Priscilla, in its last, largely degenerate form. James envisions the combination of Verena and Olive as a symbol of the power of women which could be redemptive: Verena notes, "You are my conscience," and Olive replies, "You are my form—my envelope" (p. 946).

By contrast to those reformers whose private lives have been subsumed in their public roles, Verena's public persona is simply herself. Whether she is perfectly natural or perfectly artificial cannot be determined. The private and public, personal and political, begin to merge in the character of Verena, whose appeal is based largely on her personal appearance and charm. Despite her great exposure to publicity, she remains as enigmatic as Priscilla. In her capacity for performance, she embodies the ability to synthesize opposites which gave stature to the character of Zenobia. The first description of Verena attributes many of Zenobia's qualities to her: "she looked like an Oriental"; her hair, like Zenobia's flower, "looks as if her blood had gone into it," and her appearance is "rich . . . strong and supple" (p. 854). She also embodies some of Priscilla's traits, especially the "sibylline attributes" against which James initially protested in his commentary on *The Blithedale Romance*. But Hawthorne's rather mystical character has become in James's work a recognizable type, the young American girl. Olive realizes that despite the threat of "public exploitation," Verena has been unharmed by public exposure, entirely uncontaminated by evil.

Verena has an epicurean attitude towards experience. Unlike Priscilla, she is a thoroughly modern woman entranced by the urban spectacle, for she has the "blood of the night-walking Tarrants in her veins." Her responsiveness and sensitivity make her, for Olive, an "artist"—a typically American one, for she is "poor in experience." Verena's initial encounters with Olive seem to offer access to a realm of greater activity and knowledge: "she felt taken up as by a bird of the air." But the image shows Verena as Olive's prey. The "bright, many-coloured world" for which Verena longs is not finally what will violate her spirit. For Olive, to whom the world of society and pleasure presents itself as a "temptation," the feminist mission requires that she isolate Verena from other ties and experiences.

Love both enchants and enchains Verena in her relationship to Olive: "Verena was completely under the charm . . . The fine web of authority, of dependence, that her strenuous companion had woven about her, was now as dense as a suit of golden mail" (p. 956). In their relation, James shows the kinds of enchantment and betrayal practiced by characters in *The Blithedale Romance*. Here he sees such enchantment specifically as the result of Olive's unacknowledged sexual attraction to Verena. But the imprisoning web, Olive's charm literalized, also arms Verena as a latter-day Joan of Arc. The delicate imagery of Olive's "web of authority" eventually yields to the more violent image of Basil as "lion-tamer." In the conflict between Basil and Olive for Verena, we see the final fate of the New England spirit which Verena seems to represent. Verena's "essence," which both Olive and Basil claim to preserve, is simply the "extraordinary generosity with which she could . . . give herself away" (p. 1152). When Olive makes Verena rehearse her speeches, Verena loses her spontaneous "inspiration," the final name for her spirit.

Despite her modern, urban background, Verena is often described in pastoral terms. In *The Bostonians,* except for a penultimate sequence on Cape Cod (the "Italy of Massachusetts"), pastoral is present only by allusion or intermittently. Even when Basil and Verena temporarily escape New York's bustle in Central Park, they see at the park's edge a reminder of urban poverty, "groups of the unemployed, the children of disappointment from beyond the seas" (p. 1116). Olive, in an extremely artificial pastoral vision, yearns to place Verena indoors, under a tree. To Basil she seems untouched by the world: "she reminded him of . . . vales of Arcady" (p. 1007). Verena is an Arcadian figure in a democratic pastoral, a free and sensuous maiden of rigid, repressed Boston. She embodies an eternal type in nineteenth-century form, the rebirth of the spirit of the golden age in unexpected guise. Her name and youth imply that she is the spring itself, a source of life in her own person: "everything fresh and fair renewed itself in her with extraordinary facility, everything ugly and tiresome evaporated as soon as it touched her" (p. 962). Olive thinks of her as maintaining direct contact with divinity: "holding from far-off ancestors, or even perhaps straight from the divine generosity, much more than from . . . ugly or stupid progenitors" (p. 908). While Olive gives her greater social mobility, Basil offers her the freedom of young love expressed in the language of Cavalier poetry: "Come out, come out with me" (p. 1094). Verena and Basil habitually meet out-of-doors, in such public settings as Central Park, and their discourse has the freedom of tone "in which happy, flower-crowned maidens may have talked to sunburnt young men in the golden age" (p. 1009). But their pastoral retreat soon becomes an excessively insulated private bower.[28]

In her last reported speech, Verena envisions a reintegration of the public and private realms which will reconcile men and women. Verena claims that women can only attain freedom by closer friendship with men. She pleads for a politics of intimacy in which the genius of women will become, in a phrase taken from Hawthorne, the "elixir of life." Like the Utopians of Blithedale, Verena foresees a new Paradise as the result of her ideas: "You would think you were in Eden" (p. 1048). In Verena's view, the reintegration of women into the public and political realms will bring about peace. Their fate will determine, on a national as well as a personal scale, "whether the world shall be a place of injustice or a place of love" (p. 858).

Verena's speech describes a feminist Utopia, a future in which the battle of the sexes will cease. Basil responds to Verena's plea for a "union far more intimate" with a singularly unsympathetic conviction: "She was meant for something divinely different—for privacy, for him, for love" (p. 1049). By personalizing what is supposed to be a political message, Basil exercises a power of his own. In interpreting her virtues as useful only to him, he "attributed to Miss Tarrant a singular hollowness of character" (p. 857). It is not surprising that once the feminist movement has sought a savior in Verena, who is appealing primarily as an attractive and charismatic speaker, the feminist issue should be displaced into the personal realm. Love has become the central arena for struggles of power, not only between rivals for the same loved one but between lovers themselves.

In showing the personalization of politics, James does not betray the feminist movement but rather underlines one of its themes: that the personal is also political. Hawthorne shows the abandonment of political ideals because of selfish desires, while James treats the effect of public politics on individual desires. James shows the discrepancy between imagination and reality by demonstrating the contrast between feminist ideals and the reality of male-female relations as defined by socially constructed sexuality. The idealized, romantic dreams of the feminists are subverted by what is generally taken to be a "true romance" of heterosexual love, though, as James shows, the political issues are simply reconstituted in that realm. What in conventional terms should be the romantic side of James's book, the love relationship (surrounded by often-ironic pastoral imagery), becomes instead the "grim reality" of an unhappy marriage: there is no fulfilled desire, as romance confronts reality.

The courtship of Verena and Basil, which follows the fortunes of his political ideas and is largely composed of his exposition of them, becomes a reenactment of the Civil War in which the original loser becomes the winner. Basil wants to free Verena from Olive, the women's movement, and modern cant, as Olive sought to sever her from all other attachments—to "detach her from her ties, her belongings." Finally Verena meets Basil involuntarily, under his compulsion. Basil seduces her with conservative rhetoric which Verena finds bitter and appalling. But the more she abhors his views, the more Verena becomes subject to his dominance, until the idea of women as slaves of men is literalized when Verena feels "as if she were straining at a leash" (p. 1117). Basil's original view of Verena assumes a sinister tone: "She was tremendously open to attack, she was meant for love, she was meant for him" (p. 1139). The abolitionist Miss Birdseye sees in the alleged conversion of Basil Ransom a triumph of reconstruction, without realizing that the chain pulls the other way: "It warmed her heart to see the stiff-necked young Southerner led captive by a daughter of New England trained in the right school" (p. 1140). The image of love as captivity recalls Coverdale's bitter musings in *The Blithedale Romance* about women's willingness to incur voluntarily the slavery in which men have held them for so long. In her attraction to Basil, Verena mistakes political force for love. Even as Olive displaces pride in her own talents into admiration of Verena's beauty and charm, Verena abandons the power of her gift of speech to follow a man whose ultimate attraction may be his vulnerability (as a South-

erner and a failure in business). But for Basil and Verena, the alternate vulnerability and sense of power which come with love are used not to create a bond
of mutual enhancement but to contain public struggles within private life, where
the feminist challenge to male authority will, in this case, be entirely defeated.

Basil battles ultimately not for Verena but against her, assailing the maiden
in her "cottage-fortress." His strongest opposition is provided by the proposed
"winter campaign" of the feminists, which is to commence with Verena's address at the Boston Music Hall. Basil now opposes Verena's public triumph:
"he didn't care for her engagement, her campaigns, or all the expectancy of her
friends; to 'squelch' all that at a stroke was the dearest wish of his heart. It
would represent to him his own success, it would symbolise his victory" (p.
1164). By successfully wooing Verena, Basil accomplishes a conquest in several senses—of North by South, feminine by masculine, confirmed success by
recent failure, and of her own better judgment by his will.

In the book's last section, a series of mythic allusions almost obscure the
present action. Basil's "ransoming" of Verena is associated with the freeing of
the slaves, while Olive's appearance before the audience recalls the acts of Paris
revolutionaries: "She might have suggested to him some feminine firebrand of
Paris revolutions, erect on a barricade, or even the sacrificial figure of Hypatia,
whirled through the furious mob of Alexandria" (p. 1217). As the book becomes
more enmeshed in mythic archetypes, James also draws a link to history, implying that romance and history are not opposed. But James restores us to the
present by undercutting romantic archetypes (the allusion to Verena as An-
dromeda with Basil as her noble rescuer, Perseus), showing James's realistic
subversion of romance to resist its melodramatic patterns.

Amidst the mythic references, there is a clear allusion to Hawthorne. As
the tide turns in Basil's favor, Olive achieves the martyrdom she sought from
the beginning. Waiting for Verena to return from a boat ride with Basil, Olive
"made long stations" at intervals along the shore, like Christ at the stations of
the cross (p. 1179). In this scene, as Olive finds "tragic relief" waiting for
Verena, she imagines "the boat overturned and drifting out to sea, and (after a
week of nameless horror) the body of an unknown young woman, defaced
beyond recognition, but with long auburn hair and in a white dress, washed up
in some faraway cove" (p. 1182). This passage is reminiscent of the ending of
The Blithedale Romance, in which the resurfacing of the drowned body of
Zenobia represents the darker passions which the Blithedale community has
attempted to deny. One critic notes that Hawthorne can consider Zenobia's body
only when she is dead. So in this scene, issues that have been repressed in *The
Bostonians*—death, which the characters deny in their inability to accept the
tragedy of the war; and sexuality, the implicit theme of the book—return to the
surface.

In the last meeting of Olive and Basil, Olive's momentary triumph leads her to utter a strange laugh: "there broke from her lips a shrill, unfamiliar, troubled sound, which performed the office of a laugh, a laugh of triumph, but which, at a distance, might have passed almost as well for a wail of despair" (p. 1184). At this point, Olive thinks she has won the battle; her laugh echoes that of Robin in Hawthorne's "My Kinsman, Major Molineux." Robin's laugh implies his assent to the guilt of revolution; here, by laughing, Olive succumbs to the violence and aggression of revolution. Her carefully ordered and nonpopulist reform movement gives way to a glimpse of violence and anarchy in the tragic conclusion.

The book's final scenes are laid in a setting less a battleground than an arena for martyrdom. The Boston Music Hall, seen as a Roman colosseum, is a setting for the combat of gladiators, where battle provides a victim for the mob: "He had a throb of uneasiness at his private purpose of balking it of its entertainment, its victim—a glimpse of the ferocity that lurks in a disappointed mob" (p. 1201). The book's long battle draws to a close as Basil envisions himself, in this place of performance, as another intruder into a theater—the assassin of Lincoln. Basil's private purpose has become politically sinister, at odds with the people.

Seeing Verena's pain in the conflict he causes only heightens Basil's desire to "save" her. Verena will not undergo public martyrdom; rather, Olive, facing the mob in her absence, suffers where Verena would have been applauded. Yet by being thus subjected, Olive realizes her fondest hope and exhibits her finest nature. At the end of *The Bostonians,* Olive attains the martyrdom she sought. Like Robin at the end of "My Kinsman, Major Molineux," Olive virtually joins the mob, its center as either leader or victim, absorbed into history. At the end, Olive enters into a romanticized history, achieving heroism: "she could have rushed on it without a tremor, like the heroine that she was" (p. 1217). (See figure 5.)

In the final scene of *The Bostonians,* Basil literally detaches Verena from her other ties, separating her from the embraces of her mother, Olive, and others. Basil's affection for Verena is, in his view, the "ransom" to release her from slavery. But in the last scene, Basil takes possession of Verena with the same cloaking gesture used earlier by live (and echoed from *The Blithedale Romance*). Rather than freeing her, Basil substitutes one form of domination for another. He "ransoms" Verena at the expense of her own will, which is overridden and then subtly violated.[29]

In the last paragraph, Verena's "identity," concealed by her hood, is already being effaced. She and Basil are absorbed, unrecognized, into the great crowd, and their "union, so far from brilliant" (p. 1219), seems to promise anonymity rather than privacy. The violation of Verena's selfhood, which earlier led her to sit in darkness at Marmion in a "kind of shame," now finds her "in tears" while Basil is "palpitating with his victory" (p. 1218). The element

Figure 5. Eugène Delacroix, *Liberty Leading the People,* 1830

See *The Bostonians,* p. 1217: "She might have suggested to him some feminine firebrand of Paris revolutions, erect on a barricade, or even the sacrificial figure of Hypatia, whirled through the furious mob of Alexandria."

(Courtesy Giraudon/Art Resource, N.Y.)

of domination in sexuality is made explicit in this final vignette. Distinctly, his sexual triumph represents her humiliation and defeat. The battle has been won and a new union begun. Verena's surrender, however, represents capitulation to a greater power rather than free assent to a union. Swayed by a will with which she momentarily identifies her own, Verena, James implies, will soon find herself the victim of the stronger will. This violation of Verena's individuality occurs not, like Olive's, in the name of a cause but in the name of love itself. Basil has released Verena from one form of captivity into a more permanent and intimate bondage which will stifle not only her love of experience but her "epicurean" spirit.

The violent conflicts of "those who love, or those who hate, at some acme of passion" (*The Blithedale Romance,* p. 213), inevitably end in catastrophe. Zenobia and Olive are in turn betrayed by the people they have sacrificed. The conclusions of the novels, the falls of proud women, are personal disasters, suffering both self-imposed and humiliating. The "grace of tragedy" is supplanted by the pathetic and vivid images of Olive flinging herself on the crowd and Zenobia frozen in mingled supplication and defiance. With the concluding references to a physical world to which the romance bears only the resemblance of a fairyland, we emerge from the dream worlds of *The Blithedale Romance* and *The Bostonians* into a mode of representation so realistic that it shatters the fiction.

In some ways, James reverses Hawthorne's emphasis by focusing on the love relationship rather than the reform movement. But he shows that the private relation of Verena and Basil has public implications, especially when Basil's final act is compared to an assassination. Though the ending may be read optimistically to see Olive as carrying on the lecture in Verena's place, James implies an ultimate disjunction between private and public life which will never be healed. The New England spirit represented, however ambiguously, by Verena is destroyed. Such an ending reinforces the disappearance of romance in the world of *The Bostonians* and confirms James's realism. But the force of that realism depends on the evocation of romance enchantment, pastoralism, and symbolism, through which James makes vivid the spirit that is lost.

In *The Blithedale Romance* and *The Bostonians,* Hawthorne and James use a retrospective point of view to depict the romance of reform and idealism, but this backward orientation is opposed to the plot of Utopian, futurist aspiration. Hawthorne and James do not necessarily express conservative or reactionary views. Instead, the subversion of romance by realism in these works illustrates the ultimate unreality of Utopian dreams which project a shape onto life, for such projections may veil selfish desires. Reformers seek a higher reality by continually imbuing the material world with the human spirit until reality is perfectly known. In *The Bostonians* and *The Blithedale Romance,* James and Hawthorne, unlike the reformers they describe, do not seek some absolute revelation in a vision of the future, but reflect on a moment of past crisis.[30] The romantic structure of the Utopian communities is revealed by the writers' representations, which use but subvert romance by showing the discrepancy between ideal and reality. Hawthorne and James reveal the distance between individual desire and communal goal, which suggests that the meaning of the reform movements lies not in their future goals but their past history.

While Hawthorne ultimately breaks the romantic illusion to show the spiritual emptiness of his characters, James uses Hawthorne and his generation to represent a past which continually underlies the present and shows the possibility of a more spiritual life, if only by its absence from the modern world. While the reformers of *The Blithedale Romance* and *The Bostonians* seek the increasing spiritualization of daily life in order to attain perfect knowledge of reality, the writers' use of spiritualization is very different: "By long brooding over our recollections, we subtilize them into something akin to imaginary stuff" (*The Blithedale Romance,* p. 105). An unmediated relation to the historical past is only another Utopian dream. Hawthorne concludes that his narrative cannot replace the lost reality of his Brook Farm experience. For James, the past itself has become romantic, the only locale of a fullness felt to be absent from the present; value becomes something which can only be imagined, because it does not exist anywhere.

6

"I and the Abyss":
Transcendental Romance in *The Wings of the Dove*

The elaborate details of James's Major Phase novels have led many critics to view them as triumphs of realism, while others have acknowledged their more fabular and fantastic elements. Even the title *The Wings of the Dove* suggests the parabolic nature of that book (the phrase comes from the Psalms). The title also alludes to Hawthorne's *The Marble Faun,* in which the character Hilda lives in a tower frequented by doves. Hilda, Hawthorne's American girl, resembles to some degree the "dove" of James's title, the "heiress of all the ages," Milly Theale. In *The Wings of the Dove,* James adapts and extends Hawthorne's symbols to produce a new kind of realism. The infusion of romance into realism enables James to capture a reality beyond that of the material world, one apprehended by consciousness. By creating that alternate realm, consciousness may even traverse the barrier between life and death.

As James assimilated Hawthornian romance into his own style in the 1904 Hawthorne Centenary essay, in *The Wings of the Dove* (written a few years earlier), Hawthorne has been so absorbed into James's work that he becomes part of James's method, not only a subject for allusion. In this chapter, then, rather than comparing *The Wings of the Dove* extensively to a work by Hawthorne (*The Marble Faun* is most influential here) to illustrate similarities in theme or plot, I will show how James uses particular images and symbols from that work as the basis of a new mode of narration. The inconsistencies and gaps in *The Marble Faun* which James notes and which Hawthorne himself acknowledges become for James the spaces where spirituality can be articulated. James here elaborates the surface of the novel virtually to the breaking point in order to make it reveal depths—emotional, psychological, spiritual. Thus, the mystery of romance is provided in *The Wings of the Dove* through the very details of a rich social milieu. As a result, James opens up a way for the nonmaterial to be expressed through the material world, which may be what he refers to when he describes the work in the preface as one of "indirection." If *The Marble Faun* implicitly raises mythic and religious issues through romance (for instance, the idea of the fortunate fall), this most religious of James's works addresses those issues even more fully than Hawthorne does, though through a representation in which romance is clothed in the most glittering appearances of actuality.

The Marble Faun, Hawthorne's last completed romance, probably influenced James more than any other work by Hawthorne. As James acknowledges in the 1879 *Hawthorne,* Hawthorne helped him conceive of the International Theme: "We owe him, as a contribution to the immemorial process of lively repartee between the motherland and the daughter, the only pages of the business that can be said to belong to pure literature."[1] Indeed, Marius Bewley has shown that Hawthorne's influence on James began with an early story, "The Last of the Valerii" (1868), written in the same decade as *The Marble Faun.*[2] Yet James's comments on *The Marble Faun* express ambivalence. On the one hand, he sees it as more realistic than Hawthorne's earlier works, particularly in its guidebook-like descriptions of Rome. On the other, he criticizes Hawthorne for indulging in "moonshiny romance" and for making the character Donatello "more like a strain of music than a piece of writing": "The action wavers between the streets of Rome, whose literal features the author perpetually sketches, and a vague realm of fancy in which quite a different verisimilitude prevails."[3] Indeed, the synthesis of actual and fanciful Hawthorne achieved in earlier works had deteriorated by this point, as he would not complete another romance after *The Marble Faun.* In some ways, the romance is constituted by such slippages, which constitute the mystery of the story. (See figure 6.)

In his commentary on *The Marble Faun,* James continually seeks a realism which Hawthorne did not try to provide. James especially tries to identify instances of psychological verisimilitude in Hawthorne's work. The moment of Hilda's confession and that of the murder over the abyss of the Tarpeian Rock are James's favorite scenes because they capture universal psychological truths—the efficacy of confession in ridding the soul of guilt, the universal potential for murderous impulses. In 1879, James views images like the doves as "picturesque conceits" not connected to "real psychology." Yet in his own work, he achieves "real psychology," paradoxically, by developing Hawthorne's images into symbolic patterns. What appears in Hawthorne's work as a literal place or an image (such as the abyss, based on the actual site of the Tarpeian Rock) becomes symbolic or allegorical in James. The abyss, presented as an actual place (a canyon in the Alps) in Milly Theale's first appearance, increasingly becomes an image that haunts her.

In the 1879 *Hawthorne,* James finds the "art of narration" in *The Marble Faun* more at fault than in Hawthorne's other works (as Hawthorne himself frequently comments on the inconsistency and lack of continuity of his own narrative). In the 1897 essay, however, James finds "the art of narration" the most interesting aspect of the story: the drama is "less complete than that of the almost larger element that I can only call the landscape and the spirit . . . the message, the mystery of the medium in which his actors move . . . the breath of old Rome, the sense of old Italy." The distance between the elements of fantasy and the actual setting in *The Marble Faun,* which James initially saw as disabling, becomes the chief merit of the book for him. He now sees that distance, and the more mystical elements of the book generally, as creating a romantic atmosphere which is even more important than the plot. At the end of this essay, James turns the images to which he consistently reverts—the abyss of the Tarpeian Rock or the doves of Hilda's tower—into metaphors for the creative process: "His beautiful, light imagination is the wing that on the autumn evening just brushes the dusky window. It was a faculty that gave him much more a terrible sense of human abysses than a desire rashly to sound them and rise to the surface with his report. On the surface—the surface of the soul and the edge of the tragedy—he preferred to remain."[4] Here the wings of the dove become explicitly the wings of imagination, the abyss the depths of moral and psychological understanding. For James, Hawthorne's imagination, however powerful, remains incomplete in its explorations, for he does not delve into the moral issues he identifies.

Thus James sees the gaps or discrepancies in Hawthorne's work as constituting his romantic medium, the atmosphere of distance, which dominates over the plot or "drama." In his own work, James makes the methodological issue in Hawthorne—the gap between sign and meaning—into the very subject of his plot. For his drama concerns, in several guises, the attempt of consciousness to unite with life, especially in Milly Theale's desire to "live all she can" under the sentence of death. James begins, as he recommended to Hawthorne, by taking a model from real life, his long-dead cousin Minnie Temple. But as he says in the preface, his "tenderness of imagination" about his cousin's memory causes him to make the work one of "indirection," not mimetic but mythic or parabolic representation.

Unlike Hawthorne, James plunges into the abyss which represents the problem of good and evil and especially the capacity to reveal the soul. When Milly Theale broods over the abyss near the opening of *The Wings of the Dove,* in a moment pregnant with Miltonic as well as Hawthornian associations, she is identified with James's creative spirit. Similarly, the image of the wings of the dove, which Hawthorne associates with Hilda only metonymically, becomes the appropriate "symbol" not only for Milly Theale's "spirit" but for the human spirit generally.

Milly is the central symbol of the book, and the story of her unnamed illness and death indicates the incapacity of any symbol or representation to embody what it was meant to stand for. As William James notes, quoting F. W. H. Myers, in *The Varieties of Religious Experience* (written at the same time as *The Wings of the Dove*), the soul is necessarily encountered housed in the body, but can only be known through the decay of the body: "Each of us is in reality an abiding psychical entity, far more extensive than he knows—an individuality which can never express itself completely through any corporeal manifestation. The Self manifests through the organism; but there is always some part of the Self unmanifested; and always, as it seems, some power of organic expression in abeyance or reserve."[5] Thus Milly's spirit is most clearly manifested along the line at which her body is decaying, and fully revealed only in death. The gap in James's representation, then, serves as a trace of spiritual meaning.

James adapts the Christian allegory of *The Marble Faun* in scenes involving Milly as dove which heighten Hawthorne's religious allusions, especially by reference to Milton. In the preface, he announces that the story has "a very old" motive; though this phrase has several meanings, one motive may be Hawthorne's theme of the Fall. In *The Wings of the Dove* allegory is finally linked with the light of common day. As Angus Fletcher has shown, allegory may be characterized as a particular kind of narration (which he describes in one chapter as "Progress and Battle").[6] As Carolynn van Dyke demonstrates, allegory may impel the narration by alternating between literal and figurative levels, as the drama of representation itself becomes the story.[7] In its evocation of something beyond the literal, allegory may dramatize not the connection between signifier and signified, but the distance between them. In *The Wings of the Dove,* James translates the issue of representation—the gap between symbol and meaning in allegory—into a dramatic one, a question of life and death. The struggle to unite consciousness with life is the basis of the love affair of Merton and Kate, Milly Theale's effort to live, and the interactions between the three of them. It is clearly James's effort, too, as he announces in the preface, where he states that he has sought "to make my medal hang free," so that "its obverse and its reverse, its face and its back, would beautifully become optional for the spectator" (p. 294). This implies that James seeks to combine idea and reality, image and what it represents.

James turns resemblances which Hawthorne suggests as metonymies in *The Marble Faun*—especially the wings of the dove—into symbols or allegories. Thus he tries to repair the "gaps" in Hawthorne's writing, the distance between symbols and what they stand for.[8] Nevertheless, the spiritual reality he seeks to capture is apparent only in the gaps in his own representation, known by its absence. In the death of Milly Theale, the gaps are the only testament to the soul. The ultimate limit of his representation is recorded in the preface and enacted in the plot as Milly Theale's spirit manifests itself only after her death. But James eventually values art over life even more than Hawthorne does; in the last section of the book he asserts the power of consciousness to create its own world or transfigure this one without the need to copy an already-existent reality.

In the preface to *The Wings of the Dove,* James announces that the story is based on a "very old—if I shouldn't perhaps say a very young—motive; I can scarce remember the time when the situation on which this long-drawn fiction mainly rests was not vividly present to me."[9] This phrase has usually been taken to refer to James's "model" for his story of a woman dying young: his cousin Minnie Temple, who died in her twenties of tuberculosis. She is also mentioned at the end of his *Autobiography,* as a symbol of James's own lost youth. James seeks not so much to reincarnate Minnie Temple as restore to her "the sense of having lived."

This subject, James fears, is inherently motionless and static, because it uses a "sick young woman" as the "central figure." Yet he soon realizes that such a character is only more deeply engaged in the "panting pursuit of life," his definition of romance in the preface to *The American.* The other characters at once flesh out Milly's story and constitute the "opposition" to her: "If this longing can take effect only by the aid of others, their participation (appealed to, entangled, and coerced as they find themselves), becomes their drama too" (p. 291). Milly's longing for life can take effect only by "the aid of others"; that aid, however, becomes a deadly trap. If the other characters form a trap for Milly Theale, she is the "shipwreck" which draws everything to destruction like the "pool of a Lorelei."

As James realizes, his "tenderness of imagination" for his dead cousin paradoxically leads him not to revivify but entomb her in his novel, by treating her constantly at "second-hand," James sees her only through the perspectives of others, which constitute the literary architecture which makes Milly a Princess: "What I find striking, charming and curious, [is] the author's instinct everywhere for the indirect presentation of his main image . . . all as if to approach her circuitously, deal with her at second hand . . . as an unspotted princess is ever dealt with. . . . All of which proceeds, obviously, from her painter's tenderness of imagination about her, which reduces him to watching her, as it were, through the successive windows of other people's interest in her" (p. 306). James participates in the same indirection towards Milly which within the novel constitutes the deadly trap "prepared for" her by Kate and Merton.

Milly Theale, like the God whose circumference is everywhere and center nowhere, is always absent, though she is the "center" of the novel. She becomes "what we never can directly know" (James's definition of the romantic), reflected only through the consciousness of others. That very absence becomes the sign of her value. James notes that we can know some things only along the margin of their disappearance: "The process of life gives way fighting, and often may so shine out on the lost ground as in no other connexion" (pp. 289–90). In rereading his work, James finds the gaps in the story the clearest evidence of Milly Theale's spirit, so that he deliberately seeks "to mark the gaps and the lapses . . . the absent values, the palpable voids" (pp. 296–97). Milly Theale's spirit is internalized in the mind of the reader, as it is in the memory of Merton Densher. For reading is an art of "imparting to patches the value of presences." For James, leaving a gap becomes an aim as well as the limit of representation. At the end of the preface, he emphasizes the incompleteness of his description: "I become conscious of overstepping my space without having brought the full quantity to light. The failure leaves me with a burden of residuary comment of which I yet boldly hope elsewhere to discharge myself" (p. 306). Art captures life only through the marks of its absence, which become the evidence of an elusive reality.

Especially at points where James evokes *The Marble Faun* explicitly or implicitly, he transcends Hawthorne's representation in the capacities of language and art to touch the ineffable spirit. The story of *The Wings of the Dove* is that of the attempt to incarnate the human spirit in the body, the world, and language, the problem James confronts in the preface. The unencumbered consciousness of Milly Theale enters the London world characterized by the "drag of a related state" of realism to inform it with transfiguring love. At the end of the London section, Milly separates herself from the world of social relations back into romantic isolation in Venice. Only at the end of this section, with her death, can Milly's spirit affect the society of London. After Milly's separation from bodily form, her spirit touches Merton Densher in memory, as Minnie Temple's originally touched James. The romantic spirit combines with a realistic world only by transforming it in retrospect.

In the preface, James describes London society as the world "prepared for" Milly Theale. It is literally "prepared for her" in the structure of the novel, sketched in the first two books before Milly appears. In his extensive description of objects, in this part of the book James appears to write in the mode of Dickensian realism. However, making explicit what is implicit in Dickens, James shows the poverty of a physical world untransformed by consciousness. In this case, the "drag of a related state"—the limitations imposed by objects, family ties, and especially financial constraints—does not so much tie the individual to reality as dissociate him or her from it. Such alienation from reality is seen in the consciousness of Kate Croy, as described in the novel's first sentence. The very syntax manifests a split in her identity: "She waited, Kate Croy, for her father to come in, but he kept her unconscionably, and there were moments at which she showed herself, in the glass over the mantel, a face positively pale with the irritation that had brought her to the point of going away without sight of him."[10] When Kate looks in the mirror, we see no reflection but a ghostly shadow, a "face positively pale." The material world has taken over her consciousness to such a degree that her very emotions become dingy: "She tasted the faint, flat emanation of things, the failure of fortune and of honour." The extensiveness of the description empties out its objects. We are left with the feelings evoked by objects rather than objects themselves ("the effect of the purplish cloth"). There is no outlet even for consciousness on the "small balcony to which the pair of long windows gave access." The "vulgar little room" is reflected in the "vulgar little street" in an inescapably self-contained reflection (I, 3). Reality dissolves into a series of reflections—Kate's face in the mirror, the street in the room. James implies that without a transforming consciousness, the real is inaccessible.

In Kate's initial encounter with Merton Densher, she momentarily escapes her restrictive situation to enter the realm of romance. Their meeting represents Merton and Kate's momentary and partial ascent to that uplifted state:

> She had observed a ladder against a garden wall, and had . . . climb[ed] it . . . to see over into the probable garden on the other side. On reaching the top she had found herself face to face with a gentleman engaged in a like calculation . . . and the two inquirers had remained confronted on their ladders. The great point was that for the rest of that evening they had been perched—they had not climbed down; and indeed, during the time that followed, Kate at least had had the perched feeling—it was as if she were aloft without a retreat. (I, 53)

She escapes from the "drag of a related state" into the elevation of romance, of "experience disengaged, disembroiled, disencumbered, exempt from the conditions that we usually know to attach to it, and . . . drag upon it" (*AN* 33). The image of the ladder indicates the temporary and fragile nature of this moment. The initial meeting place of Kate and Merton becomes an artificial form of the Edenic garden, Hyde Park, where they meet not spontaneously but by arrangement, under the eye of Kate's aunt, Mrs. Lowder. The Edenic imagery of their love soon takes on sinister overtones.

When Miriam and Donatello frolic in the Borghese Gardens near the beginning of *The Marble Faun,* Hawthorne notes that "the scene is like Eden in its loveliness" (*CE* IV, 73). Similarly, Kate and Merton's love is associated with green spaces—the garden, Hyde Park, the garden "temple" of marriage—but the spaces are limited and enclosed. Deprived of the usual paths of transition in courtship, Merton and Kate arrive at their goal too soon: "Marriage was somehow before them like a temple without an avenue. They belonged to the temple and they met in the grounds" (I, 59). Kate's insistence on controlling the relationship and trying to guarantee financial security prevents the fulfillment of their love. Whereas in the case of Miriam and Donatello, knowledge causes the loss of Eden, for Kate and Merton the absence of sexuality because of the limits imposed by Kate's aunt becomes the "snake in the garden" of their love.

Kate identifies Merton with consciousness, as he identifies her with life; their relationship seems to promise the union of these opposites, which is James's aim throughout the book: "He represented what her life had never given her and . . . never would give her; all the high, dim things she lumped together as of the mind. . . . He had rendered her in especial the sovereign service of making that element real." For Kate, Merton seems to reconcile thought and life (a form of combining the imaginary and actual) and so to make the intellectual "element real" (I, 50–51). Kate represents to the passive Merton exactly the opposite element, life itself: "Life ... was what he must somehow arrange to annex and possess." Thus the union of Kate and Merton promises to result in the "whole soft breath of consciousness meeting and promoting consciousness."

But the love of Kate and Merton swiftly degenerates from an innocent to a sinful one, for it lacks a language through which it can be expressed. When Merton visits Mrs. Lowder's house and views its furnishings, he finds his own capacities for expression obliterated.

> These things finally represented for him a portentous negation of his own world of thought—of which, for that matter, in presence of them, he became as for the first time hopelessly aware. They revealed it to him by their merciless difference. . . . It was the language of the house itself that spoke to him. . . . (I, 79)

The "language of the house" resembles the voice of the alienating objects in the opening scene. The asserted presence of the material world seems to Densher to annihilate his "world of thought." Rather than elaborating surfaces in order to reveal depths, the effect of the "language" of the furniture is to conceal or destroy deeper meaning.

While Mrs. Lowder's furniture expresses the "merciless difference" between her wealth and Merton's poverty, or between consciousness and material things, Kate and Merton's love requires a language or means of expression through which consciousness can be linked to the material world. Merton and Kate believe that their situation can be resolved, their love realized, only through the infusion of an outer spirit. Kate sees that spirit represented in Milly Theale, who is American and ineffably "romantic."

James certifies the reality of Milly by exhibiting her through the eyes of Susan Shepherd Stringham, the "ordinary subscriber to the Boston Evening Transcript." To Susan, Milly is the "real thing, the romantic life itself' (I, 107). In the preface, James vouches for Susan as a reliable register, whose perceptions forerun the reader's. In a letter to Howells, James described the American millionaire as embodying the "romance of the real," a highly fantastic situation which is nonetheless a reality.[11] So Milly stands for a life which, however fantastic, is authentic. James attributes to Milly the qualities he associates with romance, largely as a result of her wealth—extreme freedom, disconnection, and elevation (*AN* 305 and 292): "It was a New York legend of affecting, of romantic isolation, and a set of New York possibilities."

In Milly's first appearance, she wanders along an Alpine trail, leaving behind her a "Tauchnitz volume" (I, 123), implying her transcendence at once of linguistic representation and the picturesque mode of tourism. Susie attempts to communicate with her by writing in the book, but Milly never retrieves it. Instead, she enters the realm of meaning beyond language which James figures by the abyss. "Uplifted and thrown forward" over the Alpine chasm, Milly "broods o'er the abyss," like the dove of the Holy Spirit in Milton.

When Susie realizes that Milly is not contemplating suicide but rather "looking over the kingdoms of the earth with a view to conquering them," Susie resolves the sublime awe of the scene into the picturesque view of the tourist: "The dangerous, rocky path resolved into a 'view' pure and simple" (I, 123). But Milly's perspective here is less that of an observer in an Asher Durand painting, calmly contemplating Nature from a safe perch, than the mountain-borne spectator in a work by Caspar David Friedrich, suspended over the abyss. Though Milly does not contemplate suicide, her vantage point here is not calmly detached but precipitous, "thrown forward and vertiginous" (I, 123). The scene contains both the fear and the majesty of the sublime, as Milly looks down into "whatever was beneath" in a "state of uplifted and unlimited possession" (I, 123–24).

The conflicting Miltonic echoes suggest the ambiguity of the abyss. On the one hand, it represents the world about to be informed by creativity, over which the spirit broods. On the other hand, it represents the kingdoms of the world which Satan uses to tempt Christ. In this case, James implies that the temptation for Milly would be to resist plunging into the "whole assault of life." Milly must descend into the abyss to realize her consciousness.[12] James notes the necessity for his representation to unite with the actualities of European civilization. In James's criticism, he claimed that Hawthorne did not explore the abysses he described, the problems of morality and psychology. For James, the solution of those problems requires immersion in a social world.

Milly clearly resembles Hawthorne's Hilda in her elevation as well as her almost other-worldly innocence. In *The Marble Faun,* Hilda loses her innocence because of what she witnesses at the Tarpeian Rock (the glance between Miriam and Donatello that seems to authorize the murder of Miriam's "model"). For Milly, an abyss looms in her life before her loss of innocence or witnessing of wrongdoing. In this aspect, Milly is more like Miriam, haunted from the beginning by a figure alternately referred to as "the shadow," "the model," or "the monk." James seems to take that figure symbolically by showing Milly Theale, like Miriam, constantly shadowed by a threat. In addition, Milly here becomes the deep diver, not just a witness to a plunge into the abyss. Implicitly, her experience will not be only vicarious but actual.

When Milly Theale does face the "assault of life" in entering London society, she encounters not life but art, a "situation really romantic" (I, 145). Her initiation into society is so sudden and magical that Susie seems to have arranged it like a fairy godmother: "Susie . . . had only had to wave a neat little wand for the fairy tale to begin at once" (I, 145). With its bright lights, careful arrangement, and people who talk like characters in a play, Maud Lowder's dining room seems more a stage set than a real place: "The smallest things . . . were all touches in a picture and denotements in a play" (I, 148).[13]

In London, European social life remains inaccessible to Milly, mediated continually by representation. When she enters the National Gallery, Milly thinks she would like to be a lady-copyist—Hilda's profession: "[They] seemed to show her for the time the right way to life. She should have been a lady-copyist—it met so the case" (I, 288). Hawthorne uses this profession to indicate Hilda's retreat from artistic originality: "No doubt the girl's early dreams had been of sending forms and hues of beauty into the visible world out of her own mind. . . . [But] Hilda had ceased to consider herself as an original artist" (*CE* IV, 56). The reference to Hilda reflects Milly's desire to remain aloof from life as person, not artist. In visiting the National Gallery, she first encounters Merton Densher, the person she has ostensibly come to London to see, as a representation. As she stands in a gallery of Dutch pictures, Milly hears someone comment on a picture in the "English style" (I, 291). She turns away from the Dutch pictures—which for James, as for George Eliot, were images for realism—to encounter an image which she recognizes after a moment as her friend Merton Densher. She also refuses to see the meaning of the conjunction of Merton and Kate, the double portrait of their intimacy revealed to her.

Milly's refusal to confront life except as mediated by representation culminates at Matcham, where she reaches the "high water-mark of her imagination" (I, 210), as life becomes a vivified painting. But Milly herself becomes the subject of a comparison between art and life at this point, as Lord Mark notes her resemblance to the Bronzino portrait. When she views the Bronzino, Milly comprehends the ultimate effect of taking life as representation—freezing into death.[14] The portrait said to resemble her shows a woman of great status who is nevertheless "dead, dead, dead." The image resembles that of Minnie Temple in James's memory. At the high point of life, Milly glimpses her own mortality. As William James says in *The Varieties of Religious Experience,* "Life and its negation are inextricably bound up together"; the abyss which represents the kingdoms of the earth in the Alpine scene is here the abyss of death. Milly's foreknowledge of her death dooms her.

Milly, like Hilda as James described her, has eaten of "the tree of bitter knowledge," in this case because she is given foreknowledge of her own death.[15] Unlike Hilda, Milly seeks a physical rather than religious cure, when she visits the doctor, not the priest. Nevertheless, the religious implications of this visit are clear when James includes a specific reference to *The Marble Faun.* After her visit to Luke Strett, Milly "feels—I can't otherwise describe it—as if I had been, on my knees, to the priest. I've confessed and I've been absolved. It has been lifted off" (I, 134). At this moment, which Milly "can't otherwise describe," James clearly alludes to one of his favorite scenes in *The*

Marble Faun, Hilda's confession to the priest in St. Peter's. The religious connotations of Milly's visit are implied by the name of her physician, which is that of one of the apostles.

When Milly visits Sir Luke Strett, her major fear is that he will see her as "romantic" and so not take her seriously. But in this scene James realizes romance, as Milly's visit to the doctor finally enables her to touch reality, when she wanders through Regent's Park afterwards.[16] Near the end of *The Marble Faun,* Hawthorne speculates that Miriam may be "no real artist"; in coming to Rome as a painter, she was "stepping out of her native sphere only for an interlude, just as a princess might alight from her gilded equipage to go on foot through a rustic lane" (*CE* IV, 285). James's scene occurs in Regent's Park (aptly named), as Milly symbolically descends from her royal carriage: "She had come out . . . at the Regent's Park, round which . . . her public chariot had solemnly rolled. But she went into it further now; this was the real thing" (I, 250). The scene is a tableau of human life, like the "field full of folk" in *Piers Plowman.* Milly sees that her "sickness" is a version of the universal anxiety of mortality: "Their box, their common anxiety, what was it, in this grim breathing-space, but the practical question of life" (I, 250).

After Hilda's witnessing of the murder and confession, her knowledge of life makes art seem meaningless to her: "she had known such a reality, that it taught her to distinguish inevitably the large portion that is unreal, in every work of art" (p. 270). But art becomes the means for Milly to realize her vision of life. Milly finds a spiritual reality, though ultimately at the price of separation from life, by immersing herself in a world of art.

In the last part of the novel, representation is controlled by the projections of desire, James's definition of romance: what can be known "only through the beautiful circuit and subterfuge of our thought and our desire." While, in the preface, James claims that the consciousness of Merton Densher "remains entwined upon the reel," in the penultimate section of *The Wings of the Dove,* set in Venice, the consciousness of Milly Theale is unentwined, projected onto a world that embodies her vision. Milly becomes a copyist in a different way than Hilda, in the sense that she recreates famous paintings—notably a Veronese—as living tableaux. But here, "art makes life," a transformation completed in Milly's recreation of a Veronese painting in a party at her Venetian villa.

The symbolic drama begins when Mrs. Lowder applies to Milly what will become the name for her spirit: "She's a dove." As applied by Mrs. Lowder, the term is meant to keep Milly in her place, passive and self-effacing. But it becomes instead the source of her power, providing her with a definition of her role as creator. It gives her a role which shields her, underneath which her spirit can be preserved.[17] Milly resolves to "study . . . the dovelike" to "avert all inquiry into her own case."

When Milly takes up residence in a Venetian palazzo, her resemblance to

Hilda becomes clear. James makes his heroine not only virginal but religious, the "priestess of the worship" (II, 135). James calls her palace "the ark of her deluge" (II, 143), associating Milly with the dove of Noah's ark. Milly withdraws from the world to transform it by projecting her visions:

> Oh, the impossible romance—! The romance for her, yet once more, would be to sit there for ever, through all her time, as in a fortress; and the idea became an image of never going down, of remaining aloft in the divine, dustless air, where she would hear but the splash of the water against stone. (II, 147) (See figure 7.)

Hawthorne's Hilda is elevated in her tower not only physically but emotionally, isolated from others. James's description of Milly's palazzo, though, seems closer to Hawthorne's description of Donatello's villa, a more sensual place that is ornately decorated. Despite her elevation, Milly does not place herself above the moral and emotional problems of this world. Hilda's gaining of knowledge leads to her rejection of others, but in Milly James wishes to show how innocence can be preserved even after knowledge has been attained.

Milly arranges the palazzo in Venice according to her visions until it seems an artistic creation rather than a physical entity: "where hard, cool pavements took reflections in their lifelong polish, and where the sun . . . played over the painted 'subjects' in the splendid ceilings" (II, 132). If Milly cannot bring her spirit into contact with actuality, she can nonetheless create a representation by which to bestow it on the material world. Milly reforms the worldly Venetian society in the image of her spirit. Lord Mark suggests a painterly parallel to her life in Venice: "There ought of course always to be people at top and bottom, in Veronese costumes, to watch you do it" (II, 147). By projecting her consciousness into artistic tableaux, Milly seeks not to escape but to embrace reality. In the use of these tableaux vivants, the narrative here resembles the pictorialism of romance. But here the pictures serve not to freeze but realize reality. While Hawthorne evokes actual works of art, James translates such works into moving images of his own drama.

The Veronese painting constituted at Milly's party is *The Marriage at Cana,* a clearly religious work, in which Christ himself appears in the background at the center, surrounded by a halo of light. Though the figure is in the background, its presence transforms the elegant scene of Venetian court life. The painting establishes a contrast between worldly flesh and spirit, but the theme of marriage implies a reconciliation of the two.[18] (See figure 8.) The tableau of romance becomes in James's work a fully arranged work of art in which the distance between actual and fanciful is bridged. The realized painting is at once a complete representation of society and fully symbolic.

In this scene, James fulfills the religious connotations of the dove image by associating Milly Theale explicitly with the Holy Ghost. The guests in

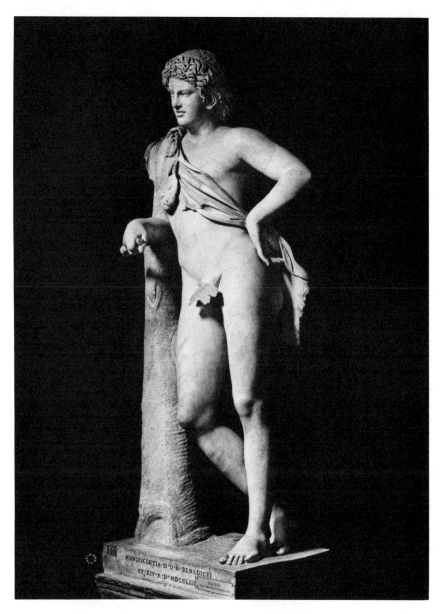

Figure 6.   Praxiteles, *Faun,* Fourth Century B.C.
(Courtesy Alinari/Art Resource, N.Y.)

Figure 7.   Alvin Langdon Coburn, *The Venetian Palace*, 1907
Frontispiece to *The Wings of the Dove* (volume XX of the
New York Edition).
*(Courtesy International Museum of Photography at George
Eastman House.)*

Milly's palace feel suspended in a warm, watery bath, like the waters warmed by the brooding of the dove in Genesis. Like the dove, Milly becomes a mediating spirit, the benevolent "genius" of the party: "Milly, let loose among them in a wonderful white dress, brought them somehow into relation with something that made them more finely genial" (II, 213). At this point, Merton feels that "the Veronese picture of which he had talked with Mrs. Stringham was not quite constituted." It will not be completed until he and Kate enter the picture.

When Kate and Merton enter Milly's aesthetic frame, they are finally touched by her spirit. Kate and Merton take the place of the marrying couple in the Veronese, talking in the foreground about their plan to deceive Milly for her money, which they finally articulate to each other at this moment. Here, as they gossip, Milly appears in the background, like Christ in the Veronese, and draws their gazes. Milly finally becomes a "symbol," as her spirit finds the embodiment James sought throughout. To Kate, Milly's pearls represent the vast gap between the two women in financial status, which Kate's marriage will not lessen:

> Milly's royal ornament had—under pressure now not wholly occult—taken on the character of a symbol of differences, differences of which the vision was actually in Kate's face. It might have been in her face too that, well as she certainly would look in pearls, pearls were exactly what Merton Densher would never be able to give her. Wasn't *that* the great difference that Milly tonight symbolized? (II, 219)

To Kate, Milly seems to represent the insufficiency of Kate's impending marriage. But Merton recognizes that "the dove" is "the figure" for Milly's "spirit," as Milly becomes "embodied poetry" (II, 217), James's ideal from the preface realized. Milly's figurative aspect here evokes not the gap which divides her from others but the intrinsic value of her own spirit. When Milly looks back at Kate and Merton, they see in her not a "symbol of differences," but the mediating spirit of love itself: "Milly, from the other side, happened at the moment to notice them, and sent across towards them in response all the candour of her smile, the lustre of her pearls, the value of her life, the essence of her wealth. It brought them together again, with faces made fairly grave by the reality she put into their plan" (II, 229). Milly, as the third term of their desire, becomes a possible intermediary. Only when Kate regards Milly does Kate see herself as Merton's wife.

At this point, the Veronese is fully constituted, as the placement of James's characters echoes its arrangement. Milly, dressed in white, assumes the position of Christ, as Merton and Kate take the place of the wedding couple. The picture is completed when Milly looks across at Merton and Kate and the shadowy Lady Mills finally reaches them to conclude the sequence. For a moment, as book 8 ends, the action is frozen into an image. The point of the painting—

the full integration of the worldly and spiritual—is enacted, as Milly's spirit temporarily transforms the Venetian scene as well as the love of Merton and Kate.

Milly's aesthetic, poetic existence turns her into "embodied poetry" for Merton Densher, at once ideal and real. Her identification with stillness and silence implies for Merton her access to invisible worlds, providing intimations of something beyond reality: "Her welcome . . . her disconcerting poetry . . . had, to his imagination . . . meaning that hung about it like . . . mere ghosts of sound" (II, 184–85). Milly infuses the visible world with the invisible spirit, as an absent presence. By contrast, Merton's attempt to make Kate fully present to him results in a different kind of absence. Merton seeks a "proof" of Kate's love by making her visit him in his room—the subject they are discussing at the party. Densher feels that Kate's full physical "presence" to him will affirm the "reality" of their relation, which, in the absence of contact between them, he is beginning to doubt. We see not the actual sexual encounter but its aftermath. After this experience, Merton is consumed by memories of Kate. But all he has are memories; Kate's invisible presence in his rooms turns her into a ghost. In his unmediated possession of her, Densher has reduced rather than heightened her presence to him. What remains within his walls is only a remnant of her. His attempts to preserve her image only increase her exclusion: "When he closed the door . . . he always shut her in. Shut her out . . . rather" (II, 238). This segment resembles Hawthorne's description of Miriam haunting Donatello's home like a shadow after the tragedy (the murder over the abyss) which has made them both guilty.

By making Kate fully present to him, Merton has made her into a less than human ghost. By contrast, Milly implies to Densher "ghosts of sound," intimations of something beyond reality. With Kate, Merton seeks to grasp the real through absolute knowledge of the loved one: "For the knowledge of what she was he had absolutely to see her now . . . stand there for him in all the light of his admirable, merciless meaning" (II, 208). Yet the knowledge which demands pure lucidity and visibility deprives the object of its fullness. After this act of possession, Densher's "realities" grow "shabby" (II, 207). In the actual enactment of his desire, desire falters (the passage refers to his writing, but its double meaning is unavoidable): "It was partly what he had moved into rooms for, only to find himself, almost for the first time in his life, stricken and sterile" (II, 208).

While in relation to Kate, Merton tries to turn a "luminous conception" into an "historic truth" (II, 236), in his relation to Milly things take the opposite turn. When Milly absents herself from him in her final illness, Merton is irrevocably haunted by a mental image. Here, as James implies in the preface, spiritual reality becomes not what is fully present but what is absent. When Merton is barred from Milly's door during her final illness, Milly disappears from his sight for a period equivalent to that of Christ's entombment—three days. Again,

James echoes a passage in *The Marble Faun,* the chapter near the end when Hilda disappears for four days. During this period, Kenyon reflects on his love for her, and realizes that the spirit is greater than the body: others have tried to "kidnap the mortal body, for the sake of the immortal spirit that might otherwise be lost forever" (*CE* IV, 299). Merton's separation from Milly enables him to realize not only his love for her but the existence of a spiritual realm. In the last section of the book, Merton, originally identified with the passive lover Donatello in relation to Kate (who resembles Miriam, the more experienced woman), becomes more like Kenyon, a figure for the artist, in relation to Milly. While the love of Kenyon and Hilda is realized in marriage, that of Merton and Milly (as of James and Minnie Temple) is by definition unrealizable. James addresses Hawthorne's theme of the fortunate fall to emphasize that something is recovered from suffering and tragic knowledge, though the larger question of whether anything triumphs over death remains unanswered.

When Milly turns her face to the wall, and the tragedy of the book descends with Lord Mark's sudden revelation of Merton and Kate's engagement, the work approaches the pitch of romance. Venice becomes the symbol of civilization itself, the "drawing room of Europe": "It was a Venice all of evil" (II, 259). As in a Shakespearean romance, the outer weather becomes a mirror of Densher's inner state; storm breaks out, turning the city into "a Venice all of evil" (II, 259). Milly's absence breaks the harmony of the world itself, as Merton perceives "the broken charm of the world." Yet Venice appears "new-dyed" when Merton emerges after the storm: "Venice glowed . . . the scattered pinks, yellows . . . were like a hanging-out of vivid stuffs, a laying down of fine carpets" (II, 294). So, too, through her suffering, Milly Theale emerges through a sea-change, new-born.[19]

Merton blames Lord Mark for Milly's illness: "The weather had changed, the rain was ugly, the wind wicked, the sea impossible, *because* of Lord Mark" (II, 263). Yet Merton soon realizes that the cause of the disaster was not Lord Mark's directness but his own indirection, shown even in his view of Lord Mark, seen behind the pane of glass at Florian's. What has doomed Milly, he realizes, is not Lord Mark's revelation of the truth, but his and Kate's constant evasion of the facts not only of their engagement but of Milly's illness, which has led Milly to suffer in silence for months.

Like Merton's lies by omission, *The Wings of the Dove* itself is a "ring of expensive fictions" which omits the central facts of Milly's illness and death. The fiction intended to save or immortalize Milly here looks like the lies that have betrayed her, the most damaging of lies in the guise of beauty. Milly dies of the inability to find a surface to reflect her. Ultimately there is no representation that can reflect the single ultimate fact of life, death:

> He hadn't only never been near the facts of her condition—which counted so as a blessing for him; he hadn't only, with all the world, hovered outside an impenetrable ring fence, within which there reigned a kind of expensive vagueness made up of smiles and silences and beautiful fictions and priceless arrangements, all strained to breaking; but he had also . . . actively fostered suppressions. . . . It was a conspiracy of silence . . . to which no one had made an exception, the great smudge of mortality across the picture, the shadow of pain and horror, finding in no quarter a surface of spirit or of speech that consented to reflect it. (II, 299)

Though death may be incapable of embodiment in the surfaces of the world, we can reach awareness of something beyond mortality by means of this world, particularly through memory. Such spiritual awareness is first attained by Merton in Venice, and then fulfilled in London. In London, the material of the physical world is in the service of romance for Merton Densher, as he can catch intimations of Milly Theale from every aspect of the visible world. In a state of extreme attention, he breaks through to the spiritual level which constantly underlies the material realm. Merton lives in presence of "that marked element of the rare," on the border between the spiritual and physical worlds— the locale of romance for Hawthorne. As Milly becomes a perfectly preserved image, Merton Densher himself has finally been absorbed into the picture. His last meeting with her is shown only as reproduced in Merton's memory: "He himself for that matter took in the scene again at moments as from the page of a book. He saw a young man far off and in a relation inconceivable. . . . It was his own face Densher had known" (II, 342).

In his heightened awareness, Merton "turns the very pulses of the air into revelations." Merton catches a revelation even from the presence of Aunt Maud's brougham before Sir Luke's door. When Mrs. Lowder speaks of Milly as "our dear dove," "the words fitted an image deep in his own imagination" (II, 356). Merton finds an objective correlative for his quasi-religious mood, on the day of Milly's death, in the Brompton Oratory (she dies on Christmas, linking her again to Christian birth). Though his spiritual exaltation is not precisely religious, a place of worship will embody it sufficiently: "At the door then . . . his idea was really . . . consecrated. . . . It didn't match his own day, but it was much less of a discord than some other things actual and possible" (II, 361–62).

Merton's ultimate vision occurs through the destruction of Milly's communication. This final message of the spirit is burned by Kate in the fire of a room like that in which the book began, implying that she has become complicit with the spirit-killing qualities of her family and the realm of material objects. In James's work, though, imagination works best when confronted by an absence, not a presence. At this point, Merton achieves a revelation no less one because it is the loss of a revelation:

He should never, never know what had been in Milly's letter. The intention announced in it he should but too probably know. . . . The part of it missed for ever was the turn she would have given her act. This turn had possibilities that, somehow, by wondering about them, his imagination had extraordinarily filled out and refined. It had made of them a revelation the loss of which was like the sight of a priceless pearl cast before his eyes . . . into the fathomless sea. . . . (II, 396)

The image of the pearl here associates Milly's pearls of the party scene with both the pearl of great price of *Matthew* and the "pearls that were his eyes" of *The Tempest*. The allusion to *Matthew* makes clear Merton's willingness, like the merchant of the parable, to sacrifice Milly's money for her spirit. The rebirth of *The Tempest* is evoked in other images here as well: "a pearl . . . into the fathomless sea" indicates the outstripping of a romance revelation ("Full fathom five") by a Christian one. Merton becomes attuned to unheard music, seeing things unseen: "something that, for the spiritual ear, might have been audible as a faint far wail. . . . He sought and guarded the stillness, so that it might prevail there till the inevitable sounds of life, once more, comparatively coarse and harsh, should smother and deaden it" (II, 396). For Merton, hearkening to the almost inaudible sounds of the spirit finally means blocking out the sounds of current life.

James's use of the pearl image here may have been provoked by a passage near the beginning of *The Marble Faun*. Looking at a statue of a pearl fisher in the same gallery as the statue of the faun, one of the characters comments, "But what a strange efficacy there is in death! If we cannot all win pearls, it causes an empty shell to satisfy us just as well" (*CE* IV, 90). So Merton's satisfaction not with the pearl itself, the fullness of Milly's spirit, but the "empty shell" of representation, shows the "strange efficacy" of death. Similarly, Minnie Temple's death, sadly, was the means by which her spirit became most clearly evident to James.

Kate's refusal to acknowledge the reality of her life, the conditions of her existence with her family, means that her romance with Merton cannot be fully realized. James notes that romance, to be convincing, must reform its ties to "communities," but Kate's denial of her family indicates her unwillingness to accept the "related state." The ties which would complete Kate and Merton's romance are left unforged, as Kate sees in Merton's turned back "the missing links" (p. 436). If Merton has learned of spiritual love through Milly, he cannot reunite it with the physical world. The link supposed to provide the connection between Kate and Merton, Milly's money, instead severs it.

In the last scene of *The Wings of the Dove*, we see the final attempt to make the ideal penetrate the ordinary, to gain a communication from the spirit. Merton's supreme "test" of Kate is to see if she can repudiate the gift of Milly's money; if so, he feels that the material and spiritual can be reunited in their marriage. For he wishes to gain the gift of Milly's spirituality and not her material bequest. But for Kate money is the only possible means of realizing their union. Merton finally retreats from life into the spiritual world: "Her memory's your love. You *want* no other" (II, 405). His insistence that Kate return the letter "intact and inviolate" denies the history of their relationship and the fact that she is no longer "intact" (II, 398). Merton's desire to leave the decision about the money to Milly's lawyers, "the good people in New York," the "authors of our communication" (II, 398), without the vehicle of the letter itself, seeks a communication based on the author's intention before its incarnation in language.

But this intention is never fully enacted; as James admits, writing in the preface as the author of the New York Edition, his desire to produce "embodied poetry" by bringing the spirit of Minnie Temple into representation was never fulfilled. At the end of the novel, money—the Jamesian vehicle of "realization"—is incapable of operation, reduced to a "floating signifier." In the absence of the union of Kate and Merton, money has no function or power. Rather than informing life, the memory of Milly separates Merton from ordinary existence into a purely spiritual realm, while consigning Kate to a pragmatic reality now apparently incapable of union with the spirit. As the author of this communication, James may be sorrowing at the spectacle of a message never received.

The ending of *The Wings of the Dove* recalls an incident at the end of *The Marble Faun* when Miriam seeks to have a packet delivered. It affirms that the mystery of Miriam's identity can be known only in retrospect, for "the packet, to be delivered long after her departure, contained a reference to this design, besides certain family documents, which were to be imparted to her relative as from one dead and gone" (*CE* IV, 332). Milly's love makes her Christ-like: "She died for you that you might understand her." But instead of redeeming Kate and Merton's love, the spreading of her wings, the gift of her spirit, does not uplift but "cover" them, making them subject to her power (II, 404). Merton is left in permanent stasis; Kate, embracing life, can only register the irrevocable transformations of time: "We shall never again be as we were" (II, 405). In the fallen world, even a spiritual visitation cannot reunite consciousness and reality, though it can have a destructive effect. In the modern world, the spirit can be known only by its absence.

By turning Hawthorne's images into an allegory of the creative imagination, James manages to embody a spiritual reality which Hawthorne felt powerless to describe. Nevertheless, as James notes, that reality is known only along the margin of its disappearance. Given a physical world which can provide no surface which fully reflects the spirit, James acknowledges the inevitable gap of all representation—the abyss of death, perhaps, which means that "words never reach their objects."[20] As Hawthorne's postscript implies that his communication will fail to reach the ears of his single "gentle reader" (whom he imagines may be dead—*CE* IV, 463–64), James's work ends with a failed communication. Milly's unread letter represents the intention of the "author of the communication," an intention which, as soon as enacted in representation, is doomed to be realized only incompletely.

Figure 8. Paolo Veronese, *The Marriage at Cana,* 1563
(*Courtesy Alinari/Art Resource, N.Y.*)

The Golden Bowl: Henry James's Romance of the Real

"Nature's world is brazen, the poets only deliver a golden."
—Sir Philip Sidney, "An Apology for Poetry"

In *The Golden Bowl*, James accomplishes the fusion of romance and realism which remains incomplete in *The Wings of the Dove*. As in *The Wings of the Dove*, James makes use of a series of linked figures, though in this work he eschews allegorical narration. Nonetheless, *The Golden Bowl* is in many ways a symbolic drama—in its repetition of a central image which represents the narrative as a whole and the use of characters elevated far above the ordinary, including a prince and princess. In *The Golden Bowl*, direct echoes of Hawthorne are more distant, though the use of a quartet of characters and a Roman prince is reminiscent of *The Marble Faun*. Instead, James here uses the symbolic form of Hawthornian romance but gives it a different meaning, using it to present a convincing simulacrum of the world rather than to invent a new reality. In *The Wings of the Dove*, the problem of representation is enacted in the plot of the novel. In *The Golden Bowl*, form and subject are so intertwined that the arrangement and ordering of events become as significant as the events themselves.

The variety of readings evoked by *The Golden Bowl* testifies to the novel's almost uncanny double effect. For some critics, the book is an instance of consummate social realism in the vein of Balzac, while others see it as Christian or Swedenborgian allegory.[1] *The Golden Bowl* is unique because it captures the range of meaning of allegory without any sacrifice of verisimilitude. Both allegorical and mimetic readings refer the book to a context outside itself, that of Christian drama or Edwardian society. They thus split the powerful fusion of imagination and reality which is the source of the novel's uncanniness. In the self-contained world of *The Golden Bowl*, the forms of social life are transformed by imagination, which manipulates reality to its own ends. James does not seek to mirror an outer world but to project an inner one onto a fully-conveyed, detailed physical realm.

In *The Golden Bowl,* by inverting realistic conventions or extending them to the breaking point, James discovers the romance of reality. Here social forms do not reflect a reality outside the book but provide the vehicle for an imagination that seeks to remake the world. James presents a world malleable to desire, capturing what he identifies in Hawthorne's work as "the real romantic note."[2] When subjected to consciousness, the world we know appears as the one we desire, exhibiting a value not otherwise apparent; reality becomes "golden."

In the preface to *The Wings of the Dove,* James speaks of stretching the form of the novel to its ultimate extent, until we hear the "crack" of the pressure brought to bear on it. In *The Golden Bowl,* the mold is certainly filled to bursting with James's most elaborate plot, language, and descriptions. But its characters, James's richest and most aristocratic, are disentangled from all limits, especially financial, and even for the most part from any social background; though their homes bear the name of London streets, the locales are so abstract that they could be anywhere. In the much-analyzed elaborate figures of James's late style (also seen in *The American Scene,* the *Autobiography,* etc.), the foreground or literal action is nearly usurped by the elaborate metaphorical action. Language ceases to be referential, as in the preface James continually refers to the writer as the "poet." In the process of stretching the mold of the novel to its ultimate extent, in a work which seems replete with detail, James in fact inverts the referential bias of the realistic novel. His descriptions do not so much locate as isolate his characters.

In *The Golden Bowl,* James casts doubt on the notion that representation is capable of mirroring a reality external to itself. He sees reality as already reflected through consciousness, making every work of representation necessarily one of "re-representation."[3] In life as in art, the real cannot be perfectly captured, though it can be evoked through the construction of beautiful golden bowls—artistic and other structures—which contain it imaginatively. Penetration to the depths of the real, through the combination of romance and realism, calls a halt to language, vision, and almost to the novel form itself.

We can interpret *The Golden Bowl* in light of two essays which James wrote about romance shortly afterwards—the essay for the Hawthorne Centenary of 1904 and the preface to *The American* of 1907. In the Hawthorne essay, James notes that Hawthorne transforms reality in the act of perceiving it, without lessening his accuracy of depiction: his romance presents "the very application of the spectator's, the poet's mood, in the kind of reflection the things we know best and see oftenest may make in our minds." By preserving romance's sense of adventure without its artificial trappings (settings distant in time or place, supernatural beings), Hawthorne produces the "real as distinguished from the artificial romantic note." In his works, "'The light that never was on land or sea' keeps all the intimacy and yet adds all the wonder. . . . This very freedom of the spell remains all the while truth to the objects observed—truth to the very Salem in which the vision was born" (1904, p. 28).

When we read medieval romances, we feel an uncanny familiarity with events that replicate primal urges and wishes, although in displaced, symbolic form. When the satisfaction of such wishes is depicted without the veil of distance in time or place, in adventures of human beings rather than of mythical creatures, our primal urges grow accessible as elements permeating everyday life. Properly executed, as it is in Hawthorne's works, romance presents "something deeply within us, not . . . something infinitely disconnected from us" (1904, p. 27). The uncanny—the recognition of something forgotten and repudiated—merges with our grasp of the everyday world.[4] Faithful depiction of the outer world as shaped and transformed by the inner one captures the essence of the real. Such depiction reflects back to us an image of ourselves from the world; we become aware that the reality we perceive is a product of the mixing—often unconscious—of self with world. That is, reality is always represented or reflected to us through consciousness; by exhibiting that reflection, artistic representation restores to us a sense of our presence in the world. The satisfaction of desire reveals the romantic in the real and so enables us to recognize the romantic as familiar rather than alien. As James notes of Hawthorne's *The House of the Seven Gables* in the 1904 Hawthorne essay, Hawthorne's work "takes up the New England Real . . . and so invests and colors it . . . by that artistic economy which understands *values* and uses them" (1904, p. 28). James discovers the excitement and intensity of romance within everyday life, to be attained not by escaping reality but penetrating to its heart.

As James implies in the preface to *The American,* the things we know through realism and those we know through romance are interdependent. The real "represents the thing we cannot possibly *not* know, sooner or later, in one way or another," while the romantic "stands, on the other hand, for the things that . . . we never *can* directly know; the things that can reach us only through the beautiful circuit and subterfuge of our thought and our desire." The best writers combine these strains to produce "intensity" and "richness": "The interest is greatest . . . when he [the novelist] commits himself in both directions . . . by the law of some rich passion in him for extremes" (*AN* 31–32). In *The Golden Bowl,* James's realism becomes the vehicle for romance. The elaborate descriptions of social manners and physical objects become symbolic of melodramatic adventures. By showing the world refracted through consciousness, James turns manners into abstract forms. Through such reflection, Maggie Verver transforms her world without violating its surfaces, reshaping reality to fit her desires without sacrificing her connection to life (unlike Milly Theale). The "reality" of social forms is now subject to the "circuit . . . of thought and desire" of romance. Thus the forms themselves become illustrative of a drama in which thought has the power to influence reality.

Romance is present in the early sections of *The Golden Bowl* principally by allusion, as the book's figures frequently describe romantic works by such artists as Wagner, Keats, and Poe. Though the action of the book is restrained and the civilized surface preserved, its extended figures (comparable to epic similes) typically allude to extreme adventures or savage conflicts.[5] These figures, most pronounced in the middle of the novel, become less prevalent at the end, as they are realized in the actual landscape. Maggie's book begins with the elaborate image of a pagoda; near the end of it, an actual pagoda in a garden appears. Most of the figures are presented as devised in the consciousness of a character; they are therefore "figures of thought" rather than action. The effect is to blur the line between literal and metaphorical, actual and imagined events. The figure and its referent become less easily distinguished, even interchangeable. Thus James manages to absorb the most far-flung meaning evoked in figures into the texture of ordinary life. James does not need to penetrate below the surface of reality to reach its meaning; here life at its most rich and intense is found on the surface.

In the preface to *The Princess Casamassima,* James noted that this novel was inspired by elements of his actual experience:

> This fiction proceeded quite directly during the first year of a long residence in London, from the habit and the interest of walking the streets. . . . The attentive exploration of London, the assault directly made by the great city upon an imagination quick to react, fully explains a large part of it. (*AN* 59)

But in the preface to *The Golden Bowl,* James disclaims the possible influence of the physical world. Rather, he claims, here his imagination created autoch- thonously, and later found real "objects" (*AN* 346) to confirm his vision. By imagining the house in Portland Place, the Bloomsbury shop, and other settings, he gave them life as places, or at least as images which could be found in actuality. Describing his search for scenes to "illustrate" the work with the photographer Coburn, James thinks London will "illustrate" his work as examples illustrate a truth. Thus the photographs are precisely "images always confessing themselves mere optical symbols or echoes, expressions of no particular things in the text, but only of the type or idea of this or that thing" (*AN* 333).[6] James reverses the traditional Platonic hierarchy here. His text becomes the ideal type for which London provides reflections. James's seemingly humble claim that his and Coburn's task was "not to 'create' but simply to recognize" in fact gives his imagination primacy over the physical world. Now, the imagination finds actual objects to confirm its vision: "The prodigious city . . . does on occasion meet halfway those forms of intelligence that *it* recognizes" (*AN* 335).

The illustrations, which were perhaps intended to provide documentation for James's imaginative creation, have the opposite effect. Coburn's hazy, romanticized photographs rather turn the reality of London itself into an image. We can follow a similar progression in the course of the novel. On the first page, reality appears as "objects massive and lumpish." The visions of the characters, particularly those of Maggie Verver, increasingly shape the world to their desires. By the end of the book, Maggie's world is largely remade by her projections, though the question of whether her imagination can conquer reality entirely remains unresolved.

In *The Golden Bowl,* as he says in the preface, James continually subjects objects to imagination by making the work one of "representation" (*AN* 335). This term may refer to the fact that many of the novel's events happen twice, first in the Prince's book, then in Maggie's. The Matcham party, for instance, occurs spontaneously in the first part and is recreated by Maggie's deliberate design in her book.[7] In the preface, James distinguishes between revision as rewriting and, what the term literally means, simply the "act of seeing it [the novel] again," by means of which the objects of consciousness are transformed (*AN* 337). In *The Golden Bowl* the act of reseeing—or especially redoing—also produces changes. Such reflection reveals the value of actuality, which cannot otherwise be known. It is not so much that things happen twice as that they are seen twice; the second seeing produces the gold. Only the second view shows us the "value" of the ordinary, everyday, and intimate. In *The Golden Bowl,* where the action is also that of artistic vision, arrangement, and reporting, revision and reaction uncover the deepest emotions.

The use of romance can be traced particularly in the three figurative quests of the book, signaled by the use of ship imagery.[8] The Prince's search for satisfaction with little conscious reflection is described as a quest for a "greenwood of romance" in his affair with Charlotte. Adam Verver's quest is more epic than romantic; he seeks to assert his will over things and people to achieve a conquest through superior financial or aesthetic power. Maggie must combine her husband's desire to escape reality with her father's exertion of control over it. She accomplishes this aim especially by intuiting and internalizing her husband's desire, through which she becomes aware of her own desire for him.[9] She makes unconscious desire subject to consciousness to compete the "circuit . . . of thought and desire." Through the mediation of such social forms as dinner parties and bridge games, Maggie reconstructs the Prince's romance not as an escape from reality but as a fulfillment attainable within accepted social structures: the satisfaction of desire in marriage, not adultery. Maggie thus incorporates romance into realism, recovering adventure and passion within the highly developed forms of civilized life, of which the chief representative here is the "sacred form" of marriage. Thus she gives reality heightened "value."

As Janet Gabler-Hover notes, "Maggie ... temporarily sustains fictions so as ultimately to transcend the conventionalized situation of adultery in which ... she discovers herself."[10] She, unlike the Prince and Charlotte, uses social forms while understanding their fictiveness, using form to move beyond it. By eschewing melodramatic confrontation and maintaining, with great strain, an unbroken surface, Maggie attains passionate intensity within equilibrium. The preservation of the wildest desires within the fabric of civilization constitutes the romance of reality.

I. The Prince

The Golden Bowl is epic in intent and scope, if not in subject. The opening of the story presents a prince meditating on empire like an epic hero:

> The Prince ... was one of the modern Romans who find by the Thames a more convincing image of the truth of the ancient state than any they have left by the Tiber ... If it was a question of an *Imperium,* he said to himself, and if one wished, as a Roman, to recover a little the sense of that, the place to do so was on London Bridge, or even . . . at Hyde Park Corner.[11]

The Prince appears to meditate on the transfer of empire from Rome to London; in fact, at the time James is writing, the beginning of the twentieth century, the real imperial power is American. The Prince is inadequate as epic hero, for his desires are far more limited in scope. He moves quickly from political sites—London Bridge and Hyde Park Corner—to the place of commerce, Bond Street, where all desire is reduced to desire for commodities: "He had strayed, simply enough, into Bond Street, where his imagination, working at comparatively short range, caused him now and then to stop before a window in which objects massive and lumpish, in silver and gold ... applied to a hundred uses and abuses, were as tumbled together as if, in the insolence of the Empire, they had been the loot of far-off victories" (I, 3). The imagination of this hero, like the world at which he gazes, is spiritually "bankrupt"; he sees in the spoils of empire only "objects massive and lumpish." Reality appears to him a jumble of meaningless signs. Alienated from his original context, the Prince can see no visions, attain no greater hope or ambition than "undirected thought."

While the Prince's imagination can operate only at "comparatively short range," the Ververs' imaginations apparently encounter no resistance from actuality. The Prince himself is acquired by them in a marriage enacted on the book's opening pages, primarily as a business transaction between lawyers. *The Golden Bowl* begins where most novels end, with a marriage, and the somewhat hasty courtship implies that the Prince's work of knowing Maggie is yet to begin, despite Fanny Assingham's blithe assurance that "'you're in port—the port ... of the Golden Isles'" (I, 27). But the Prince understands that his romantic quest is only beginning, despite the financial and sexual security of the marriage implied in Fanny's metaphor. (Whether the Prince's motives are to know Maggie or only to conform to the role of husband because of her wealth is difficult to assess; perhaps the Prince himself does not know his motives at this point.) His figure for his quest expresses the difficulty of knowledge for the husband of Maggie Verver. In comparing himself to Pym at the end of Poe's *Narrative of A. Gordon Pym,* the Prince sees himself confronted, in the Ververs, by a mystery of formlessness that seems to belong to another order of existence. The Prince sees the Ververs as peculiarly innocent, immune to the social constraints and traditions which have shaped him:[12]

> These things, the motives of such people . . . were obscure. . . . They contributed to that element of the impenetrable which alone slightly qualified his sense of his good fortune. He remembered to have read, as a boy, a wonderful tale by Allan Poe, his prospective wife's countryman—which was a thing to show, by the way, what imagination Americans *could* have; the story of the shipwrecked Gordon Pym, who, drifting in a small boat further toward the North Pole—or was it the South?—than anyone had ever done, found . . . before him a thickness of white air that was like a dazzling curtain of light, concealing as darkness conceals, yet of the colour of milk or of snow. There were moments when he felt his own boat move upon some such mystery. The state of mind of his new friends . . . had resemblances to a great white curtain. (I, 22)

James here alludes to perhaps the most bizarre example of American romance, Poe's *Narrative of A. Gordon Pym;* implicitly, the Prince's quest is identified with that of Pym, who seeks the ultimate source of mystery without any guideposts.

Maggie initially cannot employ the traditional forms—of language and social roles—which comprise the Prince's background. When she tries to match him verbally with figures for her affection, she produces the unfortunate image of the "steamliner" (I, 15), which not only emphasizes her wealth and Americanness but is full of references to "water-tight compartments," as if to assert her sexual inaccessibility to him. The Prince's view of the Ververs as "impenetrable" implies that Maggie, the mother of his child, in some ways remains virginal emotionally.

By contrast, when Charlotte Stant enters, she represents to the Prince no mystery but the "already known" (I, 46). Charlotte has mastered the social and linguistic forms in which the Prince has been bred. Their relation depends on a Kate Croy-like manipulation of such forms. But their affair, while enabled by the manners of civilized society at the beginning of the twentieth century, exposes the emptiness of that world. Despite the fact that the Prince initially sees Charlotte in sexual and financial terms (he envisions her as a filled purse), and that their affair begins in a store, the Prince and Charlotte seek to infuse their world with a meaning and spiritual richness felt to be absent. They try to make forms such as language magical, as if forms alone could create spiritual meaning. Their affair occurs in the gaps left by the disappearance of Christianity (Matcham, the site of their rendezvous, is an "Easter rite"), but their search for enchantment produces only further emptiness.

The enchanted places of romance become the long, blank front of the house at Matcham.[13] In the presence of the Prince and Charlotte, the complex life of the English country house dwindles to a sordid affair. At the end of the interlude at Matcham, the house is deserted except for Lady Castledean and her lover, Mr. Blint. The Prince and Charlotte base their affair on a fantasy of perfect union. Their resistance to social rules and to the limitations of reality generally tends to rob the world around them of meaning. By refusing to accept the boundaries of social forms, the adulterous lovers put pressure on the forms of language and social interaction which they cannot sustain. The Prince and Charlotte's attempts at magic become sheer repetition, and their "spiritual" communion is reduced simply to physical contact at the cathedral town of Gloucester, where the adultery is apparently consummated.

The Prince seeks to use language as magical invocation: at Matcham he repeats "Gloucester, Gloucester" (I, 358). But the words alone will not transport him there; he and Charlotte must take the 11:22 train (I, 362). The fiction of their spontaneity is exposed by the elaborate arrangements to which they must resort to maintain it. Their rejection of the containment of accepted social behavior leaves them to rely on other, mechanical forms of manipulation. The Prince and Charlotte fail to respect the ultimate mystery of otherness in human beings and in language itself. The Prince attempts to replace the obscurity of the Ververs with an easier and more direct satisfaction, a romance which severs the ties to reality. As a result, he and Charlotte separate language and passion from their necessary connections to "communities."

The Prince considers his love for Charlotte an oasis which transforms the arid places of life into the enchanted spaces of romance: "a meaning that their associated sense was to drain even as thirsty lips . . . might drink in at last the promised well in the desert. There had been beauty . . . in the exploration of which, as in that of the sun-chequered greenwood of romance, his spirit thus, at the opening of a vista, met hers" (I, 347). The Prince and Charlotte almost succeed in thinking themselves into their mental image of a romantic retreat: " 'It only wants a moon, a mandolin, and a little danger to be a serenade' " (I, 357). But their romance is a kind of mirage. As the form of the house party at Matcham breaks down, "things . . . melted together almost indistinguishably" (I, 351). Among the distinctions lost in the Prince's all-encompassing sense of beauty are moral ones. He sees the cathedral of Gloucester as scene-painting, reducing the religious sense to a "wash of far-away water colour" (I, 357).

What the Prince considers a "certain sweet intelligibility" at Matcham is actually an extreme confusion of social classes and morality. The Prince and Charlotte necessarily deny the truth, with the result that their seeming transcendence actually leads to a slippage below ordinary reality.

The illusion of mystical spirit actually results from a sense of absence or lack of form, a confusion articulated in Lady Castledean's need, in order to conceal her adultery, of "the presence—which really meant the absence—of a couple of other friends" (I, 352). The Prince seeks to enhance his diminished sense of self through his affair with Charlotte. But, as he dimly realizes, the affair has robbed him of his identity even more than his marriage has, turning him into a mere tool for Lady Castledean:

> the very relinquishment, for his wife's convenience, of his real situation in the world; with the consequence thus that he was, in the last analysis, among all these so often inferior people, practically held cheap and made light of. But though all this was sensible enough there was a spirit in him that could rise above it, a spirit that positively played with the facts . . . from that of the droll ambiguity of English relations to that of his having in mind something quite beautiful and independent and harmonious, something wholly his own. (I, 353)

Despite the Prince's conviction that he can manipulate reality, "play with the facts," in his affair with Charlotte he has relinquished rather than gained control over reality. The "spirit in him" which he perceives only represents his loss of contact with the "facts" of reality.

In Adam Verver, James presents an opposite and somewhat appalling portrayal of someone whose spirit is seemingly dominated by "facts." Adam uses his imagination as a form of power, a way to impose his will on reality. In the moment of his transformation from businessman to connoisseur, he does not so much transcend the material world as import it into imagination:

> He had, like many other persons, in the course of his reading, been struck with Keats's sonnet about stout Cortez in the presence of the Pacific; but few persons, probably, had so devoutly fitted the poet's grand image to a fact of experience . . . His "peak in Darien" was the sudden hour that had transformed his life, the hour of his perceiving, with a mute, inward gasp akin to the low moan of apprehensive passion, that a world was left him to conquer and that he might conquer it if he tried. . . . To rifle the Golden Isles had, on the spot, become the business of his future, and with the sweetness of it—what was most wondrous of all—still more even in the thought than in the act. (I, 241)

Adam's vision, unlike the Prince's, is decidedly long-ranging. In Adam's consciousness, buttressed by the money and industry lost by the Prince's Roman family, objects are transformed into beautiful aesthetic works. By comparing Adam to Keats's Cortez (in "On First Looking into Chapman's Homer"), James also transforms the romantic vision of the classical world into the epic imagination. Adam Verver, like the poet in Keat's poem, also reaches a world beyond material bounds, but one made possible by and contained within the realm of finance. Keats's term "realms of gold" refers ambiguously either to the material realm or the world of classical poetry. But Adam does not abandon the worlds Keats repudiates. Instead, he applies the terms "realms of gold" quite literally to the imaginative enterprise, as imaginative discovery becomes "rifling," romantic vision a "business."

For Adam, vision becomes conquest, as indicated by the misreading which makes Cortez the subject of Keats's sonnet rather than the vehicle of one of its similes. In recalling his first marriage, Adam sees women as a limit to vision, speculating that he would never have reached his revelation if his wife were still alive. Unlike the Prince, Adam seeks Charlotte not as partner in a courtly romance but as an object of conquest. Like an epic hero, he begins, like Aeneas, by "polishing and piling up his arms" (I, 144); then, like Jason, he launches his ships to capture the golden fleece, which is Charlotte. His proposal to her occurs shortly after a successful transaction with a Brighton merchant, which concludes with Adam eating some cake; James implies that for Adam, marriage is another form of consumption. Adam's passion seems to be reserved rather for the thrill of conquest than for Charlotte herself. When Adam proposes to Charlotte, he feels that he has "burned his ships" behind him. When she asks him, "Do you think you've known me?", he responds not with thoughts of her but a retrospective meditation on his own desires. He does not seek to know her but only to "push . . . harder . . . his fixed purpose":

> He hesitated, for the tone of it, and her look with it might have made him doubt. Just these things in themselves . . . with his fixed purpose now . . . the fine pink glow, projected forward, of his ships, behind him, definitely blazing and crackling—this quantity was to push him harder than any word of his own could warn him. All that she was herself, moreover, was so lit, to its advantage, by the pink glow. (I, 221)

The light here is not the golden light of fulfilled desire. Instead, in the "pink glow" Adam sees in Charlotte only a reflection of his own desire. In the childless marriage of Adam and Charlotte, absence of mutual desire leads to the sterile expenditure of energy in opposed wills. Adam's narcissism is indicated by the description of his first marriage, in which he saw his wife as a burden, and the fact that she quickly languished. His attachment at the time of her mother's death to the ten-year-old Maggie has clear incestuous overtones and indicates that Adam is incapable of loving anyone unless he or she is a reflection of himself.

Thus, though Adam has won the goal of his quest as epic hero, the goal of satisfied desire in marriage is yet to be achieved. Almost as soon as Adam's quest is completed, the Prince subverts it. Although his congratulatory telegram to Adam and Charlotte is a concession of defeat in terms of battle, as a message to Charlotte it keeps open the possibility of their continued adultery, claiming victory in terms of love: "*à la guerre comme à la guerre* then. We must lead our lives as we see them: but I am charmed with your courage and almost surprised at my own" (I, 290). The quests of Adam as epic conqueror and the Prince as courtly lover are equally unrealized and unrealizable at the end of book 1.

II. The Princess

Maggie Verver must combine the epic and romantic quests of her father and husband to become an epic heroine herself. She must do so without breaking the decorum which reigns at the various Verver establishments (Portland Place, Eaton Square, and Fawns). Maggie considers the forms of language and social life more foreign and fictitious than the European Prince and Europeanized Charlotte do. But Maggie deliberately invokes these forms, following them punctiliously, in order to create and evoke the intimacy they are meant to create. Maggie, unlike the Prince and Charlotte, understands that forms in themselves cannot create meaning, but may serve as the adequate means for its expression. While they claim spontaneity (and even sanctity) for their affair, Maggie's preservation of her marriage is deliberately artificial.

In the aftermath of the second marriage, adultery is legitimated rather than excluded by marriage, for the Prince and Charlotte's affair now is justified and protected by their familial relationship as in-laws, giving marriage a "counter-meaning" it was not intended to have. The adulterous affair subverts all social conventions, even as the Prince and Charlotte supposedly fulfill them for the Ververs by representing the family at public gatherings. They exploit apparently innocent appearances to cover a sordid reality.

Maggie's response is not to break apart the false appearances to reveal underlying corruption but to dwell even more undeviatingly on those glittering surfaces. The difference is that while the Prince and Charlotte can only respond, Maggie can make social forms, in part through her financial capacities but also through her decision to be active rather than passive. Maggie reaches the depths of intimacy by scrupulously remaining on the level of appearances, which may be, after all, the only level on which such issues can be addressed. Maggie's manipulation is intended primarily to uncover rather than conceal deception, and her actions are governed by the lawful desires of marriage rather than the lawless ones of adultery. James shows that similar materials used for different purposes have different moral valences. Maggie can use the instruments of the adulterers' corruption—the manipulation of social forms—without losing her innocence, for "to the pure all things are pure"; Maggie combines knowledge with goodness to achieve an innocence that does not shun but rises above knowledge of evil. Maggie may use the tools of evil, but in her hands they have a different moral import. Unlike Charlotte, she even maintains sympathy for her rival throughout.

Maggie must dispel and then recreate the deceptive surface harmony without disturbing it, by reforming the forms. Though she does not express her emotion directly, it is reflected in an efflorescence of passion and adventure in the figures in her book, which become grotesque and elaborate. Maggie uses increasingly formal and abstract forms, from the social gathering of the dinner party to the ritual of a card party to the purely literary form of exchanging one volume of a novel for another in her last encounter with Charlotte. Maggie is clearly associated with the artist, and by the end of the novel form and subject tend to collapse as James virtually elides the distinction between literary and actual acts (as he does in the preface). By using surfaces, Maggie attains her deepest desires; at the end of the novel, the artificial surface drops away to leave us looking into the "unmediated vision" of the heart's innermost wishes.

Hawthorne's Hilda, once initiated into life, abandons art. Milly uses art to shape, then finally abandon life. Maggie alone achieves the satisfaction of the artist within life, and attains both love and power—indeed, earns the former because of the latter. Maggie adapts some of the mechanisms of Kate Croy— especially a control of representation and an understanding of the ambiguity of language—to accomplish more acceptable goals, notably the preservation of her marriage. Maggie's art is, like James's definition of "the real romantic note," "continuous with the very life we are leading"; her realization of desire takes place within the structures of civilized society, notably marriage. To preserve appearances, Maggie must lie incessantly and completely; her plan depends on "never deviating into truth." Despite its deceptiveness, her design never escapes into fantasy. Thus, again, her acts resemble those of James the artist; her creation is a perfect artifice. James implies that his art, like Maggie's, is ultimately a sort of lie, but a lie that finally uncovers and even establishes the truth. As Maggie dispels the false harmony which conceals the adultery to reestablish the order of marriage, James's art may through its artifice uncover the reality that is often concealed in daily life.

As James proclaims in the preface his desire to "get down into the arena with his characters," Maggie is clearly the author's surrogate, the center of consciousness. By contrast to the opening of the Prince's book, Maggie's book begins with her growth in consciousness. In this scene, she is waiting (in this case for her husband's return from Gloucester), like Kate Croy at the beginning of *The Wings of the Dove,* but she waits to better effect. Her passion for her husband is expressed in the figures she uses, one of which evokes the quester's cup: "You've seemed these last days . . . more absent than ever before. . . . There comes a day when something snaps, when the full cup, filled to the very brim, begins to flow over. That's what has happened to my need of you. . . . I'm as much in love with you now as the first hour, except that there are some hours

. . . that show me I'm even more so" (II, 18). But it is precisely "some such words as those" which "were what didn't ring out." Maggie's romantic image is never articulated. Instead, the absence of direct expression is the sign of Maggie's passion and devotion; her silence enables the Prince to see "that his wife was *testifying,* that she adored and missed and desired him" (II, 19). Rather than expressing her desire, Maggie internalizes it. Waiting permits the entrance of consciousness in the "lapse" of time: "Such things . . . played, through her full after-sense, like lights on the whole impression" (II, 20).

Here, her waiting gives her a heightened "sense of possession." It also enables the first intuitions to arise which will lead to her suspecting her husband's adultery. For the "second wait" for him proves "of not inconsiderable length . . . to her later and more analytic consciousness," as she waits a long time while he dresses. Later in the book, she recognizes this moment as the first clue to his infidelity. Maggie's long wait becomes interpretable when her unconscious impression is subjected to conscious reflection. His desire eventually becomes subject to her consciousness, which will fill the gap between desire and its objects (it is a "circuit of *thought* and desire"). Through the acquisition of consciousness, Maggie turns the apparent signs of her subjection and helplessness—waiting, passivity—into ways to achieve power.

By repeating the events of the Prince's book, Maggie reveals the reality behind his illusions. Her recreation of the Matcham gathering exposes it as "the Easter revels at that visionary house" (II, 49). While at Matcham, the Prince sought to "play with the facts," to deny the reality of his adulterous situation, Maggie uses the Matcham people to confirm her suspicions of his infidelity. The uneasy party virtually reveals the fact that the country-house gathering was merely a cover for the adultery of Lady Castledean and of Charlotte and the Prince.

When she reconstructs the adventures of the Prince and Charlotte, paradoxically, Maggie achieves legitimate fulfillment of the desire they pursued illicitly. The most notable example of this pattern is the selling of the golden bowl. Charlotte's initial attempt to buy it from the Bloomsbury dealer is incomplete, perhaps because her motives are impure and she cannot see the crack in it. The Prince, who sees the crack, is somewhat contemptuous of Charlotte for her blindness, which seems to signify that she cannot understand that adultery is wrong, that it rends not only marriage but the social fabric generally. But the bowl is eventually sold to Maggie, and its meaning becomes apparent in this second transaction. Because of his "personal liking" for Maggie, the vendor of the bowl visits her house to inform her of the imperfection in the bowl after she has bought it. There he discovers the photographic portraits of Charlotte and the Prince, which remind him of his earlier encounter with them—their visit to his shop on the eve of the Prince's wedding. Maggie thus learns not just of the crack but what it represents—the adultery within her marriage. By gaining this awareness, she pays the price of the bowl, which is knowledge.[14] James suggests that as knowledge constitutes the effort of marriage, the possibility of adultery must be encompassed within that knowledge to make the marriage complete. Only awareness of what threatens the stability of marriage can insure that stability.

In the rest of the novel, Maggie acts much like the golden bowl's vendor. James uses a similar figure, the owner of a shop, as an image for the artist, who trades his goods in the "back-shop of the imagination" (in the preface to *The Portrait of a Lady, AN* 47). Like the Bloomsbury shop owner, Maggie is motivated not by revenge but by love—not so much love of any particular individual, as she tells Fanny, as "love itself" (II, 116). As the shop owner was able to reveal the meaning of the bowl to her by means of representation (the photographs), Maggie fulfills her desires through the mediation of social forms translated into artistic representations. Once Maggie comes into possession of the bowl, she becomes the artist of the book as well as of her own fate.

When Fanny deliberately and dramatically breaks the bowl, she is seeking to deny the adultery and its consequences. But in this act she not only releases Maggie's anger but shatters the false surfaces of harmony, hiding a crack, which have characterized Maggie's life. Maggie struggles to pick up the separate pieces and reform the original unity. Thus, while she strives to put the social order back together, she also resolves not to forget the adultery. The crack in the bowl remains and is multiplied, but Maggie holds the pieces together nevertheless. Her ideal is to complete the "circuit of desire" through the intervention of artistry and social forms to produce a reconstruction more perfect than the original construction: "A brilliant, perfect surface . . . the golden bowl as it was to have been. The bowl with all our happiness in it. The bowl without the crack" (I, 216–17). The image implies that the polished surface of the bowl contains depths, as Maggie seeks to create a perfectly artificial world which contains all depths of meaning within it. The crack can never be erased. To do so would require achieving a happiness that has never yet existed within the book, for the marriage of Maggie and the Prince was imperfect from the outset. But Maggie's construction of an artificial realm may offer the closest approximation to the ideal. The bowl "as it was to have been" captures in the future what has never been in the past, with the effect of retrospectively healing the failures and transgressions of the past.

Maggie accomplishes the realization of her desires first through social, then more purely artistic forms. The first such form is the bridge game, in the languid setting at Fawns which seems the height of civilized formality. As the game begins, Maggie sits outside as a spectator (reading what appears to be a journal of the aesthetic movement, often seen as espousing "art for art's sake"), "the last salmon-coloured periodical" (II, 231). The allusion reinforces Maggie's emphasis on forms, which would seem to make her immune from passion. But through the surface of mannered ceremonies, a raw, instinctual conflict looms.

When Maggie leaves the room, Charlotte pursues her like a wild animal: "the splendid shining supple creature was out of the cage" (II, 239). But Maggie repudiates rather than engages in such savage conflict:

> The rights of resentment, the rages of jealousy, the protests of passion . . . figured nothing nearer to experience than a wild eastern caravan, looming in view with crude colours in the sun . . . all a thrill, a natural joy to mingle with, but turning off short before it reached her and plunging into other defiles. (II, 236–37)

By internalizing rather than enacting this "impossible romance," Maggie does not repress her feelings but controls them, turning the raw energy of instinct into a power of command: "She had found herself . . . thrilling with the idea of the prodigious effect that . . . she had at her command" (II, 233). Here, then, the internalization of romance becomes the sublimation of instinct, the very formative basis of civilization.

While Maggie avoids direct conflict with Charlotte, Charlotte doesn't hesitate to attack Maggie. Her conversation with Maggie ends with a kiss of forgiveness, a Judas-kiss which "took on, with their [the others'] arrival, a high publicity" (II, 252). Maggie plays her part, covering herself with a hood in an apparent sign of humility, as if assuming the role of "scapegoat." But Maggie's humility here is only an act of "humbugging"; her seeming passivity again provides her with a strength through the accumulation of consciousness. By exposing herself in her treachery, Charlotte loses face. By repudiating "high publicity," by contrast, Maggie gains intimacy, which is private, not public. She grows closer to her husband during this scene, while Charlotte soars off into the unreal:

> They were together thus, he and she, close—close together—whereas Charlotte, though rising there radiantly before her, was really off in some darkness of space that would steep her in solitude and harass her with care. The heart of the Princess swelled accordingly even in her abasement. (II, 250)

As she achieves the reality of intimacy, Maggie also fulfills her romantic role as Princess, as she is given that title here.

Many critics see the elegant surface of the novel as a cover for violent feelings which are repressed rather than resolved. Instead, the surface itself reveals the pressure of such emotions, which are contained only at the price of "arrangements strained to breaking." But, as Fanny says, "the forms are two-thirds of conduct," perhaps all we have of morality. As James notes in the preface to *The Golden Bowl*, artistic acts have consequences even more than ordinary deeds; they comprise "conduct minutely attested, conduct with a vengeance." Artistic acts "help reconstitute the whole chain of connections." Maggie's artistry, then, does not remove her from reality but links her to it. Maggie, unlike Kate Croy, realizes her romance by reconnecting the ties of family, those to her husband as well as those to her father. The realization of romance is also indicated by the gradual dissolution of the figures which appeared earlier in the book, some of which become actual objects within the story. The ship imagery which began with allusions to epic and modulated into romance finally subsides into the final boat image, a canoe, as Maggie's quest becomes domestic idyll.

Maggie's relation with her father, as we have seen, begins as a somewhat incestuous one. Her new independence and connection to her husband necessarily separate her from her father. But the separation finally results in a new connection to him as adult woman rather than the dutiful daughter who also served as surrogate wife. While their long colloquies early in the novel were inappropriately extended, by the end of the book Adam and Maggie can embrace a moment of intimacy by understanding that it is temporary.

In one of the book's last scenes, Adam joins Maggie in her "boat"; the identity of their perceptions is suggested by a reference to their imaginations as one: "It was wonderfully like their having got together into some boat and paddled off from the shore where . . . luxuriant complications made the air too tropical. Why . . . couldn't they always live, so far as they lived together, in a boat? . . . They needed only *know* each other, henceforth, in the unmarried relation" (II, 255). The image of perfect unity here might seem to imply the Ververs' search to recapture their old intimacy. But the figurative construction here shows their own recognition of the fictitiousness of such intimacy. The recovery of affection between father and daughter, purged of incestuous overtones, makes them laugh at former anxieties:

> It might have been funny to them now that the presence of Mrs. Rance and the Lutches . . . had once, for their anxiety and their prudence, constituted a crisis; it might have been funny that these ladies could ever have figured, to their imagination, as a symbol of dangers vivid enough to precipitate the need of a remedy. (II, 253–54)

As their ugly, unadorned names indicate, Mrs. Rance and the Lutches (the former an apparent admirer of Mr. Verver, whom he seeks to escape by marrying Charlotte) represent the reality principle itself. For the Ververs, reality is no longer something threatening which must be transformed into figures or symbols but something amusing. For reality now confirms and includes the imaginative vision.

In the last part of the book, allusions to gold proliferate, as if the characters were seeking to reestablish the harmony of the golden age. During this encounter between the Ververs, James locates the "golden air" in the actualities of time and space: "They had meanwhile been tracing together, in the golden air that, towards six o'clock of a July afternoon, hung about the massed Kentish woods, several features of the social evolution of her old playmates, still beckoned on, it would seem, by unattainable ideals" (II, 256). There lingers a "finer tone" in reality which draws us toward, not away from, the actual, in the hope of realizing ideals. Maggie's vision approaches that of the author, as James describes his revisionary act in the preface: "She might have been wishing, under this renewed, this still more suggestive visitation, to keep him with her for remounting the stream of time and dipping again, for the softness of the water, into the contracted basin of the past" (II, 258). James refers to his own authorial act of revision as an attempt to "remount the stream" of time (*AN* 97).

Revision can recover a lost originality known only through representation. Here the ultimate source of life is rediscovered in a description of the individual as a sea creature, as if in the original oceanic environment "the suggestion as of a creature consciously floating and sinking in a warm summer sea, some element of dazzling sapphire and silver, a creature cradled upon depths, buoyant among dangers, in which fear or folly or sinking otherwise than in play was impossible." (II, 263). The "great extension" of consciousness reaches its furthest fulfillment, extending to awareness of a primordial realm of unrestricted freedom and "play."[15] Thus the fall into consciousness is converted into a gain, as it enables us to imagine the unfallen state: "He sat awhile as if he knew himself hushed . . . yet it was an effect that might have brought before him rather what she had gained than what he had missed. The beauty of her condition was keeping him, at any rate, in sight of the sea, where though his personal dips were over, the whole thing could shine at him, and the air and the plash and the play become for him too a sensation." The elaborate figurative structure of ships breaks down to the original tenor of such vehicles, the ocean associated with death and birth, consciousness of which is the next best thing to heaven: "It could yet pass very well for breathing the bliss . . . for tasting the balm" (II, 263).

This vision of absolute satisfaction is mostly that of Adam, who seeks a world of perfect unity and formlessness. But Maggie seeks satisfaction within the forms of everyday life. She considers the reality principle the means to fulfillment rather than frustration of desire. The final encounters of *The Golden Bowl* preserve the ultimate desire—the wish for pure union—with the forms which at once mediate and realize that desire, notably the form of marriage. In the last part of the novel, words and actions become both literal and metaphorical. Doubleness becomes fusion, resulting in a vision at once lovely and horrible.

The romance of the Prince and Charlotte—their disconnection from social forms—looks increasingly tragic and even deadly. Maggie sees them as Tristan and Isolde locked in a *liebestod*. At the furthest reach of Maggie's imagination, she captures the figure of the greenwood with which the Prince had pictured the enchantment of romance in their affair. Maggie finds romance "deeply within" her, as by internalizing the figures she discovers the literal meaning to which they refer:

> There had been . . . few quarters in which the Princess's fancy could let itself loose; but it shook off restraint when it plunged into the figured void of the detail of that relation. This was a realm it could people with images—again and again with fresh ones; they swarmed there like the strange combinations that lurked in the woods at twilight; they loomed into the definite and faded into the vague, their main present sign being that they were always . . . agitated. Her earlier vision of a state of bliss made insecure by the very intensity of the bliss—this had dropped from her; she had ceased to see, as she lost herself, the pair of operatic or high Wagnerian lovers (she found, deep within her, these comparisons) interlocked in their wood of enchantment, a green glade as romantic as one's dream of an old German forest. (II, 280)

The images of fairy tales are traced back to their source, the child's unconscious grasp of sexuality. Maggie views the relation of the Prince and Charlotte as ao primal scene (the "strange combinations"), the meaning of which she does not consciously understand. By penetrating to the depths of her unconscious, the desire for which the figures stand, she achieves a realization of her own sexuality which inspires these images of romance.

Maggie's "vision of . . . bliss made insecure by the very intensity of the bliss" recalls James's fear, in the "Preface" to *The American,* that an excess of happiness, in the elevation of romance, may lead to disconnection from reality: "The dream of an intenser experience easily becomes rather some vision of a sublime security like that enjoyed on the flowery plains of heaven, where we may conceive ourselves proceeding in ecstasy from one prodigious phase and form of it to another" (*AN* 32). But Maggie maintains the intensity of passion without losing contact with reality. By contrast, the figures of romance lock the Prince and Charlotte into a "dream." James notes that the spectacle of an imprisoned figure in romance can result in the greatest sense of freedom for the reader: "Beguile the reader's suspicion of *his* being shut up, transform it for *him* into a positive illusion of the largest liberty, and the success will ever be proportionate to the chance" (*AN* 39). Charlotte's imprisonment in a disconnected world becomes the very focus of Maggie's vision.

Maggie's apparent willingness to tolerate Charlotte's imprisonment is balanced by the depth of Maggie's sympathy for her, a sympathy far greater than that of her father or the Prince. In some ways Maggie allows her father to act cruelly towards Charlotte for her, but at several points Maggie seems to ask her father silently whether this is necessary. In any case, the "halter" around Charlotte's neck is only a figurative one, so that even Adam Verver cannot necessarily be dismissed as cruel. Charlotte's "quaver" may be the expression of the instincts she has never been able to tame, as in some ways she makes her own prison.

When she hears the voice of Charlotte reduced to a cicerone, which "sounded . . . like the shriek of a soul in pain" (II, 292), Maggie's simultaneous sympathy for and triumph over Charlotte results in an access of vision: "There was . . . an awful mixture in things. . . . This snatched communion yet lifted Maggie as on air" (II, 292). The physical, external union of Charlotte and the Prince is replaced by an unspoken, almost unseen intimacy between the Prince and Maggie. Every act of restraint by the Prince becomes the sign of his devotion: "She kept reading not less into what he omitted than into what he performed a beauty of intention that touched her fairly the more by being obscure. It was like hanging over a garden in the dark; nothing was to be made of the confusion of growing things, but one felt they were folded flowers, and their vague sweetness made the whole air their medium" (II, 295). This passage echoes the climactic stanza 5 of Keats's "Ode to a Nightingale." Here, as in Keats, the darkness implies the lack of full revelation, though the sweets are all the richer for needing to be "guessed." Maggie cannot yet sustain the vision of the Prince's intention; its intensity requires her to obscure her sight deliberately: "she blinded her eyes from the full glare of seeing that his idea could only be to wait" (II, 295). Maggie, like the poet in the Nightingale Ode, hangs over a garden, which represents the Prince's love, growing but as yet unseen and undeveloped. This union between Maggie and her husband occurs over the "high coerced quaver" of Charlotte. In Keats's poem, the nightingale's song occasions Keats's communion with his own imagination; here, Charlotte's "quaver" enables a communion between Maggie and the Prince of intimate love.

While Keats's Ode ends by posing the alternatives of a "vision" or a "waking dream," James turns Maggie's vision into a waking reality, romance into the real. Immediately after Maggie's vision, the figurative nighttime garden becomes an actual one, the site of Maggie's final encounter with Charlotte. This encounter occurs in a garden which has not been described previously, one which contains a small ornamental structure, like the figure of the pagoda with which Maggie's book begins.

Maggie now looks out on the garden in total illumination: "She hung over . . . the gardens and the woods—all of which drowsed below her . . . in the immensity of light" (II, 306). Charlotte's retreat from the light illustrates her attempt, by contrast, to escape into the wood of enchantment she sought throughout the Prince's book: "Maggie had quickly recognized the white dress and the particular motion of this adventurer. . . . Charlotte . . . had chosen the glare of noon for an exploration of the gardens . . . and she could be betaking herself only to some unvisited quarter deep in them, or beyond them, that she had already marked as a superior refuge" (II, 307). Charlotte carries a book with her with which to "cultivate romance in an arbour" (II, 308). The arbor is like the embodiment of the image of Maggie's love as a rich garden: "several wide alleys . . . densely over-arched with the climbing rose and the honeysuckle and . . . converging . . . at a sort of umbrageous temple" (II, 308–9). Here the echoes of Keats are more direct, as James includes several of the flowers mentioned in stanza 5 of the Nightingale Ode. Charlotte's retreat into the garden which serves as the figure for the Prince's love illustrates her desire to supplant Maggie. She attempts to take Maggie's place in another way, by carrying with her the second volume of a novel, as if she were appropriating Maggie's book, the second part of *The Golden Bowl*.[16]

But Charlotte's swift movement reveals her desperation: "Maggie . . . knew her doomed . . . and in the very sight of her uncontrollable, her blinded physical quest of a peace not to be grasped, something of Mrs. Assingham's picture of her as thrown . . . beyond the great sea and the great continent had at first found fulfillment" (II, 311–12). Charlotte's romance is reduced to a "blinded physical quest," while her affair with the Prince now exists only figuratively. By contrast, the inner communion Maggie has achieved with the Prince leads to the bright illumination of this scene, as if love had provided the light. Maggie's pursuit not of a "physical quest" but an inner, mental one results in her realization of romance not in a confined garden but everywhere.

Maggie follows Charlotte to give her the first volume of the novel in exchange for the second. Here the action is purely formal, a restoration of sequential order. The earlier efforts of formal arrangement in Maggie's book here end in an entirely literary act. In returning the first volume to Charlotte, Maggie in effect isolates her permanently within the first part of *The Golden Bowl,* completing her revision of the Prince's section and claiming her own, the second part; Maggie has now entirely incorporated Charlotte's romance. She no longer needs figures which allude to something other than the present reality but can rely on the surface she has constructed, the adequate vessel and expression of her "intention and her desire."

The final encounter of the major characters emphasizes the representationality not merely of Maggie's arrangements but of James's. Here the surfaces are clearly representations, the characters transformed into two-dimensional, storybook figures. While the tale begins with the Prince's remark that Adam "has no form," by the end of the novel there is nothing but form: "The form of their reunion was at least remarkable" (II, 354). The visit of Charlotte and Adam is like "some stiff official visit" (II, 354): "He received Royalty, bareheaded . . . in the persons of Mr. and Mrs. Verver" (II, 356). Characters which have been rather fully developed here become allegorical. The description works in the opposite way from most allegories; rather than representations standing for human vices or virtues, the human characters become representations. Reality grows shadowy as the symbolic level becomes dominant. Maggie's entire house at Eaton Square becomes a shadowy series of reflections: "The high cool room . . . with the perfect polish of its wide floor reflecting the bowl of gathered flowers . . . drew from her a remark in which this whole effect was mirrored" (II, 354).

At the end of this scene, as Charlotte and the Prince are viewed as works of art, we seem to see the chilling power of the Ververs' aestheticism to turn people into pictures. James makes extensive use here of the language of financial acquisition and appreciation associated throughout with Adam Verver and given some sinister overtones when, for instance, Adam looks at his daughter as if she were a statuette he were going to buy. Here, though, terms used earlier—"value," "possession"—become entirely ambiguous, referring equally to art and love. James suggests that aestheticism may be not a repudiation of love but a form of it. Adam's wedding gift to Maggie, one of his favorite *objets d'art*, represents his love for her, and even his view of her as a statuette may simply be a transference of loving attention from the realm of art to that of life.

The characters view representations here—as Adam takes a last look at the paintings and objects of Portland Place—not only in order to possess them, but to reckon their value. Ultimately their value is not financial or even aesthetic but moral and personal, as the aesthetic view symbolizes the moral one: "[Adam's looking at objects] signified . . . almost a special view of these devices . . . together with an independent, a settled appreciation of their general handsome adequacy" (II, 358). Adam is regarding Maggie's possessions, but his view of their "general handsome adequacy" might apply equally to the Prince. While, in the beginning of the work, the Prince seemed primarily a possession acquired by Adam for Maggie, now Adam acknowledges that Maggie possesses her husband in a different way, through the bond entailed by mature sexual love.

Form and subject are united, as aesthetic form and framing no longer contain or repress human feelings but provide their most adequate expression: "The beauty of his sentiment looked out at her . . . from the beauty of the rest, as if the frame made positively a window for his spiritual face" (II, 359). As Maggie realizes in this colloquy with her father, "He had applied the question to the great fact of the picture . . . but it was as if their words for an instant afterwards symbolized another truth" (II, 359–60). Language becomes symbolic, every word freighted with figurative as well as literal meaning, referring at once to surface appearances and spiritual depths. The surfaces are no longer a barrier but a window to the depths. In his 1879 *Hawthorne,* James criticized symbolism as "apt to spoil two good things—a story and a moral, a meaning and a form" (50). But here James reunites those pairs, capturing symbolism's range of meaning without losing the tie to reality. Thus he produces a particularly rich and intense vision.

According to James in the 1904 Hawthorne Centenary essay, combining "freedom of the spell" with "truth to the objects observed," romance and realism, produces a sense of value, "that artistic economy which understands *values* and uses them" (28). Charlotte and the Prince illustrate the value, the "rare power of purchase," not just of Adam's money but of Maggie's love:

> Mrs. Verver and the Prince fairly "placed" themselves . . . as high expressions of the kind of
> human furniture required, aesthetically, by such a scene. . . . The fusion of their presence with
> the decorative elements . . . was complete and admirable; though, to a longer view . . . they
> almost might have figured as concrete attestations of a rare power of purchase. (II, 360)

The compositional and descriptive aspects, form and subject, are fused; Charlotte and the Prince seem purely "decorative elements." Some critics view with horror what appears to be a scene of human beings transformed into furniture.[17] But in the preface, James speaks of Maggie herself as in part a decorative element: she is "a compositional resource, and of the finest order, as well as a value intrinsic"; in this way, she "duplicates, as it were, her value." Similarly, only when they fit the compositional scheme and are fully placed do Charlotte and the Prince reveal their human value. James does not deny the coercive aspects of his own representation or of Maggie's arrangements, which is why this final scene is so deliberately artificial. But he shows that fictions, despite their artifice, may reveal or even create "values" not otherwise knowable.

Maggie's sympathy for Charlotte does not prevent Maggie from seeking her own happiness and doing what social law proclaims to be right—preserving her marriage. If maintaining civilized forms requires a brutality reminiscent of the animal instincts civilization is meant to control, recognizing that fact and accepting that knowledge is for James at once the reward and price of civilization, like the crack in the golden bowl, which cannot be eradicated or denied. As James says in the preface that by the artist's act, "with a touch the whole chain of connexion is constituted," at the end of the novel Maggie reconstitutes all the connections that tie her to others. As she gives the final touches to the form, the "value" glitters in it. Form and meaning have become identified, as Maggie's arrangements sustain the weight of her love. The "longer view" reveals that the final tableau of the Ververs and their *sposi* is not only a scene of formal arrangement but one made possible not primarily by financial but personal power, Maggie's capacity for love, which only these two creatures have enabled her to know and illustrate. If some sacrifice has been entailed on her part as well as theirs, that is, James implies, the necessary cost of knowledge and of love, which purchases the bowl because it acknowledges the crack of imperfection. Maggie and Adam Verver, having reckoned the value of their love and its fruits, can now part company: they "were parting . . . absolutely on Charlotte's value—the value that was filling the room out of which they had stepped as if to give it play" (II, 365).

For James, values can be expressed or understood only through the mediation of physical representation, "furniture" of one sort or another, for values themselves are beyond articulation. Like the Keatsian garden in which beauty is a function of darkness, the fulfillment of Maggie's desire, the attainment of the object of the quest, includes blindness or horror at its heart—at the pain inflicted or the pain in the midst of love itself: "Everything . . . struck her as meaning so much that the unheard chorus swelled. She knew at last . . . how she had been inspired and guided . . . how, to her soul, all the while, it had been for the sake of this end. Here it was . . . the golden fruit that had shone from afar; only what *were* these things in the fact . . . when tested, when tasted—what were they as a reward?" (II, 367). "Value" cannot be assigned to objects, only to actions or desires. Maggie's long quest is fulfilled, as she tastes the golden apples of Paradise. Yet the fulfillment of romantic vision sounds like a tragedy, occurring in "pity and dread": " ' "See"? I see nothing but *you*.' And the truth of it had, with this force, after a moment, so strangely lighted his eyes that, as for pity and dread of them, she buried her own in his breast" (II, 369). Maggie can not confront her own guilt or the shame she may see reflected in the Prince's eyes, or even perhaps the vision of satisfaction itself. Vision is also blindness, success failure, in an acknowledgment of the inseparable mixture of morality in all human affairs.

For Keats, desire deludes in its tendency to imagine a world that never was, a realm of transcendence like that of the nightingale or the "unheard . . . melodies" of the "Ode on a Grecian Urn" (echoed in the "unheard chorus" in Maggie's mind here). James shows that, even when satisfied in reality rather than projected onto a visionary realm, desire remains incapable of uniting with its objects. For James, even fulfilled desire cannot confront reality entirely; Maggie cannot meet her husband's eyes. No wonder, then, as the attainment of the romantic quest for fulfilled love and vision resulted in blindness and tragedy, James, with his last finished novel, had written what was, for the nineteenth century at least, the "novel to end all novels."

While *The Wings of the Dove* strongly suggests the possible existence of a spiritual realm beyond this one, however inaccessible or unprovable, in *The Golden Bowl*, James's focus is squarely on this world, though the world presented often as if it were the dream of individual imagination or desire. For James, as he notes in 1904, the field of romance has widened to a whole side of life, and indeed a perspective that can be applied to any aspect of life. For James, romance becomes not so much a literary genre as a way of perceiving and understanding. It no longer needs to be set apart from this world in a special precinct like that Hawthorne claims for romance in his prefaces.

Indeed, in *The Golden Bowl*, James inverts not only Hawthornian romance but the form of the novel itself. Hawthorne uses romance to envision alternate possibilities, to unsettle ordinary existence and project images closer to the "truth of the human heart." Nonetheless, he often ironizes romance by showing it as susceptible to being overpowered by reality. For James, though, romance is present in reality. Romance is found within, not outside of, daily experience. Consciousness so fully shapes reality that desire becomes a mode of knowing. In a work which emphasizes throughout the power of the artist's craft, James sees vision as the product of revision. Romance, he suggests, may stem from unconscious longings but is realized through conscious thought and action. The romance of the real is present all around us, and is revealed by the heroic capacity to love with all one's powers of mind and heart.

Conclusion

In his late years, James's pursuit of romance, of the revisionary power of imagination against actuality, would extend to the massive, retrospective project of rewriting his country (in *The American Scene*), his own work (in the prefaces and revisions to the New York Edition), and the lives of himself and especially his brother (in the *Autobiography*).[1] If he had reached the limits of fictive representation in *The Golden Bowl*, James was to see the world as representation in *The American Scene*, viewing the sights and sounds of the United States as speaking monuments equally subject to his imagination as the more purely imaginative creations of his novels.[2] If romance was a whole "side of life," as James argues in the 1904 Hawthorne essay, it could be discovered in reality as well as fiction. Having analyzed Hawthorne's transformation of Salem in his fiction in that essay, an achievement apparent only to later viewers, James deliberately sets out to do the same, to transform actual appearances by the imaginative power of the writer, for all of the United States in *The American Scene*. His understanding of the United States as material for representation is seen even in the theatrical metaphor of the book's title. For him, his native country is a "world created, a stage set" (p. 15). By the twentieth century, having exhausted Europe as a theme, James was ready to return to the United States to consider the International Theme in reverse. For, after a twenty-year absence, at that time America rather than Europe seemed "romantic" to Henry James:

> The European complexity . . . had grown usual and calculable—presenting itself . . . as the very stuff, the common texture, of the real world. It was American civilization that had begun to spread itself thick and pile itself high. . . . Europe had been romantic years before, because she was different from America; wherefore America would now be romantic because she was different from Europe. (p.366)

Nonetheless, when he actually sees the United States he realizes that to some extent it is still as he saw it in 1879, deficient in culture. Despite the great industrial growth of the United States in the period before his return in 1904, the country remained to a great extent empty, incapable of cultural maturity. Here the gaps in experience offer the opportunity for romance, as imagination expands to compensate for scanty material. James finds that while "the romantic effect as we know it elsewhere most depends on them [details]," nonetheless "that glamour . . . so shimmered before me in their absence" (p. 149). For James, paradoxically, the romance of America inheres precisely in its lack of many things, the absence of which inspires both memory and poetic feeling: "Perpetually, inevitably . . . as the restless analyst wandered, the eliminated thing *par excellence* was the thing most absent to sight" (p. 24). For the absence of various elements—things he remembers from the America of twenty years earlier, or aspects that never existed—is precisely what awakens his imagination and allows memory to operate untrammelled: "There was a latent poetry—old echoes, ever so faint, that *would* come back. . . . Why had the inconvenience . . . of early privation become an accepted memory? All, doubtless, in the very interest, precisely, of this eventual belated romance" (pp. 28, 52).

His pursuit of romance, the revisionary power of imagination over fact, extends throughout *The American Scene*. Nonetheless, in the United States, the imagination of the "restless analyst" constantly encounters the reality of James's own personal background. If *The American Scene* illustrates the power of James's imagination to transform actuality into a series of "impressions" bathed in a retrospective light, it also dramatizes his confrontation with the facts of history and biography which engendered that imagination—his own American youth and the legacy of Hawthorne. Especially in the first half of the book, James retraces his own footsteps as he returns to the haunts of his youth in Boston, Newport, Chocorua, and other sites. In the chapter entitled "Concord and Salem," he virtually repeats Hawthorne's meanderings in "The Old Manse." James finds that his focus on the past necessarily turns his "adventure" into an "eventual belated romance" (p. 52). At the same time, he seeks in the United States a "higher reality." At one point, he describes America as if it were a Hawthorne story come to life, "a huge Rappaccini-garden" (p. 57). James seeks in the United States in *The American Scene* both the "rich real" and "the rich romantic" (p. 322). But something always escapes his grasp, as the attempt to master reality and the past leads to the discovery of a gap between his consciousness and the reality he confronts.

While Hawthorne seemed entirely assimilated to the tone of James the Master in the Hawthorne Centenary essay of 1904, on his return to Salem James discovers the still unassimilated presence of Hawthorne, the excess of power and imagination which escapes James's control. James is able, however, to claim that excess as representative of the power of the novelist in general, and so to turn the threat of Hawthorne's presence into an enhancement of his own power. The fact that Hawthorne, though a writer deeply identified with a region, escapes his local milieu, becomes a key to the art of Henry James, whose consciousness, as the preface to *The American* describes, was begotten precisely by disjunction from the American scene. In this work, which would seem to come closer to reality than James's fiction in its documentary aspect, James continually discovers his own consciousness.

Thus *The American Scene* becomes a way to question the premises of realism which, as James realizes, is often inadequate. Indeed, the "facts" may be always beyond one's grasp. Romance, which incorporates distance, may seem the ideal way to depict such a reality. As in *The Golden Bowl* and the prefaces, consciousness and vision are achieved principally through the golden light of retrospection, which recovers an otherwise illusory originality. In the prefaces, James's imagination tends to meet itself, as revision produces a circle of satisfaction in which he is both reader and writer. In this work the act of revision typically takes the form of revisiting, by which James seeks to reenact an earlier trauma and so recover it under his own control.

The intertwining of Hawthorne with James's memory and American identity reaches full expression in *The American Scene*. James's invocation of Hawthorne and the past here begins near the site where memory had overtaken him in *The Bostonians,* the Memorial Hall at Harvard (his brother's place of work for most of his life, though James hardly alludes to this). As James strives to reconnect his own personal past with the transformed America of the twentieth century, Hawthorne becomes not only his vehicle for representing America as romance, but his way of reading the realities of the United States, as James imagines Hawthorne's stories realized in the actual American environment. James refers to Hawthorne in giving his view of universities as alternatives to the money-grubbing world outside the ivory tower: "They glow, the humblest of them [the universities], to the imagination—the imagination that fixes the surrounding scene as a huge Rappaccini-garden, rank with each variety of the poison-plant of the money-passion" (p. 57). While one might expect the ivy-covered university to be associated with the enclosed garden of the scientist Rappaccini, here the relation of inside and outside, real world and imagined one, is reversed. The external world becomes the "Rappaccini-garden," infected with the "money-passion," as the university enclave becomes at once more pure and more real.

Here, as throughout *The American Scene,* imagination replaces reality with its own creations, turning the harsh actualities of twentieth-century America into a series of imagined scenes. By seeing American scenes as Hawthorne tales come to life, James turns reality into romance, romance into reality. On his return to the Memorial Hall, James finds that in that structure "the right provision had been made for the remembering mind" (p. 60). Indeed, as James meditates on Harvard, it increasingly becomes not just a place for the mind but a place of the mind, an apt image for James's imaginings. Though in this section James never mentions the brother who taught there, it is as if Harvard becomes the testing ground for his brother's theories of pragmatism, his notion that there is no reality apart from the ideas we have of it. James here feels that reality is known, as in his brother's works, rather as a leading of the mind towards truth than any fixed essence, and so feels "the instinct not to press . . . through any half-open door of the real" (p. 59).

In the area of Boston and Cambridge, looking down "over the flood of the real" (p. 68), James encounters the ghosts of a literary as well as a personal past. In the course of his confrontations with these ghosts, James comes to recognize a series of "gaps" made by the passage of time, gaps between his earlier and later selves, between himself and America generally, and between himself and the American tradition of Thoreau, Emerson, and Hawthorne. He must learn what these gaps can represent and in the process what connection exists between his life and his imagination.

For James's attempts at repetition (especially when he revisits his old home in Ashburton Place in Boston twice) tend rather to reveal discontinuity. Typically, in moments of failed repetition when he realizes the difference between the past and the present, James is struck with a feeling of emptiness, "as if the bottom had fallen out of one's biography."[3] But one might rather say that what emerge from such disconnections are, on the one hand, all of the American life James had largely repressed for twenty years, the story of his family and youth as well as that of the development of the country; and, on the other hand, the fact of his own career as writer and artist, one constituted by the disconnection between his consciousness and the American scene. In *The American Scene,* despite the disruptions, what James discovers is life, the life of his own early past in the United States and of all his subsequent career. If at the sites sacred to Hawthorne he discovers too much life, a kind of return of the dead, for James this presence of Hawthorne is finally reassuring. In acknowledging Hawthorne's difference from himself, James becomes aware of the artist's immortality and so of his own chance for immortality.[4]

In "The Old Manse," Hawthorne's religious and literary predecessors form a continuous line which extends back to the seventeenth century. In "Concord and Salem," though the "torch of history" reveals to James "the measure of his relation to the scene" (p. 227), the relation is one of disjuncture rather than connection. James's attempt to reestablish American literary connections only uncovers further gaps—between a place and its significance, the past and the present, and genius and its origins.

"Concord and Salem" is preceded by a more directly autobiographical section, on Boston. Hawthorne's presence begins to be felt even here, in James's allusion to "Rappaccini's Daughter" in the discussion of Harvard Yard, the numerous references to Hawthorne and his contemporaries as "the Weimar group," and the return to Ashburton Place, where, as James reveals in his

Autobiography, he first learned of Hawthorne's death. Ashburton Place is the "particular spot I had wished to revisit" (p. 227) because it is where he began to write. James's former home, "full both of public and of intimate vibrations" (p. 229), has become a haunted house, where James seeks to recover his earlier self: "The effort of actual attention was to recover on the spot some echo of ghostly footsteps." James seeks not only his younger self but literary inspiration itself, by projecting himself back to the moment when he first received it. Here "memory met that pang of loss," and grows more powerful in the absence of the things James remembers. While Hawthorne embroiders history with legend, for James history arises in the absence of legend. Though many elements of the scene which he remembers are now gone, one can "picture them . . . embroider them, at one's ease—to tangle them up in retrospect and make the real romantic claim for them" (p. 228). Here James uses not only Hawthorne's image for art—Hester Prynne's embroidery of the Scarlet Letter—but the phrase he used to describe Hawthorne's art in the 1904 essay ("the real romantic note"), implying that the absence of many things heightens memory. He feels this claim "in particular for the sacrificed end of Ashburton Place."

The visit to Ashburton Place seems to reestablish his link to the past and even to the "life" which lingers at his former home. But his attempt to repeat the visit proves a "justly-rebuked mistake." For on his second visit there James finds not ghostly presences but "a gaping void, the brutal effacement . . . of every related object, of the whole precious past" (p. 229). With the destruction of the house, the second visit becomes a violent break reenacting the original trauma, or "rupture," of James's youth (p. 230). Ashburton Place was not only where he began to write, but the scene of a rupture in many senses: James lived there during the great national rupture of the Civil War, which found a private equivalent for him in his "obscure wound." The "obscure wound" enforces James's separation from active life, disqualifying him from participation in the war, and ultimately estranging him from active American life in general.

The loss of origins provokes in James a radical dislocation of identity: "One plunged backward into space without meeting anything. It was . . . as if the bottom had fallen out of one's biography." Loss of his creative origins removes the very ground of James's identity. He is forced to acknowledge that alienation from the life around him was always his relation to the American scene: "the whole figure of my connection with everything about, a connection that had been sharp, in spite of brevity, and then had broken short off" (p. 229).

James recognizes that his relation to the past is one of disconnection rather than connection. After this traumatic incident, he notes the way in which the past recedes from our grasp and attempts also to reconnect with it by seeking the sources of literary genius. When he visits the places of origin of other writers, James's search for the source of literary inspiration becomes transgression, for Concord and Salem are the "central or sacred cities" of the American Romantics. To go there is to encounter the ghosts of Emerson and his contemporaries in a trespass against sacred authority, for "ghosts . . . belong only to places and suffer and perish with them" (p. 243). James goes to Concord and Salem to find the very secret of the genius of his predecessors.

Thus, entering the area of the Old Manse, James, like Hawthorne before him, feels great trepidation. The weight of authority which intimidated Hawthorne is increased by Hawthorne's own intimidating precedent. Where James most closely echoes Hawthorne in this essay, he also most attempts to suppress him. Hawthorne introduces his stories in "The Old Manse" by saying: "With these . . . withering blossoms I have intermixed some that were produced long ago—old, faded things, reminding me of flowers pressed between the leaves of a book. . . ." James uses the same image to seal up Hawthorne's book and prevent its circulation: "I might have lost . . . my good little impression, which otherwise, as a small flower plucked from a withered tree, I could fold away, intact, between the leaves of my romantic herbarium" (p. 269). While Hawthorne takes a humorous tone towards ghosts in "The Old Manse," James feels alternate "tenderness" and "terror" towards the ghost of Hawthorne. In "the Old Manse," Hawthorne's anxiety about time and influence resolves into a Wordsworthian "serene and blessed mood." While Hawthorne felt in the autumnal scene "the promise of a blissful Eternity," James feels no such renewal when visiting the same area at the same time of year. Rather, the burden of the past makes originality impossible for him, for in this place all of his reactions have been previously experienced and recorded: "Not a russet leaf fell for me, while I was there, but fell with an Emersonian drop" (p. 265).

Yet James, like Hawthorne, overthrows the past by replacing history with personal impression: "Official history . . . leaves the exquisite melancholy of everything unuttered" (p. 261). For James, one understands the past by breaking the historical line of sequence. His relation to the past is deeper and richer because it is the absence of relation. Of the "embattled farmers" at Concord Bridge, James says, "We feel . . . the *precluded* relation on the part of the fallen defenders. The sense that was theirs and that moved them we know, but we seem to know better still the sense that wasn't, and that couldn't, and that forms our luxurious heritage." Our rich tradition depends on our disconnection from our forefathers, as the full sweep of memory rushes into the gap between us. Our inheritance, the wealth of "what our forefathers produce for us," is the result of our disconnection from them, their having "so little of the conscious credit of it" (p. 262).

So, too, James finds disconnection an advantage in his search for literary origins. He is initially dismayed to find the actual sites of Concord poorer and ruder than the works they inspired. The Old Manse bears "every due similitude to the shrunken historic site in general" (p. 263). Yet, as Hawthorne discovered, disconnection may be liberating rather than disappointing. By exaggerating the disconnection between the Manse and Hawthorne's essay on it, James renews the Manse as a subject for his own pen. He metaphorically renovates the Old Manse by describing it as denuded of Hawthorne's "mosses": "the manse . . . would now appear to have shaken itself a trifle disconcertingly free of the ornamental mosses scattered by Hawthorne's light hand" (p. 263). Though James seems disappointed that such sites destroy rather than aid our attempt to reenvision the writer, in fact such "reconstitution" would be frightening to James because it would give the past new life. James's "renovation" of the manse frees it of Hawthorne's haunting presence to make it merely a "mild monument," testimony to Hawthorne's death rather than his continuing presence.

Thus James suppresses Hawthorne's ongoing presence, though he protests his "so good general intention." No wonder, then, he feels acute anxiety when he approaches the sites where he imagines Hawthorne's ghost might actually persist. When he reaches the threshold of the Salem Witch House, he is held back by a "sacred terror . . . in spite of the quite definite sturdy stamp of the attraction" (p. 268). When he is shown "the window of the room in which Hawthorne had been born," he feels that "wild horses . . . wouldn't have dragged me into it" (p. 270).

At the end of the chapter "Concord and Salem," James also visits (or rather fails to visit, looking at it from a distance) a site associated not only with Hawthorne but with even older American scenes—the House of the Seven Gables. The latter represents no apparent correspondence to Hawthorne's work. James acknowledges that it is impossible to connect genius and its origins; we cannot trace genius to its source because it is, by definition, greater than its source or surroundings. James breaks "the poor illusion of a necessity of relation between the accomplished thing . . . and those other quite equivocal things that we inflate our ignorance with seeing it suggested by." Hawthorne's "admirable book (*The House of the Seven Gables*) so vividly forgets . . . any such origin or reference, 'cutting' it dead . . . and outsoaring the shadow of its night, that the connection has turned a somersault into space, repudiated like a ladder kicked back from the top of the wall" (p. 271). James wittily turns disconnection into a social "cut." Finally, for James disconnection is not traumatic but redeeming. For genius's triumph is that it cannot be traced to its origin and so requires none—it is ultimately unhoused. James's original rupture from the active American world never healed, but the rupture constituted an identity. What originally seemed alienation has proved a legacy and "begotten . . . a consciousness" (p. 267). The levelling of Ashburton Place, then, simply literalized the necessary separation between a great writer and his origins, as genius "outsoars" its links to time and space.

The destructive renovation which concludes "The Old Manse" is, in *The*

American Scene, the preexistent condition of American life. Hawthorne's sympathies lie with neither the renovators nor the past. Though he breaks his "pact" with past authorities, whom he tries to demystify, Hawthorne also reclaims the power of the past, by attributing to his own work its "substance" and endurance. For James, sublimity still resides in the past, "the mystery of antiquity" standing for the mystery of life itself. James finds that the past retains divine inscrutability, which makes him more relieved than despairing to know that we never see the face of genius unveiled: "Endless are its ways of besetting and eluding, of meeting and mocking us" (p. 271).

James describes romance as completing "the beautiful circuit and subterfuge of our thought and our desire" which connects us to the "things . . . we never *can* directly know." James comes full circle on this issue in his own work, as can be discerned in the pattern of his essays on Hawthorne, which progress from rejection to assimilation of Hawthornian romance and implicitly of the American scene. The strain of romance and the fantastic remains strong throughout James's work, especially in the ghost stories of the 1890s (such "amusettes" as *The Turn of the Screw*). but romance is present as a counter-strain even in such purportedly "naturalistic" works as *The Bostonians*. In James's last novels, his detailed plots and descriptions would seem to represent the height of realism, while his heroines in their exalted status, the "heiresses of all the ages," resemble characters from fairy tales. The fusion of romance and reality here results in the possibility of desire being realized within such conventional forms as those of marriage and the novel. In *The American Scene,* James seeks at once to discover the "romance" of his long-lost American past and to confront a reality that he may have lost in going to Europe.

The influence of Hawthorne on James not only in plots and characters but mode of representation signals an important link in nineteenth-century American literature. Though the Civil War was in some ways the abyss James felt it to be between the two parts of the century, in this literary relation the division between romance and realism James saw early in his career was actually a defense against their underlying continuity. Romance was not repudiated by the end of the nineteenth century, but formed the very basis for modernism. Though romance fantasy might seem opposed to modernist skepticism, in fact romance dramatizes the processes of desire and the difficulty of satisfaction which are central themes of modernist literature. The presence of romance within the novel emphasized the subjective elements of representation. While the result was to unsettle the faith in a stable "reality" outside representation, the sense of enchantment in romance also provided intimations of a meaning and reality discernible only by questioning actuality. Thus if romance led to modernism by subverting certitudes through desire, it also made desire a mode of knowing. With the influence of romance in mind, the gaps or absences in modernist works may be seen not as signs of emptiness but traces of meaning that is as much created as perceived. In those gaps romance magic finds a means of expression, if now primarily within the mind rather than outside it.

Hawthorne has been seen either as inadequate in relation to James, who allegedly mastered issues Hawthorne raised but could not resolve, or as too powerful, setting a model of romance-writing which James could only overturn by adapting the new form of "realism." But Hawthorne's romance is at once more controlled and more indeterminate than critics of this relation have seen; his romance shows the difficulty of capturing "reality" in representation which James himself could not resolve. James's Hawthorne is not Melville's writer of "blackness ten times black"; as early as the 1879 *Hawthorne* James disputes Montegut's characterization of Hawthorne as a "romancier pessimiste." In light of the issues raised by Hawthorne, James was led not only to a massive reexamination of "realism," or the capacity of any representation to reflect a world outside it, but a questioning of the very nature or existence of "the real." Armed with what he always recognized as Hawthorne's penetration to the "deeper psychology," and what he came to see as Hawthorne's moral insight, James showed that we have no immediate knowledge of or way to depict reality; all we have are impressions. The search for "The Real Thing" intensifies in the novels of James's Major Phase, in which the rich details fail, as James himself acknowledged, to capture the facts of death and sexuality *(The Wings of the Dove)*, love and sexuality *(The Golden Bowl)*, industry and intimacy *(The Ambassadors)*. But James's late works show that the failure to grasp reality was not a problem for representation alone. In *The American Scene,* the prefaces, and the *Autobiography*, by transforming history, his work, and his life into romantic representations, James dramatizes our inability ever to know the real. That the consciousness of this distance survives and even triumphs over death makes this unbridgeable gap into a rich legacy for life as well as art. For James, reality was best known through romance, an admittedly fictive construct, but one which provides the best outlet for the life which otherwise seems ever escaping our grasp.

Notes

Introduction

1. See, for instance, the landmark work of Richard Chase, *The American Novel and its Tradition* (Garden City, N.Y.: Anchor-Doubleday, 1957). Chase's thesis has been extended by Joel Porte, *The Romance in America* (Middletown, Ct.: Wesleyan University Press, 1969) and Michael D. Bell, *The Development of American Romance* (Chicago, Ill.: University of Chicago Press, 1980).

2. Henry James, *Hawthorne* (1879; reprinted Ithaca, N.Y.: Cornell University Press, 1956).

3. Northrop Frye, *Anatomy of Criticism* (Princeton, N.J.: Princeton University Press, 1957), 190–206.

4. The first major essay on Hawthorne's influence on James was by another expatriate: T.S. Eliot, "The Hawthorne Aspect," *Little Review* 5 (1918), 47–53; reprinted in *The Question of Henry James,* ed. F.W. Dupee (London: Allen Wingate, 1947), 123–33. The major works on the Hawthorne influence are Marius Bewley, *The Complex Fate: Hawthorne, Henry James, and Some Other American Writers* (London: Chatto and Windus, 1952), and Robert E. Long, *The Great Succession: Henry James and the Legacy of Hawthorne* (Pittsburgh, Pa.: University of Pittsburgh Press, 1979). Both writers see James as perfecting Hawthorne by transforming romance into realism. For a similar view, see Yvor Winters, "Maule's Well, or Henry James and the Relation of Morals to Manners," in his *In Defense of Reason* (Denver, Colo.: Allen Swallow, 1937), 300–343. There is not yet a comprehensive account of the influence throughout James's career; Bewley treats a few novels and does not address the changes in James's view of Hawthorne. Long's book stops at *The Bostonians,* with no treatment of the Major Phase works.

    Studies more sympathetic to Hawthorne, which therefore see the influence as more pervasive, include R.W.B. Lewis, "Hawthorne and James: The Matter of the Heart," in *Trials of the Word: Essays in American Literature and the Humanistic Tradition* (New Haven, Ct.: Yale University Press, 1965), and Richard Poirier, *A World Elsewhere: The Place of Style in American Literature* (New York, N.Y.: Oxford University Press, 1966). For a consideration of James's relation to Hawthorne in personal terms, see Richard Ruland, "Beyond Harsh Inquiry: The Hawthorne of Henry James," *ESQ* 25 (1979), 95–117. See also F.O. Matthiessen, *American Renaissance* (New York, N.Y.: Oxford University Press, 1941), 292–305. For a complete bibliography of writings on the Hawthorne-James relation, see Thaddeo K. Babiiha, *The James-Hawthorne Relationship: Bibliographical Essays* (Boston, Mass.: G. K. Hall, 1980). An excellent review-essay is John C. Rowe's "'What the Thunder Said': James's

Hawthorne and the American Anxiety of Influence: A Centenary Essay," *Henry James Review* 4 (1983), 81–119. On Hawthorne's influence on other later writers, see John McElroy, "The Hawthorne Style of American Fiction," *ESQ* 19 (1973), 117–23; and Hyatt Waggoner, *The Presence of Hawthorne* (Baton Rouge, La.: Louisiana State University Press, 1979).

5. "Letter to the Honorary Robert S. Rantoul," 10 June 1904, in *The Proceedings in Commemoration of the One Hundredth Anniversary of the Birth of Nathaniel Hawthorne* (Salem, Mass.: Essex Institute, 1904), 55–62. The essay is reprinted in *The American Essays of Henry James*, ed. Leon Edel (New York, N.Y.: Vintage, 1956), 24–31. All subsequent references to this essay are to this edition, and will be abbreviated "1904."

6. On James as modernist, see Sergio Perosa, *Henry James and the Experimental Novel* (Charlottesville, Va.: University Press of Virginia, 1978); Stuart Hutchinson, *Henry James, an American as Modernist* (London: Vision/Totowa, N.J.: Barnes and Noble, 1983).

   On the transformation of romance into later romanticisms and then modernism, see especially Geoffrey Hartman, "False Themes and Gentle Minds," in *The Fate of Reading* (Chicago, Ill.: University of Chicago Press, 1975), 283–97; and Harold Bloom, "The Internalization of Quest-Romance," in *The Ringers in the Tower* (Chicago, Ill.: University of Chicago Press, 1971), 13–35. On romanticism and modernism in the novel, see Charles Schug, *The Romantic Genesis of the Modern Novel* (Pittsburgh, Pa.: University of Pittsburgh Press, 1979); David Thorburn, *Conrad's Romanticism* (New Haven, Ct.: Yale University Press, 1974); Allon White, *The Uses of Obscurity* (London: Routledge and Kegan Paul, 1981). Schug and White include extended analyses of James.

7. Chase, p. 13 and p. xi.

8. See especially the first two chapters of Michael Bell's *The Development of American Romance*.

9. Frye, *Anatomy of Criticism,* p. 193. Other works on romance I have found particularly useful for matters of definition are: Gillian Beer, *The Romance* (London: Methuen, 1970); Howard Felperin, *Shakespearean Representation* (Princeton, N.J.: Princeton University Press, 1972); Frye, *The Secular Scripture* (Cambridge, Mass.: Harvard University Press, 1979); Patricia Parker, *Inescapable Romance* (Princeton, N.J.: Princeton University Press, 1979).

10. Fredric Jameson, *The Political Unconscious: Narrative as a Socially Symbolic Act* (Ithaca, N.Y.: Cornell University Press, 1981). Subsequent page references are to this work.

11. Martin Heidegger, "The Origin of the Work of Art," in *Poetry, Language, Thought,* trans. Albert Hofstadter (New York, N.Y.: Harper and Row, 1971), 17–87.

12. 1904, p. 28.

13. Yves Bonnefoy, "Image and Presence: Yves Bonnefoy's Inaugural Address at the College de France," *New Literary History* 15 (1983), 433–51. Passages cited are from pp. 437, 441, 442, and 443 respectively.

14. Henry James, *Notes of a Son and Brother,* Vol. II of the *Autobiography,* ed. F.W. Dupee (New York, N.Y.: Criterion, 1956), 480.

Chapter 1

1. George Levine, *The Realistic Imagination* (Chicago, Ill.: University of Chicago Press, 1981).

2. Peter Brooks, *The Melodramatic Imagination* (New Haven, Ct.: Yale University Press, 1976; Donald David Stone, *The Romantic Impulse in Victorian Fiction* (Cambridge, Mass.: Harvard

University Press, 1980). Other works on the blending of romance and realism in nineteenth-century and twentieth-century novels include: Donald Fanger, *Dostoevsky and Romantic Realism* (Cambridge Mass.: Harvard University Press, 1965); Tobin Siebers, *The Romantic Fantastic* (Ithaca, N.Y.: Cornell University Press, 1984); Donald David Stone, *Novelists in a Changing World* (Cambridge, Mass.: Harvard University Press, 1972). A work that considers this issue in novels in both England and America is Edwin Eigner, *The Metaphysical Novel in England and America* (Berkeley, Ca.: University of California Press, 1978). What Eigner identifies as the metaphysical novel (Bulwer-Lytton's term) is what I call romance; he considers these works in light of their philosophical ideas, while I am interested in romance as a means of representing and commenting on the literary uses of imagination.

3. Erich Auerbach, *Mimesis* (Princeton, N.J.: Princeton University Press, 1953).

4. Barry Qualls, *The Secular Pilgrims of Victorian Fiction* (Cambridge: Cambridge University Press, 1982), 15. Qualls identifies romance with a paradigm of Biblical pilgrimage; my notion of romance is based rather on the quest of the imagination. Another work which questions the notion of realism in the Victorian novel and prose by analyzing a counter-strain of romance is Rosemary Jann, *The Art and Science of Victorian History* (Columbus, Ohio: Ohio State University Press, 1985).

5. George Eliot, Chapter 17 of *Adam Bede,* reprinted in George Becker, ed., *Documents of Modern Literary Realism,* ed. George Becker (Princeton, N.J.: Princeton University Press, 1963), 112–116. See also Charles Dickens, preface to *Bleak House* (Boston, Mass.: Houghton Mifflin, 1956), xxxii, where he claims to dwell on the "romantic side of familiar things."

6. Sir Walter Scott, "Introduction to *The Fortunes of Nigel,*" reprinted in *Novelists on the Novel,* ed. Miriam Allott (London: Routledge and Kegan Paul, 1959), 50.

7. Richard Chase, *The American Novel and its Tradition* (Garden City, N.Y.: Anchor-Doubleday, 1957).

8. Northrop Frye, *Anatomy of Criticism* (Princeton, N.J.: Princeton University Press, 1957).

9. Scott, review of Jane Austen's *Emma, Quarterly Review* 14 (1815–16), 193.

10. Review of "The Entail," *Blackwood's Magazine* 13 (1823), quoted in Michael Munday, "The Novel and Its Critics in the Early Nineteenth Century," *Studies in Philology* 79 (1982), 221.

11. Chase, *The American Novel and its Tradition,* xi.

12. Munday, "The Novel and Its Critics," 205–226. For information about the debate on romance and novel in English periodicals, see also Ioan Williams, ed., *Novel and Romance* (New York, N.Y.: Barnes and Noble, 1970); Walter Kendrick, "Balzac and British Realism: Mid-Nineteenth Century Theories of the Novel," *Victorian Studies* 20 (1976), 5–24; and James Kincaid, "The Forms of Victorian Fiction," *Victorian Newsletter* 47 (1975), 1–4. A highly influential work on romance in both England and American was Clara Reeve, *The Progress of Romance* (Colchester: William Keymer, 1785).

     On romance and novel in American periodicals, see George Dekker, "Sir Walter Scott, the Angel of Hadley, and American Historical Fiction," *Journal of American Studies* 17 (1983), 211–28; G. Harrison Orians, "The Romance Ferment After *Waverley,*" *American Literature* 3 (1932), 408–432; and Robert Winston, "Paulding's *The Dutchman's Fireside* and Early American Romance," *Studies in American Fiction* 11 (1983), 47–60.

     A recent book of essays which considers the use of romance in writers of the age of "realism" in America (the late nineteenth century) is *American Realism,* ed. Eric Sundquist (Baltimore,

Md.: Johns Hopkins University Press, 1982). See especially Sundquist's introduction, "The Country of the Blue," 3–24, in which he states that for American writers of the late nineteenth century, "The gulf between the 'real world' and their own isolated imaginative selves often remained a conspicuous one or, on the contrary, collapsed altogether and left them in the bluest of countries, the country of American romance" (p. 31). I am in accord with Sundquist's revisionary notion that romance was perpetuated rather than suppressed in the latter part of the nineteenth century.

For works that argue against the English/American, novel/romance distinction, see Christopher Caudwell, *Romance and Realism* (Princeton, N.J.: Princeton University Press, 1970); Robert Falk, *The Victorian Mode in American Fiction* (East Lansing, Mich.: Michigan State University Press, 1965); Harold Kolb, *The Illusion of Life: American Romance as a Literary Form* (Charlottesville, Va.: University Press of Virginia, 1969); Nicolaus Mills, *American and English Fiction in the Nineteenth Century* (Bloomington, Ind.: Indiana University Press, 1973). While I generally agree with this perspective, I would not want to claim that all fiction is either realistic or romantic, but rather to emphasize the interrelation between the two modes.

13. Brownson, *Democratic Review* 12 (1843).

14. Simms, in *The Theory of the American Novel,* ed. George Perkins (New York, N.Y.: Holt, Rinehart and Winston, 1970), 41.

15. Nathaniel Hawthorne, *The Centenary Edition of the Works of Nathaniel Hawthorne,* ed. William Charvat et al. (Columbus, Ohio: Ohio State University Press, 1962–). Subsequent references to Hawthorne are to this edition, by volume and page number.

On Hawthorne's prefaces and theory of romance, see, among articles: Darrel Abel, "'A More Imaginative Pleasure': Hawthorne on the Play of Imagination," *Emerson Society Quarterly* 55 (1969), 63–71; Abel, "Giving Lustre to Gray Shadows: Hawthorne's Potent Art," *American Literature* 41 (1969), 373–88; Abel, "Hawthorne, Ghostland, and the Jurisdiction of Veracity," *American Transcendental Quarterly* 24 (1974), 30–38; Kent Bales, "Hawthorne's Prefaces and Romantic Perspectivism" *ESQ* 23 (1977), 55–69; Nina Baym, "Concepts of the Romance in Hawthorne's America," *Nineteenth-Century Fiction* 38 (1984), 426–43; Jesse Bier "Hawthorne on the Romance: His Prefaces Related and Examined," *Modern Philology* 53 (1955), 17–24; Evan Carton, "Hawthorne and the Province of Romance," *ELH* 47 (1980), 331–54; Maurice Charney, "Hawthorne and the Gothic Style," *New England Quarterly* 34 (1961), 36–49; Jeffrey Duncan, "The Design of Hawthorne's Fabrications," *Yale Review* 71 (1981), 51–71; Dan McCall, "Hawthorne's Familiar Kind of Preface," *ELH* 35 (1968), 422–39; Walter Benn Michaels, "Romance and Real Estate," *Raritan* 2 (1983), 66–81; Thomas Pauly, "Hawthorne's Houses of Fiction," *American Literature* 48 (1976), 71–91. I have found most useful those which discuss the blending of opposites in the prefaces (Abel, Carton, Charney, Michaels) and those which emphasize the development in the course of the prefaces (Abel, Bales, Bier, Duncan. In my view, Hawthorne's use of the blending of opposites is not just an image for romance but a way of indicating the interpenetration of romance and reality.

Among discussions in books, see Michael D. Bell, *The Development of American Romance* (Chicago, Ill.: University of Chicago Press, 1980); Millicent Bell, *Hawthorne's View of the Artist* (Albany, N.Y.: State University of New York Press, 1962); Richard Brodhead, *Hawthorne, Melville, and the Novel* (Chicago, Ill.: University of Chicago Press, 1973), 1–43; Edgar Dryden, *Nathaniel Hawthorne: The Uses of Enchantment* (Ithaca, N.Y.: Cornell University Press, 1977), 147–52; Rita Gollin, *Nathaniel Hawthorne and the Truth of Dreams* (Baton Rouge, La.: Louisiana State University Press, 1979); Richard Jacobson, *Hawthorne's Conception of the Creative Process* (Cambridge, Mass.: Harvard University Press, 1965); Claudia Johnson, *The Productive Tensions of Hawthorne's Art* (University, Ala.: University of Alabama Press, 1981); Terence Martin, *Nathaniel Hawthorne* (New Haven, Ct.: College and University Press, 1965), 38–48; Hyatt Waggoner, "Art and Belief," *Hawthorne Centenary Essays,* ed. Roy Harvey Pearce (Columbus, Ohio: Ohio State University Press, 1964), 167–195. I find Martin's treatment particularly helpful for illuminating some possible relations of Hawthorne to James in their definitions of fiction. Several of these critics emphasize the mythic aspects of Hawthorne's representation. Michael Bell sees Hawthorne as having a "conservative" view of romance. Both views, finally, tend to isolate romance from reality, whereas I think Hawthorne uses romance here as a subversive stance which transforms reality.

16. Angus Fletcher, *Allegory* (Ithaca, N.Y.: Cornell University Press, 1964), 253.

17. Martin Price, *To the Palace of Wisdom* (Carbondale, Ill.: Southern Illinois University Press, 1964), 364.

18. Henry James, "The Art of Fiction" (1884), in *Partial Portraits* (1888; reprinted Westport, Ct.: Greenwood, 1970), 375–408. Subsequent page references are to this edition.

    On James and impressionism, see especially Paul Armstrong, *The Phenomenology of Henry James* (Chapel Hill, N.C.: University of North Carolina Press, 1983); Darilyn Bock, "From Reflective Narrators to James: The Coloring Medium of the Mind," *Modern Philology* 76 (1979), 259–72; Suzanne Ferguson, "The Face in the Mirror: Authorial Presence in the Multiple Vision of Third Person Impressionist Narration," *Criticism* 21 (1979), 230–50; John C. Rowe, "Re-Marking the Impression," *Criticism* 24 (1982), 233–60; Peter Stowell, *Literary Impressionism: James and Chekhov* (Athens, Ga.: University of Georgia Press, 1980). For an argument against seeing James as impressionist, see Quentin Anderson, *The American Henry James* (New Brunswick, N.J.: Rutgers University Press, 1957). While I generally agree with the critics who view James as an impressionist writer, I wish to balance the emphasis on subjectivity in his works with a sense of the way mental impressions depend on the incorporation of experience. Some critics see James's imagination as entirely self-reflexive.

    On "The Art of Fiction," see Armstrong, 37–68; Sarah Daugherty, *The Literary Criticism of Henry James* (Athens, Ohio: Ohio University Press, 1981), 113–24; Richard Hocks, *Henry James and Pragmatistic Thought* (Chapel Hill, N.C.: University of North Carolina Press, 1974), 101–2; Marcia Jacobson, *Henry James and the Mass Market* (University, Ala.: University of Alabama Press, 1983), 10–11; Viola Hopkins Winner, *Henry James and the Visual Arts* (Charlottesville, Va.: University Press of Virginia, 1970), 46 and 59–60. See also William Veeder, *Henry James—The Lessons of the Master* (Chicago, Ill.: University of Chicago Press, 1975), 93–105, on gesture.

    Most of these critics read the essay as James's manifesto of realism, a view I contest. I am more in accord with Winner and Armstrong, who emphasize the subjectivity of the artist's consciousness. I am particularly indebted to Armstrong's extended treatment of the essay, but again feel that he tends to isolate the experience James discusses to a purely mental realm. The essay rather invokes an interaction between the mind and the world.

19. Preface to *The American, The Art of the Novel: Critical Prefaces by Henry James,* ed. R.P. Blackmur (New York, N.Y.: Scribner's, 1934), 20–39 (henceforward abbreviated *AN*). Subsequent page references are to this edition. On James's theory of realism, see especially John Bayley, "Formalist Games and Real Life," *Essays in Criticism* 31 (1981), 271–81; Millicent Bell, "Henry James: Meaning and Unmeaning," *Raritan* 4 (1984), 29–46; Dale Peterson, *The Clement Vision: Poetic Realism in Turgeney and James* (Port Washington, N.Y.: Kennikat, 1975). Instead of seeing James's transformations of representation as "poetic realism," like Peterson, I view them as the result of the interaction between romance and novel in James. Whereas for some critics James's formalism is opposed to his realism, I feel that the form of

romance enables James to unite artistic form with depiction of reality. I am particularly in agreement with Bell's treatment of the uncertainty of meaning in James.

On the preface to *The American* and other prefaces, see Charles Anderson, *Person, Place, and Thing in Henry James's Novels* (Durham, N.C.: Duke University Press, 1977), 68–79; Laurence Holland, *The Expense of Vision* (Princeton, N.J.: Princeton University Press, 1964); Susanne Kappeler, *Writing and Reading in Henry James* (New York, N.Y.: Columbia University Press, 1980), 174–90; Dorothea Krook, *The Ordeal of Consciousness in Henry James* (Cambridge: Cam-bridge University Press, 1962), 399–411; Terence Martin, *Nathaniel Hawthorne,* 42–48; Daniel Schneider, *The Crystal Cage* (Lawrence, Kan.: University Press of Kansas, 1978), 152–68; D. Seed, "The Narrator in Henry James's Criticism," *Philological Quarterly* 60 (1981), 501–21. I am indebted to Holland here and for his treatment of the prefaces generall, as well as to Schneider and Kappeler, and to Martin on the Hawthorne connection. The other critics view this preface primarily in biographical terms. I differ from earlier critics here in viewing romance as something praised, not condemned, in this preface, and thus seeing the preface as a clue to James's work as a whole, not just to the book it precedes. The presence of romance in other works of James besides *The American* is apparent in his extensive use of the term "romance" to describe his own works in other prefaces as well; see, for example, the prefaces to the volumes containing "The Aspern Papers" (including "The Turn of the Screw") and "The Altar of the Dead," *AN* 159–79 and 241–66, respectively.

20. "To H. G. Wells," 10 July 1915, Henry James: Letters, ed. Leon Edel (Cambridge, Mass.: Harvard University Press, 1974–84), IV, 770.

Chapter 2

1. The earliest sustained treatment of the Hawthorne essays as a group, emphasizing James's progressing sympathy to Hawthorne, is by Peter Buitenhuis, "Henry James on Hawthorne," *New England Quarterly* 32 (1959), 207–225. More recently, see Sarah Daugherty, *The Literary Criticism of Henry James* (Athens, Ohio: Ohio University Press, 1981), esp. pp. 86–101 and 153–57, which treat James's responses to Hawthorne and other romancers. See also, on Hawthorne's influence on James and later writers, Hyatt Waggoner, *The Presence of Hawthorne* (Baton Rouge, La.: Louisiana State University Press, 1979). Also see, on *Hawthorne,* John Carlos Rowe, "'What the Thunder Said': James's *Hawthorne* and the American Anxiety of Influence: A Centenary Essay," *Henry James Review* 4 (1983), 81–119; on the *Autobiography,* Richard Ruland, "Beyond Harsh Inquiry," *ESQ* 25 (1979), 95–117.

   The pattern of change in James's view of Hawthorne was apparently typical of his critical response to other writers, especially those who influenced him deeply. See, for instance, his response to Balzac: Daugherty, *The Literary Criticism of Henry James,* 61–70 and 168–92.

2. Henry James, *Hawthorne* (1879; reprinted Ithaca, N.Y.: Cornell University Press, 1956). Subsequent page references are to this edition. For commentary on this work, see especially Richard Poirier, *A World Elsewhere: The Place of Style in American Literature* (New York, N.Y.: Oxford University Press, 1966), and Rowe, "What the Thunder Said"; see also Buitenhuis, *The Grasping Imagination* (Toronto: Toronto University Press, 1970), and Terence Martin, *Nathaniel Hawthorne* (New Haven, Ct.: College and University Press, 1965), 108–116.

3. Preface to *The Marble Faun, The Centenary Edition of the Works of Nathaniel Hawthorne,* ed. William Charvat et al. (Columbus, Ohio: Ohio State University Press, 1962–), IV, 3. See also the similar complaints by Cooper, Simms, and Brockden Brown in *The Theory of the American Novel,* ed. George Perkins (New York, N.Y.: Holt, Rinehart and Winston, 1970).

4. "To Mrs. Humphry Ward," 26 July 1899, *Henry James:* Letters, ed. Leon Edel (Cambridge, Mass.: Harvard University Press, 1974–84), IV, 110.

5. See especially Bloom, *The Anxiety of Influence* (New York, N.Y.: Oxford, 1975), and many subsequent works.

6. "Hawthorne's French and Italian Journals," *Nation,* March 14, 1872, reprinted in *The American Essays of Henry James,* ed. Leon Edel (New York, N.Y.: Vintage, 1956), 3–11. Subsequent page references are to this edition.

7. William Dean Howells, "James's Hawthorne," reprinted in *William Dean Howells as Critic,* ed. Edwin Cady (London: Routledge and Kegan Paul, 1973), 53.

8. Samuel Taylor Coleridge, *Biographia Literaria,* Chapter 13, reprinted in *The Portable Coleridge,* ed. I. A. Richards (New York, N.Y.: Viking-Penguin, 1950), 514–16.

9. Charles Feidelson, *Symbolism and American Literature* (Chicago, Ill.: University of Chicago Press, 1953).

10. Angus Fletcher, *Allegory* (Ithaca, N.Y.: Cornell University Press, 1964); see also Maureen Quilligan, *The Language of Allegory* (Ithaca, N.Y.: Cornell University Press, 1979); Carolynn van Dyke, *The Fiction of Truth: Structures of Meaning in Narrative and Dramatic Allegory* (Ithaca, N.Y.: Cornell University Press, 1985); and the essays collected in *Allegory and Representation,* ed. Stephen Greenblatt (Baltimore, Md.: Johns Hopkins University Press, 1981).

11. Poirier, *A World Elsewhere,* pp. 93–104. See also Rowe, "What the Thunder Said." For Rowe, James shows the lack of detail in Hawthorne in order to replace Hawthorne's romance with realism. My contention is that James's own work is dependent on the very aspects of romance he criticizes.

12. "Nathaniel Hawthorne," in *A Library of the World's Best Literature,* ed. Charles Dudley Warner (New York, N.Y.: 1896–97), XII, 7053–61, reprinted in *The American Essays,* ed. Edel, pp. 11–23. Subsequent page references are to this edition.

13. "Letter to the Honorary Robert S. Rantoul," 10 June 1904, in *The Proceedings in Commemora- -tion of the One Hundredth Anniversary of the Birth of Nathaniel Hawthorne* (Salem, Mass.: Essex Institute, 1904), 55–62, reprinted in *The American Essays,* ed. Edel, pp. 24–31.

Chapter 3

1. On Hawthorne and the form of romance, see especially John C. Stubbs, *The Pursuit of Form: A Study of Hawthorne and the Romance* (Urbana, Ill.: University of Illinois Press, 1970).

2. See especially Roy Harvey Pearce, "Romance and the Study of History," in *Hawthorne Centen- -ary Essays,* ed. Pearce (Columbus, Ohio: Ohio State University Press, 1964), 221–244; and Larzer Ziff, "The Artist and Puritanism," *Hawthorne Centenary Essays,* 245–269. See also Michael D. Bell, *Hawthorne and the Historical Romance of New England* (Princeton, N.J.: Princeton University Press, 1971) and Robert H. Fossum, *Hawthorne's Inviolable Circle: The Problem of Time* (Deland, Fla.: Everett/Edwards, 1972).

3. The Spenser critics whose works I have found most useful in the treatment of romance as narrative include: Paul Alpers, *The Poetry of the Faerie Queene* (Princeton, N.J.: Princeton University Press, 1967); Judith Anderson, *The Growth of a Personal Voice: Piers Plowman and the Faerie Queene* (New Haven, Ct: Yale University Press, 1976); John Arthos, *On the*

Poetry of Spenser and the Form of Romance (Freeport, N.Y.: Books for Libraries Press, 1956); John Bender, *Spenser and Literary Pictorialism* (Princeton, N.J.: Princeton University Press, 1972); Harry Berger, *The Allegorical Temper* (New Haven, Ct.: Yale University Press, 1957); A. Bartlett Giamatti, *The Play of Double Senses* (Englewood Cliffs, N.J.: Prentice-Hall, 1975); John Guillory, *Poetic Authority: Spenser, Milton, and Literary History* (New York, N.Y.: Columbia University Press, 1983); Isabel MacCaffrey, *Spenser's Allegory* (Princeton, N.J.: Princeton University Press, 1976); Rosemond Tuve, "Spenser and Medieval Romances," in *The Faerie Queene: A Casebook*, ed. Peter Bayley (London: Macmillan, 1977). All treat Spenser's use of allegory, voice, and pictorialism in a way which illuminates how they could be adapted by Hawthorne.

4. A. C. Hamilton, "Elizabethan Romance: The Example of Prose Fiction," *ELH* 49 (1982), 287–299.

5. John Bender, *Spenser and Literary Pictorialism*, p. 35.

6. *The Faerie Queene*, in *The Poetical Works of Edmund Spenser*, ed. E. de Selincourt (London: Oxford, 1912).

7. On Spenser's influence on Hawthorne, see especially Buford Jones, "Hawthorne and Spenser: From Allusion to Allegory," *Nathaniel Hawthorne Journal* 5 (1975), 71–90; David Van Leer, "Roderick's Other Serpent: Hawthorne's Use of Spenser," *ESQ* 27 (1981), 73–84. Van Leer includes a complete bibliography on this subject in his footnotes.

8. "Hawthorne's French and Italian Journals" (1872), in *The American Essays of Henry James*, ed. Leon Edel (New York, N.Y.: Vintage, 1956), 4–5, 10–11. See especially *The American Notebooks, The Centenary Edition of the Works of Nathaniel Hawthorne*, ed. William Charvat et al. (Columbus, Ohio: Ohio State University Press, 1962–).

9. "The Haunted Mind," *Centenary Edition* IX. On this sketch, see Nina Baym, *The Shape of Hawthorne's Career* (Ithaca, N.Y.: Cornell University Press, 1976), 65; Richard Brodhead, *Hawthorne, Melville, and the Novel*, (Chicago, Ill.: University of Chicago Press, 1976), 36; Edgar Dryden, *Nathaniel Hawthorne: The Poetics of Enchantment* (Ithaca, N.Y.: Cornell University Press, 1977); Rita Gollin, *Nathaniel Hawthorne and the Truth of Dreams* (Baton Rouge, La.: Louisiana State University Press, 1979), 98–102; John Holsberry, "Hawthorne's 'The Haunted Mind,' The Psychology of Dreams, Coleridge, and Keats," *Texas Studies in Literature and Language* 21 (1979), 307–31; Norman Hostetler, "Imagination and Point of View in 'The Haunted Mind,'" *American Transcendental Quarterly* 39 (1978), 263–67; Barton Levi St. Armand, "Hawthorne's 'Haunted Mind': A Subterranean Drama of the Self," *Criticism* 13 (1971), 1–25; Terence Martin, "The Method of Hawthorne's Tales," *Hawthorne Centenary Essays*, 7–30. The essay has been analyzed principally for its reflection of dreamstates, less for its attempt to link these states to waking reality. I am indebted to Brodhead, Baym, and Martin for seeing the essay as key to Hawthorne's art, though I have not seen it treated, as I do here, as dramatization of allegoresis.

10. On the imagination as mirror, see Dryden, 156.

11. "The Old Manse," *Centenary Edition* VI. On "The Old Manse," see especially Stephen Adams, "Unifying Structures in Mosses," *Studies in American Fiction* 8 (1980), 147–63; Baym, *The Shape of Hawthorne's Career*, 113–17; Brodhead, *Hawthorne, Melville, and the Novel*, 31–32; John J. McDonald, "'The Old Manse' and Its Mosses: The Inception and Development of *Mosses from an Old Manse*," *Texas Studies in Literature and Language* 16 (1974), 77–108; Teresa Toulouse, "Spatial Relations in 'The Old Manse,'" *ESQ* 28 (1982), 154–66. Toulouse suggests the interesting possibility of reading the entire landscape allegorically. Brodhead sees

the essay as a rejection of novel-writing; I would say it rather breaks down the romance-novel distinction. Hawthorne wishes to challenge traditional notions of what constitutes "substantial" writing; his initial notion that a "novel" would be the best he could do in this vein is revised by the essay's end.

12. Ralph Waldo Emerson, "Nature," in *Complete Works,* ed. Edward W. Emerson (1903–4; reprinted New York, N.Y.: AMS, 1968), I, 25.

13. *The Scarlet Letter, Centenary Edition* I, 37. On "The Custom-House" and its relation to *The Scarlet Letter,* see especially Brodhead, *Hawthorne, Melville, and the Novel,* 32–36; James Cox, *"The Scarlet Letter:* Through the Old Manse and the Custom-House," *Virginia Quarterly Review* 51 (1975), 432–47; Paul John Eakin, "Hawthorne's Imagination and the Structure of 'The Custom-House,'" *American Literature* 43 (1971), 346–58; John Franzosa, "'The Custom-House,'" *The Scarlet Letter,* and Hawthorne's Separation from Salem," *ESQ* 24 (1978), 57–71; David Stouck, "The Surveyor of the Custom-House: A Narrator for *The Scarlet Letter,*" *Centennial Review* 15 (1971), 309–29; Marshall van Deusen "Narrative Tone in 'The Custom-House' and *The Scarlet Letter,*" *Nineteenth-Century Fiction* 21 (1966), 61–71; Larzer Ziff, "The Ethical Dimension of 'The Custom-House,'" *Modern Language Notes* 73 (1958), 338–44. Brodhead, Cox, Stouck, and Van Deusen emphasize the role of Hawthorne as narrator/character. Franzosa's identification of the narrator with Hawthorne as individual in relation to biographical background illuminates the drama of repression and its release here. Generally, I differ from previous critics in viewing the preface not so much as an alternative version of *The Scarlet Letter* or the representation of an opposite mode as a preparation for the way of reading Hawthorne calls romance. The relations between scenes in "The Custom-House" and scenes in *The Scarlet Letter* itself indicate that the preface not only complements but anticipates the action of the story.

14. See Brodhead, *Hawthorne, Melville, and the Novel,* p. 33, and my "The Symbol as Symptom: Romance and Repression in *The Scarlet Letter,*" in *The Psychoanalytic Study of Literature, Volume I,* ed. Joseph Reppen and Maurice Charney (Hillsdale, N.J.: Analytic Press, 1985), 149–66.

15. On the moonlit room, see especially Brodhead, 33–36.

16. On *The Scarlet Letter,* I have found the following most useful for discussions of romance and narrative: (Articles): Jonathan Arac, "Reading the Letter," *Diacritics* 9 (1979), 42–52; Millicent Bell, "The Obliquity of Signs: *The Scarlet Letter,*" *Massachusetts Review* 23 (1982), 9–26; Watson Branch, "From Allegory to Romance: Hawthorne's Transformation of *The Scarlet Letter,*" *Modern Philology* 80 (1982), 47–67; Paul Lewis, "Mournful Mysteries: Gothic Speculation in *The Scarlet Letter,*" *American Transcendental Quarterly* 44 (1979), 279–93; Michael Ragussis, "Family Discourse and Fiction in *The Scarlet Letter,*" *ELH* 49 (1982), 863–88; John C. Rowe, "The Internal Conflict of Romantic Narrative: Hegel's *Phenomenology* and Hawthorne's *The Scarlet Letter,*" *Modern Language Notes* 95 (1980), 1203–31.

(Books and chapters in books): Baym, *The Development of Hawthorne's Career,* 123–43 (on inner drives versus repression and the role of the artist); Brodhead, *Hawthorne, Melville, and the Novel,* 43–68 (on the method of alternating symbol and interpretation); Frederick Crews, *The Sins of the Fathers: Hawthorne's Psychological Themes* (New York, N.Y.: Oxford University Press, 1966); Kenneth Dauber, *Rediscovering Hawthorne* (Princeton, N.J.: Princeton University Press, 1977), 87–117, especially on Hawthorne's use of tableaux; Dryden, *Nathaniel Hawthorne: The Poetics of Enchantment,* on enchantment and the distance of romance; Charles Feidelson, *Symbolism and American Literature* (Chicago, Ill.: University of Chicago Press, 1953), 6–16; Feidelson, *"The Scarlet Letter,"* in *Hawthorne Centenary Essays,*

31–77; Harry Levin, *The Power of Blackness* (New York, N.Y. Knopf, 1958), 6–27 and 72–79; Terence Martin, *Nathaniel Hawthorne* (New Haven, Ct.: College and University Press, 1965), 42–48 and 108–127. In general, I have found the above works most helpful because they demonstrate the symbolic aspects of Hawthorne's depiction and his attempt to use these for detailed depiction of character. I have sought to unite the analysis of characters as romancers of Baym and Brodhead with the phenomenological and formalist emphases of Dauber and Dryden. The growing application of recent theory of language and the sign to Hawthorne in recent years, especially in the articles mentioned above, has influenced my view of the way signification operates in his works. This has led to my sense of the presence of a Jamesian drama of gesture in Hawthorne, though at a more implicit level than in James.

17.   On the relation of private and public meanings, see also Dauber, *Rediscovering Hawthorne*, pp. 97–100; and Brodhead, *Hawthorne, Melville, and the Novel* especially pp. 37 and 49. Both tend to see the meaning of the work emerging in the oscillation between romance and realism, while in my view it is located in Hawthorne's ironic invocation of romance itself. Hawthorne clearly uses the conventions of romance, such as supernaturalism and symbolism. Hawthorne recognizes the psychological accuracy of the ancient romancers, but seeks to capture their effects without endorsing the fanciful representations by which they are achieved. See as well Baym, *The Shape of Hawthorne's Career, passim,* and Dryden, *The Uses of Enchantment,* p. 88, on enchantment.

On tableaux, see Malcolm Cowley, "The Five Acts of *The Scarlet Letter,*" *College English* 19 (1957), 11–16; Ronald Gervais, "A Papist Among the Puritans: Icon and Logos in *The Scarlet Letter,*" *ESQ* 25 (1979), 11–16; Rita Gollin, *Nathaniel Hawthorne and the Truth of Dreams,* 140–151; Mark Kinkead-Weekes, "The Letter, the Picture, and the Mirror: Hawthorne's Framing of *The Scarlet Letter,*" in *Nathaniel Hawthorne: New Critical Essays,* ed. A. Robert Lee, (London: Vision/Totava, N.J.: Barnes and Noble, 1983), pp. 68–87. According to Dauber (p. 96), "the effect is to render story as scene."

18.   On the opening chapters and the render of scene as symbol, see Feidelson, *Symbolism and American Literature,* pp. 6–16; Brodhead, pp. 44–5; and Baym, p. 132. Again, I feel that Hawthorne ironizes not only allegory but symbolism here.

19.   On the Governor's mansion, see also Gollin; and Brodhead, p. 55.

20.   On Dimmesdale in relation to Hawthorne, see especially Baym, Brodhead, Crews, and Gollin. For a view of the perils of romance for characters as opposed to author, in relation to Hawthorne and Hester, see Daniel Cottom, "Hawthorne vs. Hester: The Ghostly Dialectic of Romance in *The Scarlet Letter,*" *Texas Studies in Literature and Language* 24 (1982), 47–67.

21.   See Dauber (p. 108): "Character, landscape, events, all are reconceived in the terms the dream-vision provides." He sees this chapter as "an allegory of the Calvinist type enunciated by Chillingworth" (p. 109). In my view, Hawthorne uses the symbol of the letter here not so much to convey abstract moral meaning as to illustrate an intimate psychological drama.

22.   See Baym, p. 137: "The voice bypasses language to become a direct expression of unmediated feeling." To some extent, however, that expression remains inarticulate.

23.   On realistic elements in the ending, see Brodhead, p. 67.

24.   See Dauber's chapter, "A Typical Illusion." I find his analysis very illuminating on the function of allegory in the work. He sees Hawthorne's irony as produced primarily by the use of self-conscious repetition, whereas I feel it emerges in the consistent undercutting of the conventions of romance. While he feels that Hawthorne "abandons" his story at the end, I see

the ending as a fitting conclusion to Hawthorne's ironizing of romance throughout. He does not so much "abandon" the story as complete it and guarantee its continued life by placing its real sphere of existence ultimately in the mind of the reader.

Chapter 4

1. On internalization, see Peter Brooks, *The Melodramatic Imagination* (New Haven, Ct.: Yale University Press, 1976), and Bersani, *A Future for Astyanax* (Boston, Mass.: Little, Brown, 1976), especially p. 138. Both emphasize the freedom of consciousness. In my view, this freedom is valued not for its own sake but for its capacity to give its possessor deeper connections to experience.

2. Harold Bloom, "The Internalization of Quest-Romance," in *The Ringers in the Tower* (Chicago, Ill.: University of Chicago Press, 1971), 13–35.

3. Laurence Holland, *The Expense of Vision* (Princeton, N.J.: Princeton University Press, 1964), 21.

4. Henry James, *Hawthorne* (1879; reprinted Ithaca: Cornell University Press, 1956), 87–88.

5. On picture and drama, see Charles Anderson, *Person, Place, and Thing in the Novels of Henry James* (Durham, N.C.: Duke University Press, 1980); and Robert Caserio, *Plot, Story, and the Novel* (Princeton, N.J.: Princeton University Press, 1979); on static versus "processive" portrai--ture, see William Veeder, *Henry James—The Lessons of the Master: Popular Fiction and Personal Style in the Nineteenth Century* (Chicago, Ill.: University of Chicago Press, 1975), 207; and Viola H. Winner, *Henry James and the Visual Arts* (Charlottesville, Va.: University Press of Virginia, 1970).

    On pictorialism in the novel generally, see Jay Bochner, "Life in a Picture Gallery: Things in *The Portrait of a Lady* and *The Marble Faun*," *Texas Studies in Literature and Language* 11 (1969), 761–77; Edgar Dryden, "The Image in the Mirror: The Double Economy of James's *Portrait*," *Genre* 13 (1980), 31–49; J.T. Laird, "Cracks in Precious Objects: Aestheticism and Humanity in *The Portrait of a Lady*," *American Literature* 52 (1981), 643–48.

6. "Nathaniel Hawthorne" (1897), reprinted in *The American Essays of Henry James*, ed. Leon Edel (New York: Vintage, 1956), 16.

7. J.A. Ward, *The Search for Form: Studies in the Structure of James's Fiction* (Chapel Hill, N.C.: University of North Carolina Press, 1967), 35.

8. On picture versus scene, see especially Winner, *Henry James and the Visual Arts*, and James's prefaces to *The Wings of the Dove* and *The Ambassadors* in *The Art of the Novel: Critical Prefaces by Henry James*, ed. R.P. Blackmur (New York, N.Y.: Scribner's, 1934).

9. Caserio, *Plot, Story and the Novel*, p. 201.

10. *The Art of the Novel*, p. 57.

11. *The Art of the Novel*, p. 32.

12. Brooks, *The Melodramatic Imagination*, p. 5.

13. *The Marble Faun, The Centenary Edition of the Works of Nathaniel Hawthorne*, ed. William Charvat et al. (Columbus, Ohio: Ohio State University Press, 1962–), IV, 455.

    See Charles Feidelson, "The Moment of *The Portrait of a Lady*," *Ventures* 8 (1968), 47–55. See also the image of the tapestry in relation to representation in James's preface to *Roderick Hudson*, in *The Art of the Novel*.

14. *The Portrait of a Lady*, in *Henry James: Novels 1881–1886* (New York, N.Y.: Library of America, 1985). Subsequent page references are to this edition and are given parenthetically within the text. This volume reprints the text of the 1881 version of the novel rather than the revised text of the New York Edition. I have chosen to follow the earlier version since my argument is based on a view of the development of James's career. I note some important New York Edition revisions later in these notes.

15. On Gardencourt, see Philip Grover, *Henry James and the French Novel* (London: Paul Elek, 1973), and Robert Stallman, "The Houses that James Built—*The Portrait of a Lady*," *Texas Quarterly* 1 (1958), 176–96.

16. Holland, *The Expense of Vision*, p. 21.

17. On Isabel as "romancer," see Richard Chase, *The American Novel and its Tradition* (Garden City, N.Y.: Anchor-Doubleday, 1957), 117–37. Unlike Chase, I consider romance here primar-ily in terms of narrative form, the relation of picture to drama. On the Hawthorne aspect, see Richard Brodhead, *The School of Hawthorne* (New York, N.Y.: Oxford University Prss, 1986), which has deeply influenced me. Brodhead's focus is on the cultural significance of the Hawthorne-James relation, while my concerns are more formalistic. Brodhead sees *The Portrait of a Lady* as a "Hawthornesque form of tragedy" in which Isabel is doomed by her own desires (p. 139). In my view, desire may lead to limitations but also provides the only way to know reality. See also Carren Kaston, *Imagination and Desire in the Novels of Henry James* (New Brunswick, N.J.: Rutgers University Press, 1984); and Richard Poirier, *The Comic Sense of Henry James* (New York, N.Y.: Oxford, 1960).

    On the novel generally, the interpretations I have found most useful are those which empha-size the power of imagination to heal as well as distort: Edwin Fussell, "Sympathy in *The Portrait of a Lady* and *The Golden Bowl*," *Henry James Reivew* 2 (1981), 161–66; Dorothea Krook, *The Ordeal of Consciousness in Henry James* (Cambridge: Cambridge University Press, 1962); Naomi Lebowitz, *The Imagination of Loving* (Detroit, Mich.: Wayne State University Press, 1965), esp. pp. 66–74; Ellen Leyburn, *Strange Alloy: The Mixture of Comedy and Tragedy in the Works of Henry James* (Chapel Hill, N.C.: University of North Carolina Press, 1968), 20–39; Manfred Mackenzie, "Ironic Melodrama in *The Portrait of a Lady*," *Modern Fiction Studies* 12 (1966), 7–23; Donald Mull, *Henry James's Sublime Economy* (Middletown, Ct.: Wesleyan University Press, 1973), 48–114; Philip Weinstein, *Henry James and the Requirements of the Imagination* (Cambridge, Mass.: Harvard University Press, 1971), 31–71.

    On the New York Edition revisions of the novel, see *Henry James: The Portrait of a Lady*, ed. Robert Bamberg (New York, N.Y.: Norton, 1975), 495–575; see also, in that volume, F.O. Matthiessen, "The Painter's Sponge and Varnish Bottle," 577–96; and Anthony Mazzella, "The New Isabel," 597–619.

18. *The Art of the Novel*, p. 46.

19. Charles Feidelson, "The Moment of *The Portrait of a Lady*," *Ventures* 8 (1968), 59.

20. On the melodramatic transformations of consciousness, see especially Brooks, *The Melodra-matic Imagination*.

21. In the New York Edition, this line reads: "a small group that might have been described by a painter as composing well'—Henry James, *The Portrait of a Lady*, The New York Edition: *The Novels and Tales of Henry James* (New York: Scribner's, 1907–17), III, 320. On the changes from "picturesque" to "compositional" from the 1881 edition to the New York Edition, see Matthiessen, "The Painter's Sponge and Varnish Bottle." The change these terms describe

could be used to characterize the difference between Hawthorne's and James's works generally, as Hawthorne characterizes through picturesque juxtapositions, while James's emphasis on "placement" provides almost geometrical studies of relationships, especially in the late works.

22. This phrase appears only in the 1881 edition.

23. Henry James, "The Art of Fiction," in *Partial Portraits* (1888; reprinted Westport, Ct.: Greenwood, 1970), 389.

24. On chapter 42, see Charles Anderson, *Person, Place, and Thing,* 80–123; and Ross Posnock, *Henry James and the Problem of Robert Browning* (Athens, Ga.: University of Georgia Press, 1985), 163.

25. On melodrama in James, see Jacques Barzun, "Henry James: Melodramatist," *Kenyon Review* 5 (1943), 508–21; Frederick Crews, *The Tragedy of Manners* (New Haven, Ct.: Yale University Press, 1957); and Leo Levy, *Versions of Melodrama* (Berkeley, Ca.: University of California Press, 1957). More recently, see Brooks, *The Melodramatic Imagination.* While the analogy to melodrama captures James's use of gesture and strong moral oppositions, I feel such patterns are best understood in the context of romance, with which James himself associates them in the preface to *The American.* As opposed to melodrama, romance emphasizes the pictorial over the dramatic mode of composition and the ways in which both are transformed by the projecting imagination.

26. On the transformation of aesthetic to moral terms in this section of the novel, see Krook, *The Ordeal of Consciousness.*

27. *The Scarlet Letter, The Centenary Edition of the Works of Nathaniel Hawthorne,* I, 175. Subsequent references to *The Scarlet Letter* are to this edition.

28. On Isabel and Roman ruins, see Dorothy Van Ghent, *The English Novel: Form and Function* (New York: Rinehart, 1953), 227–28. See also my "The Ruins of Empire: Reading the Monuments in Hawthorne and James," *CEA Critic* 46 (1984), 48–59.

29. On the ending, see especially Feidelson, "The Moment of *The Portrait of a Lady*"; Brodhead, *The School of Hawthorne,* p. 139; Holland, *The Expense of Vision;* Poirier, *The Comic Sense.*

Chapter 5

1. On Hawthorne's influence on James in *The Bostonians,* see Robert Long, *The Great Succession* (Pittsburgh, Pa.: University of Pittsburgh Press, 1979), 117–57; Marius Bewley, *The Complex Fate* (London: Chatto and Windus, 1952), 11–30. I find Long's discussion complete and suggestive but disagree with his view of James as improving on Hawthorne's romance. Writers who emphasize the continuities between Hawthorne and James in both subject and method include Richard Brodhead, *The School of Hawthorne* (New York, N.Y.: Oxford University Press, 1986); R.W.B. Lewis, "The Matter of the Heart," in *Trials of the Word* (New Haven, Ct.: Yale University Press, 1965); Richard Poirier, *A World Elsewhere* (New York, N.Y.: Oxford, 1966). Irving Howe's introduction to the Modern Library edition of *The Bostonians* (New York, 1956), contains suggestive remarks on the relation of *The Blithedale Romance* to *The Bostonians,* vii-x.

2. Henry James, *Notebooks,* ed. F.O. Matthiessen and Kenneth Murdock (New York, N.Y.: Oxford, 1947), 47.

3. Though most critics acknowledge the Hawthorne influence on *The Bostonians,* many finally see the influence of Daudet as making James's work one of naturalism: Peter Buitenhuis, *The*

Grasping Imagination (Toronto, Ont.: University of Toronto Press, 1970); Oscar Cargill, *The Novels of Henry James* (New York, N.Y.: Hafner, 1961); Lyall Powers, *Henry James and the Naturalist Novel* (Lansing, Mich.: Michigan State University Press, 1962). As I will show, though, James shows not so much the determination of character by environment, as naturalist works tend to do, as the capacity of characters to create their own prisons through projection of deluded desires. On the occult in both works, see Martha Banta, *Henry James and the Occult* (Bloomington,Ind.: Indiana University Press, 1972); and Howard Kerr, *Mediums, and Spirit-Rappers, and Roaring Radicals* (Urbana, Ill.: University of Illinois Press, 1972).

4. "Nathaniel Hawthorne" (1897), reprinted in *The American Essays of Henry James,* ed. Leon Edel (New York, N.Y.: Vintage, 1956), 12.

5. *The Art of the Novel: Critical Prefaces by Henry James,* ed. R.P. Blackmur (New York: Scribner's, 1934), 78.

6. "Nathaniel Hawthorne" (1897), *The American Essays of Henry James,* 19.

7. *The Blithedale Romance, The Centenary Edition of the Works of Nathaniel Hawthorne,* ed. William Charvat et al. (Columbus, Ohio: Ohio State University Press, 1962–), III, 203. On *The Blithedale Romance* generally, I have found most useful one group of articles that discusses problems of mimesis in the work, often discussing the image of the veil, and a second group that treats the issue of politics. I see these issues as interrelated, whereas they have usually been treated as opposed. Hawthorne's disavowal of any political theme in the preface may be read ironically to show that romance is precisely implicated in the representation of politics, at once the appropriate mode to treat Utopian reform and itself perhaps a way of asserting power over reality. On mimesis, see especially: Kent Bales, "The Allegory and the Radical Romantic Ethic of *The Blithedale Romance,*" *American Literature* 46 (1974), 41–53; Bill Christophersen, "Behind the White Veil: Self-Awareness in Hawthorne's *The Blithedale Romance,*" *Modern Language Studies* 12 (1982), 81–92; Frederick Crews, "A New Reading of *The Blithedale Romance,*" *American Literature* 29 (1957), 147–70; Kenneth Dauber, *Rediscovering Hawthorne;* Edgar Dryden, *Nathaniel Hawthorne: The Uses of Enchantment;* Allen Flint, "'essentially a day-dream, and yet a fact': Hawthorne's *Blithedale,*" *Nathaniel Hawthorne Journal* 2 (1972), 75–83; Rita Gollin, *Nathaniel Hawthorne and the Truth of Dreams;* Roy Harvey Pearce, "Day-Dream and Fact: The Import of *The Blithedale Romance,*" in *Individual and Community,* ed. K. Baldwin and P. Kirby; C. Swann, *"The Blithedale Romance:* Translation and Transformation, Mime and Mimesis," *Journal of American Studies* 18 (1984), 237–53.

    On politics, see: Nina Baym, *The Shape of Hawthorne's Career;* Robert C. Elliott, *"The Blithedale Romance,"* in *Hawthorne Centenary Essays,* p. 103–117; David Howard, *"The Blithedale Romance* and the Sense of Revolution," in *Tradition and Tolerance in Nineteenth-Century Fiction,* ed. D. Howard, J. Lucas, and J. Goode, 55–97; Irving Howe, *Politics and the Novel* (New York, N.Y.: Horizon, 1957); Leo Levy, *"The Blithedale Romance:* Hawthorne's 'Voyage Through Chaos,'" *Studies in Romanticism* 8 (1968), 1–19; John McWilliams, *Hawthorne, Melville, and the American Character* (Cambridge: Cambridge University Press, 1984).

8. *The Bostonians,* in *Henry James: Novels 1881–1886* (New York: Library of America, 1985). *The Bostonians* was not reprinted in the New York Edition because of its failure in America. This is a readily available edition. All subsequent page references to the novel are to this edition and are given parenthetically within the text.

9. Henry James, *Hawthorne* (1879; reprinted Ithaca, N.Y.: Cornell University Press, 1956), 66.

10. Many readers, including William James, identified Miss Birdseye as Hawthorne's sister-in-law, Elizabeth Peabody, who was still active in the 1880s. James's denial of this resemblance is reprinted in Matthiessen and Murdock's edition of the *Notebooks,* 67–68.

11. Daniel Heaton, "The Altered Characterization of Miss Birdseye in Henry James's *The Bostonians," American Literature* 50 (1979), 588–603.

12. R.W.B. Lewis, "The Matter of the Heart," p. 95.

13. See Robert Elliott, *The Shape of Utopia* (Chicago, Ill.: University of Chicago Press, 1970).

14. See Levy, *"The Blithedale Romance:* Hawthorne's 'Voyage through Chaos.' "

15. Levy, p. 1.

16. Emerson, "Nature," in *Complete Works,* ed. Edward W. Emerson (1903–4; reprinted New York, AMS, 1956), I, 46.

17. On mesmerism, see Taylor Stoehr, "Hawthorne and Mesmerism," *Huntington Library Quarterly* 33 (1969), 33–60, and *Hawthorne's Mad Scientists* (Hamden, Ct.: Archon, 1978).

18. Emerson, "Historical Notes on Life and Letters in New England," *Works* X, 337–39.

19. "To Sophia Peabody," 18 October 1841, reprinted in *The Love Letters of Nathaniel Hawthorne* (1907; reprinted Washington, D.C.: NCR Microcard Editions, 1972), II, 62–65.

20. On pastoral in *The Blithedale Romance,* see Crews, Dauber, Dryden, and Judy Schaaf Anhorn, "Gifted Simplicity of Vision: Pastoral Expectation in *The Blithedale Romance," ESQ* 28 (1982), 135–53.

21. On the role of Coverdale, see Kent Bales, *"The Blithedale Romance:* Coverdale's Mean and Subversive Egotism," *Bucknell Review* 21 (1973), 60–82; Keith Carabine, " 'Bitter Honey': Coverdale as Narrator in *The Blithedale Romance,"* in A. Robert Lee, ed., *New Critical Essays on Nathaniel Hawthorne,* 110–30; John McElroy and Edward McDonald, "The Coverdale Romance," *Studies in the Novel* 14 (1982), 1–16; Irvin Stock, "Hawthorne's Portrait of the Artist: A Defense of *The Blithedale Romance," American Literature* 47 (1975), 21–36. All tend to focus on Coverdale as a character and his relation to Hawthorne, while I would emphasize the relation in terms of the role of romancer rather than seeking reflections of Hawthorne's biography in his character. McElroy and McDonald consider Coverdale not only an unreliable narrator but a liar. Richard Poirier, *A World Elsewhere,* discusses the influence of Coverdale on James's center of consciousness. On Coverdale's retrospection, see especially Baym, *The Shape of Hawthorne's Career;* Crews, "A New Reading of *The Blithedale Romance";* Dryden, *The Uses of Enchantment;* and Gollin, *Nathaniel Hawthorne and the Truth of Dreams.*

22. James, "Letter to the Honorary Robert S. Rantoul" (1904), reprint in *The American Essays of Henry James,* p. 28.

23. James, "Nathaniel Hawthorne," (1897), reprinted in *The American Essays of Henry James,*

24. On the scene in Memorial Hall, see Peter Buitenhuis, *The Grasping Imagination,* 147–48. For a view which undercuts the reverence of the scene, see Judith Fetterley, *The Resisting Reader* (Bloomington, Ind.: Indiana University Press, 1978).

25. Trilling, *The Liberal Imagination* (New York, N.Y.: Anchor-Doubleday, 1953), 55–88. On *The Bostonians* generally, see especially: Charles Anderson, introduction to *The Bostonians* (London: Penguin, 1984); Martha Banta, *Henry James and the Occult;* Judith Fetterley, *The*

Resisting Reader (Bloomington, Ind.: Indiana University Press, 1978); David Howard, *"The Bostonians,"* in *The Air of Reality,* ed. John Goode (London: Methuen, 1972); Irving Howe, Introduction to *The Bostonians* (New York, N.Y.: Random House, 1956); Lionel Trilling, *The Opposing Self* (New York, N.Y.: Viking, 1955). Most critics tend to side with either Olive or Basil, while I think both are satirized by James. I have found Richard Brodhead's subtle treatment of love and power in this novel in his *The School of Hawthorne* most helpful. Finally, though, I would interpret his view as ultimately siding with Basil; see especially Brodhead, pp. 152–53. The politics of the book and its feminist aspect are encoded in its mode of representation, which emphasizes the dangers of one character's possession of another and the interpenetration of personal and public politics.

26.   Howard, *"The Bostonians,"* p. 61. On James and the Civil War, see Barry Menikoff, "A House Divided: *The Bostonians,"* *College Language Association Journal* 20 (1977), 459–74. See also Lewis, "The Matter of the Heart," on the aftermath of the war in *The Bostonians:* "The entire country is represented as having suffered some strange and terrible reversal of fortune" (p. 91).

27.   On feminism in this novel, see especially Judith Fetterley, *The Resisting Reader.* She sees Olive as the heroine. Fetterley also critiques the melodrama of the book as casting Basil as hero and Verena as victim. I think James's ironic invocation of melodrama is rather designed to underline the feminist point she makes, by showing that Basil's "rescue" of Verena is in fact a form of victimization. By contrast, Trilling and Howe are sympathetic to Basil. Howe identifies James's conservatism with the viewpoint of Basil Ransom, though he admits that "if Ransom is expressing James's views at all, it is in a style so deliberately inflated as to carry the heaviest ironic stress (introduction to *The Bostonians,* p. xvi). In his introduction to the new Penguin edition of the novel (1984), Charles Anderson changes his earlier view of sympathy for Basil Ransom ("James's Portrait of the Southerner," *American Literature* 27 (1955), 309–31) to skepticism of his heroism. As I show, the "feminism" of this novel seems to lie in its dramatization of the ways in which the personal becomes political. Sara de Saussure Davis provides some illuminating background on sources in 1880s feminism: "Feminist Sources in *The Bostonians,"* *American Literature* 50 (1979), 570–87. Oscar Cargill suggests a connection between James's work and his sister's life, with a brief mention of *The Bostonians,* in *"The Turn of the Screw* and Alice James," *PMLA* 78 (1963), 238–49. For more background on Alice James (whose friendship with Katharine Loring might have been a partial model for the relationship of Olive and Verena), and a more sympathetic view of her life and writings, see Ruth B. Yeazell, *The Death and Letters of Alice James* (Berkeley, Ca.: University of California Press, 1981).

28.   On pastoral in *The Bostonians,* see Robert McLean, *"The Bostonians:* New England Pastoral," *Papers on Language and Literature* 7 (1971), 374–81. On the city and pastoral, see R.A. Morris, "Classical Vision and the American City: Henry James's *The Bostonians,"* *New England Quarterly* 6 (1973), 543–57.

29.   On Basil's "ransoming" of Verena, see Fetterley, *The Resisting Reader.*

30.   For a different view of the relation of politics to representation, see Catherine Gallagher, *The Industrial Reformation of English Fiction* (Chicago, Ill.: University of Chicago Press, 1986).

Chapter 6

1.   James, "Nathaniel Hawthorne" (1897), reprinted in *The American Essays of Henry James* (New York, N.Y.: Vintage, 1956), 22.

2. Marius Bewley, *The Complex Fate* (London: Chatto and Windus, 1952), 31–54. For other writings on the relation of *The Marble Faun* to *The Wings of the Dove,* see Thaddeo Babiiha, *The James-Hawthorne Relation: Bibliographical Essays* (Boston, Mass.: G.K. Hall, 1980), esp. 229–33. Most of the sources he mentions are brief and explore character relationships. F.O. Matthiessen, in *Henry James: The Major Phase* (New York, N.Y.: Oxford University Press, 1944), sees in it "poetic drama" (p. 71) and the "mood of a fairy tale" (p. 59); here I am indebted to him. But when he looks at the images of the abyss and the Edenic imagery associated with Kate and Merton, Matthiessen feels that such images exhibit "carelessness or obliviousness on James's part" which "show how far he had drifted from the Christian knowledge that Hawthorne possessed" (p. 65). I feel rather that the echoes of Hawthorne and James's transformation of them are crucial to the entire novel.

    On the metaphysical and religious aspects of *The Wings of the Dove,* see especially Quentin Anderson, *The American Henry James* (New Brunswick, N.J.: Rutgers University Press, 1957). Other critics concerned with the role of spiritual drama in the book include Dorothea Krook, *The Ordeal of Consciousness in Henry James* (Cambridge: Cambridge University Press, 1962); John Goode, "The Pervasive Mystery of Style: *The Wings of the Dove,*" in *The Air of Reality,* ed. Goode (London: Methuen, 1972), 244–300; and R. W. B. Lewis, "The Matter of the Heart," in *Trials of the Word* (New Haven, Ct.: Yale University Press, 1965). Though I would align myself with these critics rather than with those who see the book as an instance of social realism, I feel that the spirit is evoked in this novel as something absent rather than present. See Marcia Ian, "The Elaboration of Privacy in *The Wings of the Dove,*" *ELH* 51 (1984), 107–36. Ian also treats the absences of the book, but tends to see the Jamesian self as realized through negation, especially of others. I feel the book's absences are traces of a self which representation invokes but cannot embody.

    On the analogy between style and content, which I discuss here in terms of the Hawthorne influence, see especially Laurence Holland, *The Expense of Vision* (Princeton, N.J.: Princeton University Press, 1964), and Kenneth Graham, *Henry James: The Drama of Fulfillment* (Oxford: Clarendon, 1975). On romance and realism, see Martha Banta, *Henry James and the Occult* (Bloomington, Ind.: Indiana University Press, 1972) and Frederick Crews, *The Tragedy of Manners* (New Haven, Ct.: Yale University Press, 1957); both tend to see romance and realism as opposed. I am more in accord with the view suggested by Donald Crowley and Richard Hocks, in their "Editors' Commentary" to *The Wings of the Dove* (New York, N.Y.: Norton, 1978), 439–45, especially the comment that "for James the elements of romance are part of the real, the 'poetry' part of the 'monstrous'" (p. 442). The Hawthorne relation is crucial to understanding this fusion of romance and realism in James, and Crowley and Hocks mention Hawthorne as source for James's American subject (the American girl) in *The Wings of the Dove* (p. 440). On the issue of realism in the novel generally, see especially William Stowe, *Balzac, James, and the Realistic Novel* (Princeton, N.J.: Princeton University Press, 1983).

3. Henry James, *Hawthorne* (1879; reprinted Ithaca, N.Y.: Cornell University Press, 1956), 134.

4. Henry James, "Nathaniel Hawthorne" (1897), reprinted in *The American Essays of Henry James,* p. 21.

5. F. W. H. Myers, *Proceedings of the Society for Psychical Research,* VII, 305; quoted in William James, *The Varieties of Religious Experience* (New York: Random House, 1902), 512 footnote 1.

6. Angus Fletcher, *Allegory* (Ithaca, N.Y.: Cornell University Press, 1964).

7. Carolynn van Dyke, *The Fiction of Truth* (Ithaca, N.Y.: Cornell University Press, 1985).

8. Hawthorne, *The Marble Faun, The Centenary Edition of the Works of Nathaniel Hawthorne,* ed. William Charvat et al. (Columbus, Ohio: Ohio State University Press, 1962—), Vol. IV (1968). Henceforeward referred to parenthetically as *CE* IV with page number. See Hawthorne's comment on his own narrative: "Unless we attempt something in this way, there must remain an unsightly gap, and a lack of continuousness and dependence in our narrative; so that it would arrive at certain inevitable catastrophes without due warning of their imminence" (*CE* IV, 93).

   Readings of *The Marble Faun* which have influenced my interpretation here in their treatment of romance and art include; Jonathan Auerbach, "Executing the Model: Painting, Sculpture, and Romance-Writing in Hawthorne's *The Marble Faun,*" *ELH* 47 (1980), 103–120; Nina Baym, *"The Marble Faun:* Hawthorne's Elegy for Art," *New England Quarterly* 44 (1971), 355–76; Paul Brodtkorb, "Art Allegory in *The Marble Faun,*" *PMLA* 77 (1962), 254–67; Kenneth Dauber, *Rediscovering Hawthorne* (Princeton, N.J.: Princeton University Press, 1977); Edgar Dryden, "The Limits of Romance: A Reading of *The Marble Faun,*" in *Individual and Community,* ed. Kenneth Baldwin and David Kirby (Durham, N.C.: Duke University Press, 1975), 17–48; Rita Gollin, "Painting and Character in *The Marble Faun,*" *ESQ* 21 (1975), 1–10; Harry Levin, "Statues from Italy," *Hawthorne Centenary Essays,* 119–140; Sheldon Liebman, "The Design of *The Marble Faun,*" *New England Quarterly* 40 (1967), 61–78; Roy Harvey Pearce, "Hawthorne and the Twilight of Romance," *Yale Review* 37 (1948), 487–506.

9. Preface to *The Wings of the Dove, The Art of the Novel: Critical Prefaces by Henry James,* ed. R.P. Blackmur (New York, N.Y: Scribner's, 1934), 288. References to other prefaces by James are to this volume and will be abbreviated *AN.* On the role of Minny Temple, see Lotus Snow, "The Disconcerting Poetry of Mary Temple," *New England Quarterly* 31 (1958), 312–39.

10. *The Wings of the Dove,* The New York Edition: *The Novels and Tales of Henry James,* vols. 19 and 20 (New York, N.Y.: Scribner's, 1909). All subsequent references to this novel are to this edition, with volumes referred to as either I or II.

11. "To W. D. Howells," *The Letters of Henry James,* ed. Percy Lubbock (New York, N.Y.: Scribner's, 1920), II, 224.

12. On the Miltonic allusions in the novel, see Adeline Tintner, *"Paradise Lost* and *Paradise Regained* in James's *The Wings of the Dove* and *The Golden Bowl,*" *Milton Quarterly* 17 (1983), 125–31.

   On the abyss, see Jean Kimball, "The Abyss and *The Wings of the Dove:* The Image as a Revelation," *Nineteenth-Century Fiction* 10 (1956), 281–300; Stowe, *Balzac, James, and the Realistic Novel,* p. 141; and Graham, *Henry James: The Drama of Fulfillment,* p. 183.

13. See also James's account of his own initiation into London in pictorial and magical terms: "For one's self all conveniently, there had been doors that opened—opened into light and warmth and cheer . . . the number of lurking springs at light pressure of which particular vistas would begin to recede, great lighted, furnished, peopled galleries, sending forth gusts of agreeable sound" (preface to *The Princess Casamassima, The Art of the Novel,* p. 61).

14. On the Bronzino, see especially Miriam Allott, who identifies it as the portrait of Lucrezia Panciatichi in "The Bronzino Portrait in *The Wings of the Dove,*" *Modern Language Notes* 58 (1953), 23–25; see also Viola Hopkins Winner, *Henry James and the Visual Arts* (Charlottesville, Va.: University Press of Virginia, 1970), 82–4; and Laurence Holland, *The Expense of Vision,* 302–3.

15. Henry James, "Nathaniel Hawthorne," (1897), reprinted in *The American Essays of Henry James,* p. 21.

16. On this scene, see Stowe, *Balzac, James, and the Realistic Novel.*

17. See Stowe's comments on Milly's role as dove as "model for effective action" (p. 152). In his view, Milly "must . . . spend so much of her time in her representative capacity that she has preciously little left for direct contact with the 'real' " (p. 15). I feel, however, that representation and its masks become the "real" in this novel.

18. Holland, *The Expense of Vision,* 407–8. See also Winner, *Henry James and the Visual Arts,* 184–85.

19. On the storm in Venice, see also Daniel Mark Fogel, *Henry James and the Structure of Romantic Imagination* (Baton Rouge, La.: Louisiana State University Press, 1981), 81; and Carl Maves, *Sensuous Pessimism: Italy in the Work of Henry James* (Bloomington, Ind.: Indiana University Press, 1973), 115.

20. See Ralph Waldo Emerson, "Experience," in *Essays: Second Series, Complete Works,* ed. Edward Waldo Emerson (1903–4; reprinted New York, N.Y.: AMS, 1979), III, 48.

Chapter 7

1. I have taken James's definition of romance from the "Letter to the Honorary Robert S. Rantoul" (1904), reprinted in *The American Essays of Henry James* (New York, N.Y.: Vintage, 1956), 24–31 (hereafter abbreviated "1904"), and the preface to *The American,* in *The Art of the Novel: Critical Prefaces by Henry James,* ed. R.P. Blackmur (New York, N.Y.: Scribner's, 1934) (hereafter abbreviated *AN*). For other writings of James on romance, see James E. Miller, ed., *Theory of Fiction: Henry James* (Lincoln, Neb.: University of Nebraska Press, 1972), index under "romance," and the chapters "The Romancers: Sand and Hawthorne" and "Revaluations: The Romancers," in Sarah Daugherty, *The Literary Criticism of Henry James* (Athens, Ohio: Ohio University Press, 1981).

   On *The Golden Bowl* as Balzacian realism, see John Bayley, "Love and Knowledge: *The Golden Bowl,*" in *The Characters of Love* (New York, N.Y.: Collier, 1960), 175–223. On James in general as novelist of manners, see James Tuttleton, *The Novel of Manners in America* (Chapel Hill, N.C.: University of North Carolina Press, 1972). The view of the novel as Swedenborgian allegory is that of Quentin Anderson, *The American Henry James* (New Brunswick, N.J.: Rutgers University Press, 1957); for Christian views aligned with his, see Dorothea Krook, *The Ordeal of Consciousness* (Cambridge: Cambridge University Press, 1962), and Michael Gilmore, *The Middle Way: Puritanism and Ideology in American Literature* (New Brunswick, N.J.: Rutgers University Press, 1977), 195–208.

   The commentaries on the novel I have found most illuminating are by Laurence Holland, *The Expense of Vision* (Princeton, N.J.: Princeton University Press, 1964); Mark Krupnick, *"The Golden Bowl:* Henry James's Novel About Nothing," *English Studies* 57 (1976), 533–40, Naomi Lebowitz, *The Imagination of Loving* (Detroit, Mich.: Wayne State University Press, 1965); Gabriel Pearson, "The Novel to End All Novels: *The Golden Bowl,*" in *The Air of Reality: New Essays on Henry James,* ed. John Goode (London: Methuen, 1972), 301–362; and Ruth Bernard Yeazell, *Language and Knowledge in the Late Novels of Henry James* (Chicago, Ill.: University of Chicago Press, 1976). Most ultimately see the novel as realistic in its premises, or in the case of Krupnick, as entirely anti-realistic. Richard Brodhead analyzes the symbolic dimension of *The Golden Bowl* in his *The School of Hawthorne* (New York, N.Y.: Oxford, 1986). He compares *The Golden Bowl* to *The Scarlet Letter* at length. Here I wish to consider James's way of inverting the use of symbolism in Hawthorne, so that symbols are perceived as interfused with the reality they describe rather than as products of projection. For an extensive treatment of most of the published criticism on the novel, see R.B.J. Wilson, *Henry James's Ultimate Narrative: The Golden Bowl* (St. Lucia, Queensland: University of Queensland Press, 1981).

2. 1904, p. 28.

3. Preface to *The Golden Bowl, The Art of the Novel,* p. 335. Henceforward referred to as *AN,* parenthetically within the text.

4. See Freud's "The Uncanny," *The Standard Edition of the Complete Psychological Works of Sigmund Freud,* trans. James Strachey (London: Hogarth Press, 1953–74) XVII, 217–52. He claims that we encounter the uncanny in literature more frequently than in life. I feel that James uses literature to bring the uncanny out of the realm of imaginary experience into conscious, waking awareness.

5. For an analysis that makes these figures the basis of a view of the story as Darwinian conflict, see Catherine Cox Wessel, "Strategies for Survival in James's *The Golden Bowl,*" *American Literature* 55 (1983), 576–590. I feel that the displacement of savage desires into figures represents James's way of showing the power of repression, the effort and price of civilization.

6. James's way of conceiving of reality seems to have been infectious. In his *Autobiography,* Coburn, the photographer, carries the view of reality as reflection of imagination one step further; he speculates that many of the London scenes he photographed for this book no longer exist—as if the book could endure, but reality would not: *Alvin Langdon Coburn, Photographer: An Autobiography,* ed. Helmut and Alison Gernsheim (New York, N.Y.: F.A. Praeger, 1966).

7. According to Leo Bersani, "The Jamesian Lie," *Partisan Review* 36 (1969), 53–79, the first part of the book is novelistic whereas the second half offers us Maggie's "radical revision" (p. 73). My contention is that in the first half, under the guise of novelistic forms, the Prince pursues an "impossible romance." In the second half, Maggie restores the social forms to their proper meaning by reinfusing them with romance.

8. On quest themes and romanticism in the novel, see Daniel Mark Fogel, *Henry James and the Structure of the Romantic Imagination* (Baton Rouge, La.: Louisiana State University Press, 1981); and Clare Goldfarb, "An Archetypal Reading of *The Golden Bowl:* Maggie Verver as Questor," *American Literary Realism* 14 (1981), 52–61. Fogel is interested in the image of the spiral ascent, Goldfarb in an archetypal reading of the quest. Neither develops the allusions to romantic literature as fully as seems possible. On boat imagery, see Nicola Bradbury, *Henry James: The Later Novels* (Oxford: Oxford University Press, 1979), 123–96 *passim.*

9. On such internalization, see Harold Bloom, "The Internalization of Quest-Romance," in *The Ringers in the Tower* (Chicago, Ill.: University of Chicago Press, 1971), 113–35. He discusses primarily the translation of medieval quest-romance into romantic processes of imagination. For James the quest becomes one not just of thinking or even imagining but of desiring in a sexual sense.

10. "The Deconstruction of Henry James," *Texas Studies in Literature and Language* 29 (1987), 235.

11. *The Golden Bowl,* The New York Edition: *The Novels and Tales of Henry James* (New York: Scribner's, 1907–17), vols. 23 and 24. Henceforward referred to parenthetically within the text by volume number (I or II) and page number.

12. See James's objections to the ending of Poe's *Narrative* as losing form through severing connections: "The would-be portentous climax of Edgar Poe's 'Arthur Gordon Pym,' where the indispensable history is absent, where the phenomena evoked . . . are immediate and flat. . . . The result is that, to my sense, the climax fails—fails because it stops short . . . for want of connexions. There *are* no connexions; not only . . . in the sense of further statement, but of our own further relation to the elements, which hang in the void; whereby we see the effect lost, the imaginative effort wasted" (*AN* 256–57).

13. See Fredric Jameson, *The Political Unconscious* (Ithaca, N.Y.: Cornell University Press, 1981), on the use, in modernist writers such as Kafka, of "the fantastic as a determinate, marked *absence* at the heart of the secular world" (p. 134).

14. My views of this purchase are indebted to Holland's chapter "The Marriages: *The Golden Bowl*," in *The Expense of Vision*.

15. A few years later James would conjecture on the possibility of extending consciousness into the realm after death, his definition of immortality: "Is There a Life After Death?," 1910, reprinted in *The James Family,* ed. F.O. Matthiessen (New York, N.Y.: Knopf, 1947), 602–14.

16. On gardens, see also Naomi Lebowitz, *The Imagination of Loving,* 135–36.

17. The best summation of the debate for and against the Ververs is by Ruth B. Yeazell, *Language and Knowledge in the Late Novels of Henry James,* footnote 2 to Chapter 1, 131–32.

Conclusion

1. Hawthorne's presence is pervasive in all three: in "Concord and Salem" and numerous allusions in *The American Scene;* in the definition of romance in the preface to *The American* and other prefaces; and in the description of Hawthorne's death in 1864 as associated by James with his accession to adulthood (at age 21) and the death of Lincoln in the *Autobiography*.

2. *The American Scene* (1907; reprinted Bloomington, Ind.: Indiana University Press, 1968. Subsequent parenthetical page references are to this work.
   On speaking monuments, see Peter Conn, *The Divided Mind: Ideology and Imagination in America, 1898–1917* (Cambridge: Cambridge University Press, 1983). In addition to his book, the works on *The American Scene* most relevant to my discussion, for their focus on matters of representation, are: Jean-Christopher Agnew, "The Consuming Vision of Henry James," in *The Culture of Consumption* (New York, N.Y.: Pantheon, 1983), esp. 74–100; Laurence Holland, *The Expense of Vision* (Princeton, N.J.: Princeton University Press, 1964) (appendix to revised edition, 1982), 411–34; Stuart Johnson, "American Marginalia: Henry James's *The American Scene,"* *Texas Studies in Literature and Language* 24 (1982), 83–101; Richard Lyons, "In Supreme Command: The Crisis of the Imagination in James's *The American Scene,"* *New England Quarterly* 55 (1982), 517–39; F.O. Matthiessen, *Henry James: The Major Phase* (New York, N.Y.: Oxford University Press, 1944), 105–8; Mark Seltzer, *Henry James and the Art of Power* (Ithaca, N.Y.: Cornell University Press, 1984), 96–145; Gordon Taylor, "Chapters of Experience: *The American Scene,"* *Genre* 12 (1979), 93–116; Alan Trachtenberg, *"The American Scene:* Versions of the City," *Massachusetts Review* 8 (1967), 281–95.

3. Harold Bloom, following Freud, has noted that repetition may be an attempt to gain mastery, though it is more usually understood as a compulsion aligned with the death wish. But James's attempts at repetition (especially when he revisits the Ashburton Place home) rather undo repetition. Though this undoing seems involuntary, even undesirable, it can be seen as a more

helpful way of confronting the past than the attempt at mastery: "Something positive is done which, again actually or in imagination, was done before"—*The Anxiety of Influence* (New York, N.Y.: Oxford University Press, 1975), 80. See also Bloom's "Wordsworth and the Scene of Instruction," in *Poetry and Repression* (New Haven, Ct.: Yale University Press, 1978), for a pattern similar to that of James's response to Hawthorne's birthplace.

4.   See James's 1910 essay, "Is There a Life After Death?," reprinted in *The James Family* (New York, N.Y.: Knopf, 1947), ed. F.O. Matthiessen. See also Stuart Johnson, "Prelinguistic Consciousness in 'Is There a Life After Death?,'" *Criticism* 26 (1982), 245–57.

Bibliography

Primary Sources

Hawthorne, Nathaniel. *The Centenary Edition of the Works of Nathaniel Hawthorne*. Ed. William Charvat et al. Columbus, Ohio: Ohio State University Press, 1962–.
_____ . *The Love Letters of Nathaniel Hawthorne*. 1907; reprinted Washington: NCR Microcard Editions, 1972.
James, Henry. *The American Scene*. 1907; reprinted Bloomington, Ind.: Indiana University Press, 1968.
_____ . "The Art of Fiction" (1884). In *Partial Portraits*, 1888; reprinted Westport, Ct.: Greenwood, 1970, 375–408.
_____ . *The Art of the Novel: Critical Prefaces by Henry James*. Ed. R.P. Blackmur. New York, N.Y.: Scribner's, 1934.
_____ . *The Bostonians*. Ed. Irving Howe, New York, N.Y.: Modern Library, 1956.
_____ . *Hawthorne*. 1879; reprinted Ithaca, N.Y.: Cornell University Press, 1956.
_____ . "Hawthorne's French and Italian Journals." *Nation*, March 14, 1872. Reprinted in *The American Essays of Henry James*. Ed. Leon Edel. New York, N.Y.: Knopf, 1956, 3–11.
_____ . "Is There a Life After Death?" (1910). Reprinted in *The James Family*. Ed. F.O. Matthiessen. New York, N.Y.: Knopf, 1947, 602–14.
_____ . "Letter to the Honorary Robert S. Rantoul." June 10, 1904. In *The Proceedings in Commemoration of the One Hundredth Anniversary of the Birth of Nathaniel Hawthorne*. Salem, Mass.: Essex Institute, 1904, 55–62. Reprint in *The American Essays of Henry James*. Ed. Leon Edel. New York, N.Y.: Vintage, 1956, 24–31.
_____ . Letters. 4 vols. Ed. Leon Edel. Cambridge, Mass.: Harvard University Press, 1974–84.
_____ . *The Letters of Henry James*. 2 vols. Ed. Percy Lubbock. New York, N.Y.: Scribner's, 1920.
_____ . "Nathaniel Hawthorne." In *A Library of the World's Best Literature*. Ed. Charles Dudley Warner. New York, N.Y.: 1896–97, XII, 7053–61. Reprinted in *The American Essays of Henry James*. Ed. Leon Edel. New York, N.Y.: Vintage, 1956, 11–23.
_____ . The New York Edition: *The Novels and Tales of Henry James*. 26 vols. New York, N.Y.: Scribner's, 1907–17.
_____ . *The Notebooks of Henry James*. Ed. F.O. Matthiessen and Kenneth Murdock. New York, N.Y.: Oxford, 1947.
_____ . *Notes of a Son and Brother*. Vol. II of the *Autobiography*. Ed. F.W. Dupee, New York, N.Y.: Criterion, 1956.
_____ . *Henry James: Novels 1881–1886*. New York, N.Y.: Library of America, 1985.

_____ . *The Portrait of a Lady*. Ed. Robert Bamberg. New York, N.Y.: Norton, 1975.

_____ . *The Question of Our Speech; The Lesson of Balzac: Two Lectures*. Boston, Mass. and New York, N.Y.: Houghton Mifflin, 1905.

_____ . *Theory of Fiction: Henry James*. Ed. James E. Miller. Lincoln, Neb.: University of Nebraska Press, 1972.

_____ . *The Wings of the Dove*. Ed. Donald Crowley and Richard Hocks. New York, N.Y.: Norton, 1978.

Secondary Sources

Abel, Darrel. "'A More Imaginative Pleasure': Hawthorne on the Play of Imagination." *Emerson Society Quarterly* 55 (1969), 63–71.

_____ . "Giving Lustre to Gray Shadows: Hawthorne's Potent Art." *American Literature* 41 (1969), 373–88.

_____ . "Hawthorne, Ghostland, and the Jurisdiction of Veracity." *American Transcendental Quarterly* 24 (1974), 30–38.

Adams, Stephen. "Unifying Structures in Mosses," *Studies in American Fiction* 8 (1980), 147–63.

Agnew, Jean-Christophe. "The Consuming Vision of Henry James." In *The Culture of Consumption*. New York, N.Y.: Pantheon, 1983.

Allott, Miriam. "The Bronzino Portrait in *The Wings of the Dove*." *Modern Language Notes* 58 (1953), 23–25.

Alpers, Paul. *The Poetry of the Faerie Queene*. Princeton, N.J.: Princeton University Press, 1967.

Anderson, Charles. Introduction to *The Bostonians*. London: Penguin, 1984.

_____ . "James's Portrait of the Southerner." *American Literature* 27 (1955), 309–31.

_____ . *Person, Place, and Thing in the Novels of Henry James*. Durham, N.C.: Duke University Press, 1980.

Anderson, Judith. *The Growth of a Personal Voice: Piers Plowman and the Faerie Queene*. New Haven, Ct.: Yale University Press, 1976.

Anderson, Quentin. *The American Henry James*. New Brunswick, N.J.: Rutgers University Press, 1957.

Anhorn, Judy Schaaf. "Gifted Simplicity of Vision: Pastoral Expectation in *The Blithedale Romance*." *ESQ* 28 (1982), 135–53.

Arac, Jonathan. "Reading the Letter." *Diacritics* 9 (1979), 42–52.

Armstrong, Paul. *The Phenomenology of Henry James*. Chapel Hill, N.C.: University of North Carolina Press, 1983.

Arthos, John. *On the Poetry of Spenser and the Form of Romance*. Freeport, N.Y.: Books for Libraries Press, 1956.

Auerbach, Erich. *Mimesis*. Princeton, N.J.: Princeton University Press, 1953.

Auerbach, Jonathan. "Executing the Model: Painting, Sculpture, and Romance-Writing in Hawthorne's *The Marble Faun*." *ELH* 47 (1980), 103–20.

Babiiha, Thaddeo K. *The James-Hawthorne Relationship: Bibliographical Essays*. Boston, Mass.: G.K. Hall, 1980.

Bales, Kent. "The Allegory and the Radical Romantic Ethic of *The Blithedale Romance*." *American Literature* 46 (1974), 41–53.

_____ . "*The Blithedale Romance:* Coverdale's Mean and Subversive Egotism." *Bucknell Review* 21 (1973), 60–82.

_____ . "Hawthorne's Prefaces and Romantic Perspectivism." *ESQ* 23 (1977), 55–69.

Banta, Martha. *Henry James and the Occult*. Bloomington, Ind.: Indiana University Press, 1972.

Barzun, Jacques. "Henry James: Melodramatist." *Kenyon Review* 5 (1943), 508–21.

Bayley, John. *The Characters of Love*. New York, N.Y.: Collier, 1960.

————— . "Formalist Games and Real Life." *Essays in Criticism* 31 (1981), 271–81.

Baym, Nina. "Concepts of the Romance in Hawthorne's America," *Nineteenth-Century Fiction* 38 (1984), 426–43.

————— . *"The Marble Faun:* Hawthorne's Elegy for Art," *New England Quarterly* 44 (1971), 355–76.

————— . *The Shape of Hawthorne's Career.* Ithaca, N.Y.: Cornell University Press, 1976.

Beer, Gillian. *The Romance.* London: Methuen, 1970.

Bell, Michael D. *The Development of American Romance.* Chicago, Ill.: University of Chicago Press, 1980.

————— . *Hawthorne and the Historical Romance of New England.* Princeton, N.J.: Princeton University Press, 1971.

Bell, Millicent. *Hawthorne's View of the Artist.* Albany, N.Y.: State University of New York Press, 1962.

————— . "Henry James: Meaning and Unmeaning." *Raritan* 4 (1984), 29–46

————— . "The Obliquity of Signs: *The Scarlet Letter.*" *Massachusetts Review* 23 (1982), 9–26.

Bender, John. *Spenser and Literary Pictorialism.* Princeton, N.J.: Princeton University Press, 1972.

Berger, Harry. *The Allegorical Temper.* New Haven, Ct.: Yale University Press, 1957.

Bersani, Leo. *A Future for Astyanax.* Boston, Mass.: Little, Brown, 1976.

————— . "The Jamesian Lie." *Partisan Review* 36 (1969), 53–79.

Bewley, Marius. *The Complex Fate: Hawthorne, Henry James, and Some Other American Writers.* London: Chatto and Windus, 1952.

Bier, Jesse. "Hawthorne on the Romance: His Prefaces Related and Examined." *Modern Philology* 53 (1955), 17–24.

Bloom, Harold. *The Anxiety of Influence.* New York, N.Y.: Oxford, 1975.

————— . *Poetry and Repression.* New Haven, Ct.: Yale University Press, 1978.

————— . "The Internalization of Quest-Romance." In *The Ringers in the Tower.* Chicago, Ill.: University of Chicago Press, 1971, 13–35.

Bochner, Jay. "Life in a Picture Gallery: Things in *The Portrait of a Lady* and *The Marble Faun.*" *Texas Studies in Literature and Language* 11 (1969), 761–77.

Bock, Darilyn. "From Reflective Narrators to James: The Coloring Medium of the Mind." *Modern Philology* 76 (1979), 259–72.

Bonnefoy, Yves. "Images and Presence: Yves Bonnefoy's Inaugural Address at the College de France." *New Literary History* 15 (1983), 433–51.

Bradbury, Nicola. *Henry James: The Later Novels.* Oxford: Oxford University Press, 1979.

Branch, Watson. "From Allegory to Romance: Hawthorne's Transformation of *The Scarlet Letter.*" *Modern Philology* 80 (1982), 47–67.

Brodhead, Richard. *Hawthorne, Melville, and the Novel.* Chicago, Ill.: University of Chicago Press, 1976.

————— . *The School of Hawthorne.* New York, N.Y.: Oxford University Press, 1986.

Brodtkorb, Paul. "Art Allegory in *The Marble Faun.*" *PMLA* 77 (1962), 254–67.

Brooks, Peter. *The Melodramatic Imagination.* New Haven, Ct.: Yale University Press, 1976.

Brownson, Orestes. "On Imagination," *Democratic Review* 12 (1843).

Buitenhuis, Peter. *The Grasping Imagination.* Toronto: University of Toronto Press, 1970.

————— . "Henry James on Hawthorne." *New England Quarterly* 32 (1959), 207–25.

Carabine, Keith. "'Bitter Honey': Coverdale as Narrator in *The Blithedale Romance,*" in A. Robert Lee, ed., *New Critical Essays on Nathaniel Hawthorne.* London: Vision/Totava, N.J.: Barnes and Noble, 1982, 110–30.

Cargill, Oscar. *The Novels of Henry James.* New York, N.Y.: Hafner, 1961.

————— . *"The Turn of the Screw* and Alice James." *PMLA* 78 (1963), 238–49.

Carton, Evan. "Hawthorne and the Province of Romance." *ELH* 47 (1980), 331–54.

———— . "Henry James the Critic." *Raritan* 5 (1986), 118–36.

———— . *The Rhetoric of American Romance*. Baltimore, Md.: Johns Hopkins University Press, 1985.

Caudwell, Christopher. *Romance and Realism*. Princeton, N.J.: Princeton University Press, 1970.

Charney, Maurice. "Hawthorne and the Gothic Style." *New England Quarterly* 34 (1961), 36–49.

Chase, Richard. *The American Novel and its Tradition*. Garden City, N.Y.: Anchor-Doubleday, 1957.

Christophersen, Bill. "Behind the White Veil: Self-Awareness in Hawthorne's *The Blithedale Romance*." *Modern Language Studies* 12 (1982), 81–92.

Alvin Langdon Coburn, Photographer: An Autobiography. Ed. Helmut and Alison Gernsheim. New York, N.Y.: F.A. Praeger, 1966.

Coleridge, Samuel Taylor. *Biographia Literaria,* chapter 13. Reprinted in *The Portable Coleridge*. Ed. I. A. Richards. New York, N.Y.: Viking-Penguin, 1950, 514–16.

Conn, Peter. *The Divided Mind: Ideology and Imagination in America, 1898–1917*. Cambridge: Cambridge University Press, 1983.

Cottom, Daniel. "Hawthorne vs. Hester: The Ghostly Dialectic of Romance in *The Scarlet Letter*," *Texas Studies in Literature and Language* 24 (1982), 47–67.

Cowley, Malcolm. "The Five Acts of *The Scarlet Letter*." *College English* 19 (1957), 11–16.

Cox, James. *"The Scarlet Letter:* Through the Old Manse and the Custom-House." *Virginia Quarterly Review* 51 (1975), 432–47.

Crews, Frederick. "A New Reading of *The Blithedale Romance*." *American Literature* 29 (1957), 147–70.

———— . *The Sins of the Fathers: Hawthorne's Psychological Themes*. New York, N.Y.: Oxford University Press, 1966.

———— . *The Tragedy of Manners*. New Haven, Ct.: Yale University Press, 1957.

Dauber, Kenneth. *Rediscovering Hawthorne*. Princeton, N.J.: Princeton University Press, 1977.

Daugherty, Sarah. *The Literary Criticism of Henry James*. Athens, Ohio: Ohio University Press, 1981.

Dekker, George. "Sir Walter Scott, the Angel of Hadley, and American Historical Fiction." *Journal of American Studies* 17 (1983), 211–12.

Dickens, Charles. Preface to *Bleak House*. Boston, Mass.: Houghton Mifflin, 1956.

Dryden, Edgar. "The Image in the Mirror: The Double Economy of James's *Portrait*." *Genre* 13 (1980), 31–49.

———— . "The Limits of Romance: A Reading of *The Marble Faun*." In *Individual and Community*. Ed. Kenneth Baldwin and David Kirby. Durham, N.C.: Duke University Press, 1975, 17–48.

———— . *Nathaniel Hawthorne: The Uses of Enchantment*. Ithaca, N.Y.: Cornell University Press, 1977.

Duncan, Jeffrey. "The Design of Hawthorne's Fabrications." *Yale Review* 71 (1981), 51–71.

Eakin, Paul John. "Hawthorne's Imagination and the Structure of 'The Custom-House.'" *American Literature* 43 (1971), 346–58.

Eigner, Edwin. *The Metaphysical Novel in England and America*. Berkeley, Ca.: University of California Press, 1978.

Eliot, George. Chapter 17 of *Adam Bede*. Reprinted in *Documents of Modern Literary Realism*. Ed. George Becker. Princeton, N.J.: Princeton University Press, 1963, 112–116.

Eliot, T. S. "The Hawthorne Aspect," *Little Review* 5 (1918), 47–53. Reprinted in *The Question of Henry James*. Ed. F.W. Dupee. London: Allen Wingate, 1947, 123–33.

Elliott, Robert C. *"The Blithedale Romance*." In *Hawthorne Centenary Essays*. Ed. Roy Harvey Pearce. Columbus, Ohio: Ohio State University Press, 1964, 103–17.

———— . *The Shape of Utopia*. Chicago, Ill.: University of Chicago Press, 1970.

Emerson, Ralph Waldo. *Complete Works*. Ed. Edward W. Emerson. 1903–4; reprinted New York: AMS, 1968, Vols. I, III, and X.

Falk, Robert. *The Victorian Mode in American Fiction*. East Lansing, Mich.: Michigan State University Press, 1965.

Fanger, Donald. *Dostoevsky and Romantic Realism*. Cambridge, Mass.: Harvard University Press, 1965.

Feidelson, Charles. "The Moment of *The Portrait of a Lady*." *Ventures* 8 (1968), 47–55.

―――― . *"The Scarlet Letter."* In *Hawthorne Centenary Essays*. Ed. Roy Harvey Pearce. Columbus, Ohio: Ohio State University Press, 1964, 31–77.

―――― . *Symbolism and American Literature*. Chicago, Ill.: University of Chicago Press, 1953.

Felperin, Howard. *Shakespearean Representation*. Princeton, N.J.: Princeton University Press, 1972.

Ferguson, Suzanne. "The Face in the Mirror: Authorial Presence in the Multiple Vision of Third-Person Impressionist Narration." *Criticism* 21 (1979), 230–50.

Fetterley, Judith. *The Resisting Reader*. Bloomington, Ind.: Indiana University Press, 1978.

Fletcher, Angus. *Allegory*. Ithaca, N.Y.: Cornell University Press, 1964.

Flint, Allen. " 'essentially a day-dream, and yet a fact': Hawthorne's *Blithedale*." *Nathaniel Hawthorne Journal* 2 (1972), 75–83.

Fogel, Daniel Mark. *Henry James and the Structure of the Romantic Imagination*. Baton Rouge, La.: Louisiana State University Press, 1981.

Fossum, Robert H. *Hawthorne's Inviolable Circle: The Problem of Time*. Deland, Fla.: Everett/Edwards, 1972.

Franzosa, John. " 'The Custom-House,' *The Scarlet Letter*, and Hawthorne's Separation from Salem." *ESQ* 24 (1978), 57–71.

Freud, Sigmund. "The Uncanny." *The Standard Edition of the Complete Psychological Works of Sigmund Freud*. Trans. James Strachey. London: Hogarth Press, 1953–74. XVII, 217–52.

Frye, Northrop. *Anatomy of Criticism*. Princeton, N.J.: Princeton University Press, 1957.

―――― . *The Secular Scripture*. Cambridge, Mass.: Harvard University Press, 1979.

Fussell, Edwin. "Sympathy in *The Portrait of a Lady* and *The Golden Bowl*." *Henry James Review* 2 (1981), 161–66.

Gabler-Hover, Janet. "The Deconstruction of Henry James." *Texas Studies in Literature and Language* 29 (Summer 1987), 235.

Gallagher, Catherine. *The Industrial Reformation of English Fiction*. Chicago, Ill.: University of Chicago Press, 1986.

Gervais, Ronald. "A Papist Among the Puritans: Icon and Logos in *The Scarlet Letter*." *ESQ* 25 (1979), 11–16.

Giamatti, A. Bartlett. *The Play of Double Senses*. Englewood Cliffs, N.J.: Prentice-Hall, 1975.

Gilmore, Michael. *The Middle Way: Puritanism and Ideology in American Literature*. New Brunswick, N.J.: Rutgers University Press, 1977.

Goldfarb, Clare. "An Archetypal Reading of *The Golden Bowl*: Maggie Verver as Questor." *American Literary Realism* 14 (1981), 52–61.

Gollin, Rita. *Nathaniel Hawthorne and the Truth of Dreams*. Baton Rouge, La.: Louisiana State University Press, 1979.

―――― . "Painting and Character in *The Marble Faun*." *ESQ* 21 (1975), 1–10.

Goode, John. "The Pervasive Mystery of Style: *The Wings of the Dove*." In *The Air of Reality*. Ed. Goode. London: Methuen, 1972, 244–300.

Graham, Kenneth. *Henry James: The Drama of Fulfillment*. Oxford: Clarendon, 1975.

Greenblatt, Stephen, ed. *Allegory and Representation*. Baltimore, Md.: Johns Hopkins University Press, 1981.

Greenwald, Elissa. "The Ruins of Empire: Reading the Monuments in Hawthorne and James." *CEA Critic* 46 (1984), 48–59.

———. "The Symbol as Symptom: Romance and Repression in *The Scarlet Letter*." In *The Psychoanalytic Study of Literature, Volume I*. Ed. Joseph Reppen and Maurice Charney. Hillsdale, N.J.: Analytic Press, 1985, 149–66.

Grover, Philip. *Henry James and the French Novel*. London: Paul Elek, 1973.

Guillory, John. *Poetic Authority: Spenser, Milton, and Literary History*. New York, N.Y.: Columbia University Press, 1983.

Hamilton, A.C. "Elizabethan Romance: The Example of Prose Fiction." *ELH* 49 (1982), 287–99.

Hartman, Geoffrey. "False Themes and Gentle Minds." In *The Fate of Reading*. Chicago, Ill.: University of Chicago Press, 1975, 283–97.

Heaton, Daniel. "The Altered Characterization of Miss Birdseye in Henry James's *The Bostonians*." *American Literature* 50 (1979), 588–603.

Heidegger, Martin. "The Origin of the Work of Art." In *Poetry, Language, Thought*. Trans. Albert Hofstadter. New York, N.Y.: Harper and Row, 1971, 17–87.

Hocks, Richard. *Henry James and Pragmatistic Thought*. Chapel Hill, N.C.: University of North Carolina Press, 1974.

Holland, Laurence. *The Expense of Vision*. Princeton, N.J.: Princeton University Press, 1964.

Holsberry, John. "Hawthorne's 'The Haunted Mind,' The Psychology of Dreams, Coleridge, and Keats." *Texas Studies in Literature and Language* 21 (1979), 307–31.

Hostetler, Norman. "Imagination and Point of View in 'The Haunted Mind.'" *American Transcendental Quarterly* 39 (1978), 263–67.

Howard, David. "*The Blithedale Romance* and the Sense of Revolution." In *Tradition and Tolerance in Nineteenth-Century Fiction*. Ed. Howard, John Lucas, and John Goode. London: Routledge and Kegan Paul, 1978, 55–97.

———. "*The Bostonians*." In *The Air of Reality: New Essays on Henry James*. Ed. John Goode. London: Methuen, 1972.

Howe, Irving. *Politics and the Novel*. New York, N.Y.: Horizon, 1957.

Howells, William Dean. "James's Hawthorne." Reprinted in *William Dean Howells as Critic*. Ed. Edwin Cady. London: Routledge and Kegan Paul, 1973.

Hutchinson, Stuart. *Henry James, An American as Modernist*. London: Vision/Totowa, N.J.: Barnes and Noble, 1983.

Ian, Marcia. "The Elaboration of Privacy in *The Wings of the Dove*." *ELH* 51 (1984), 107–36.

Jacobson, Marcia. *Henry James and the Mass Market*. University, Ala.: University of Alabama Press, 1983.

Jacobson, Richard. *Hawthorne's Conception of the Creative Process*. Cambridge, Mass.: Harvard University Press, 1965.

Jameson, Fredric. *The Political Unconscious: Narrative as a Socially Symbolic Act*. Ithaca, N.Y.: Cornell University Press, 1981.

Jann, Rosemary. *The Art and Science of Victorian History*. Columbus, Ohio: Ohio State University Press, 1985.

Johnson, Claudia. *The Productive Tensions of Hawthorne's Art*. University, Ala.: University of Alabama Press, 1981.

Johnson, Stuart. "American Marginalia: Henry James's *The American Scene*." *Texas Studies in Literature and Language* 24 (1982), 83–101.

———. "Prelinguistic Consciousness in 'Is There a Life After Death?'" *Criticism* 26 (1982), 245–57.

Jones, Buford. "Hawthorne and Spenser: From Allusion to Allegory." *Nathaniel Hawthorne Journal* 5 (1975), 71–90.

Kappeler, Susanne. *Writing and Reading in Henry James*. New York, N.Y.: Columbia University Press, 1980.

Kaston, Carren. *Imagination and Desire in the Novels of Henry James*. New Brunswick, N.J.: Rutgers University Press, 1984.

Kendrick, Walter. "Balzac and British Realism: Mid-Nineteenth Century Theories of the Novel." *Victorian Studies* 20 (1976), 5–24.

Kerr, Howard. *Mediums, and Spirit-Rappers, and Roaring Radicals*. Urbana, Ill.: University of Illinois Press, 1972.

Kimball, Jean. "The Abyss and *The Wings of the Dove:* The Image as a Revelation." *Nineteenth-Century Fiction* 10 (1956), 281–300.

Kincaid, James. "The Forms of Victorian Fiction." *Victorian Newsletter* 47 (1975), 1–4.

Kinkead-Weekes, Mark. "The Letter, the Picture, and the Mirror: Hawthorne's Framing of *The Scarlet Letter*," in *Nathaniel Hawthorne; New Critical Essays*. Ed. A. Robert Lee. London: Vision/Totowa, N.J.: Barnes and Noble, 1982, 68–87.

Kolb, Harold. *The Illusion of Life: American Romance as a Literary Form*. Charlottesville, Va.: University Press of Virginia, 1969.

Krook, Dorothea. *The Ordeal of Consciousness in Henry James*. Cambridge: Cambridge University Press, 1962.

Krupnick, Mark. *"The Golden Bowl:* Henry James's Novel About Nothing." *English Studies* 57 (1976), 533–40.

Laird, J. T. "Cracks in Precious Objects: Aestheticism and Humanity in *The Portrait of a Lady*." *American Literature* 52 (1981), 643–48.

Lebowitz, Naomi. *The Imagination of Loving*. Detroit, Mich.: Wayne State University Press, 1965.

Levin, Harry. *The Power of Blackness*. New York, N.Y.: Knopf, 1958.

———. "Statues from Italy." In *Hawthorne Centenary Essays*. Ed. Roy Harvey Pearce. Columbus, Ohio: Ohio State University Press, 1964, 119–140.

Levine, George. *The Realistic Imagination*. Chicago, Ill.: University of Chicago Press, 1981.

Levy, Leo. *The Blithedale Romance:* Hawthorne's 'Voyage Through Chaos.'" *Studies in Romanticism* 8 (1968), 1–19.

———. *Versions of Melodrama*. Berkeley, Ca.: University of California Press, 1957.

Lewis, Paul. "Mournful Mysteries: Gothic Speculation in *The Scarlet Letter*," *American Transcendental Quarterly* 44 (1979), 279–93.

Lewis, R. W. B. "Hawthorne and James: The Matter of the Heart." In *Trials of the Word: Essays in American Literature and the Humanistic Tradition*. New Haven, Ct.: Yale University Press, 1965.

Leyburn, Ellen. *Strange Alloy: The Mixture of Comedy and Tragedy in the Works of Henry James*. Chapel Hill, N.C.: University of North Carolina Press, 1968.

Liebman, Sheldon. "The Design of *The Marble Faun*." *New England Quarterly* 40 (1967), 61–78.

Long, Robert E. *The Great Succession: Henry James and the Legacy of Hawthorne*. Pittsburgh, Pa.: University of Pittsburgh Press, 1979.

Lyons, Richard. "In Supreme Command: The Crisis of the Imagination in James's *The American Scene*." *New England Quarterly* 55 (1982), 517–39.

MacCaffrey, Isabel. *Spenser's Allegory*. Princeton, N.J.: Princeton University Press, 1976.

Mackenzie, Manfred. "Ironic Melodrama in *The Portrait of a Lady*." *Modern Fiction Studies* 12 (1966), 7–23.

McCall, Dan. "Hawthorne's Familiar Kind of Preface." *ELH* 35 (1968), 422–39.

McDonald, John J. "'The Old Manse' and Its Mosses: The Inception and Development of *Mosses from an Old Manse*." *Texas Studies in Literature and Language* 16 (1974), 77–108.

McElroy, John. "The Hawthorne Style of American Fiction." *ESQ* 19 (1973), 117–23.

——— and McDonald, John. "The Coverdale Romance," *Studies in the Novel* 14 (1982), 1–16.

McLean, Robert. *"The Bostonians:* New England Pastoral." *Papers on Language and Literature* 7 (1971), 374–81.

McWilliams, John. *Hawthorne, Melville, and the American Character.* Cambridge: Cambridge University Press, 1984.

Martin, Terence. "The Method of Hawthorne's Tales." In *Hawthorne Centenary Essays.* Ed. Roy Harvey Pearce. Columbus, Ohio: Ohio State University Press, 1964, 7–30.

———. *Nathaniel Hawthorne.* New Haven, Ct.: College and University Press, 1965.

Matthiessen, F. O. *American Renaissance.* New York, N.Y.: Oxford University Press, 1941.

———. *Henry James: The Major Phase.* New York, N.Y.: Oxford University Press, 1944.

———. "The Painter's Sponge and Varnish Bottle." In *Henry James: The Portrait of a Lady.* Ed. Robert Bamberg. New York, N.Y.: Norton, 1975, 577–96.

Maves, Carl. *Sensuous Pessimism: Italy in the Work of Henry James.* Bloomington, Ind.: Indiana University Press, 1973.

Mazzella, Anthony. "The New Isabel." In *Henry James: The Portrait of a Lady.* Ed. Robert Bamberg. New York, N.Y.: Norton, 1975, 597–619.

Menikoff, Barry. "A House Divided: *The Bostonians.*" *College Language Association Journal* 20 (1977), 459–74.

Michaels, Walter Benn. "Romance and Real Estate." *Raritan* 2 (1983), 66–81.

Mills, Nicolaus. *American and English Fiction in the Nineteenth Century.* Bloomington, Ind.: Indiana University Press, 1973.

Morris, R. A. "Classical Vision and the American City: Henry James's *The Bostonians.*" *New England Quarterly* 6 (1973), 543–47.

Mull, Donald. *Henry James's Sublime Economy.* Middletown, Ct.: Wesleyan University Press, 1973.

Munday, Michael. "The Novel and Its Critics in the Early Nineteenth Century." *Studies in Philology* 79 (1982), 205–26.

Myers, F. W. H. *Proceedings of the Society for Psychical Research,* VII, 305. Quoted in William James, *The Varieties of Religious Experience.* New York, N.Y.: Random House, 1902, p. 512, fn. 1.

Orians, G. Harrison. "The Romance Ferment After *Waverley.*" *American Literature* 3 (1932), 408–31.

Parker, Patricia. *Inescapable Romance.* Princeton, N.J.: Princeton University Press, 1979.

Paul, Thomas. "Hawthorne's Houses of Fiction." *American Literature* 48 (1976), 71–91.

Pearce, Roy Harvey. "Day-Dream and Fact: The Import of *The Blithedale Romance.*" In *Individual and Community.* Ed. Kenneth Baldwin and David Kirby. Durham, N.C.: Duke University Press, 1975.

———. "Hawthorne and the Twilight of Romance," *Yale Review* 37 (1948), 487–506.

———. "Romance and the Study of History." In *Hawthorne Centenary Essays.* Ed. Pearce. Columbus, Ohio: Ohio State University Press, 1964, 221–44.

Pearson, Gabriel. "The Novel to End All Novels: *The Golden Bowl.*" In *The Air of Reality: New Essays on Henry James.* Ed. John Goode. London: Methuen, 1972, 301–62.

Perkins, George, ed. *The Theory of the American Novel.* New York, N.Y.: Holt, Rinehart and Winston, 1970.

Perosa, Sergio. *Henry James and the Experimental Novel.* Charlottesville, Va.: University Press of Virginia, 1978.

Peterson, Dale. *The Clement Vision: Poetic Realism in Turgenev and James.* Port Washington, N.Y.: Kennikat, 1975.

Poirier, Richard. *A World Elsewhere: The Place of Style in American Literature.* New York, N.Y.: Oxford University Press, 1966.

────── . *The Comic Sense of Henry James*. New York, N.Y.: Oxford, 1960.

Porte, Joel. *The Romance in America*. Middletown, Ct.: Wesleyan University Press, 1969.

Posnock, Ross. *Henry James and the Problem of Robert Browning*. Athens, Ga.: University of Georgia Press, 1985.

Powers, Lyall. *Henry James and the Naturalist Novel*. East Lansing, Mich.: Michigan State University Press, 1962.

Price, Martin. *To the Palace of Wisdom*. Carbondale, Ill.: Southern Illinois University Press, 1964.

Qualls, Barry. *The Secular Pilgrims of Victorian Fiction*. Cambridge: Cambridge University Press, 1982.

Quilligan, Maureen. *The Language of Allegory*. Ithaca, N.Y.: Cornell University Press, 1979.

Ragussis, Michael. "Family Discourse and Fiction in *The Scarlet Letter*," *ELH* 49 (1982), 863–88.

Reeve, Clara. *The Progress of Romance*. Colchester: William Keymer, 1785.

Rowe, John C. "The Internal Conflict of Romantic Narrative: Hegel's *Phenomenology* and Hawthorne's *The Scarlet Letter*." *Modern Language Notes* 95 (1980), 1203–31.

────── . "Re-Marking the Impression." *Criticism* 24 (1982), 233–60.

────── . "'What the Thunder Said': James's *Hawthorne* and the American Anxiety of Influence: A Centenary Essay." *Henry James Review* 4 (1983), 81–119.

Ruland, Richard. "Beyond Harsh Inquiry: The Hawthorne of Henry James." *ESQ* 25 (1979), 95–117.

St. Armand, Barton Levi. "Hawthorne's 'Haunted Mind': A Subterranean Drama of the Self." *Criticism* 13 (1971), 1–25.

Schneider, Daniel. *The Crystal Cage*. Lawrence, Kan.: University Press of Kansas, 1978.

Schug, Charles. *The Romantic Genesis of the Modern Novel*. Pittsburgh, Pa.: University of Pittsburgh Press, 1979.

Scott, Sir Walter. "Introduction to *The Fortunes of Nigel*." Reprinted in *Novelists on the Novel*. Ed. Miriam Allott. London: Routledge and Kegan Paul, 1959, p. 50.

────── . "Review of Jane Austen's *Emma*." *Quarterly Review* 14 (815–16), 193.

Seed, D. "The Narrator in Henry James's Criticism." *Philological Quarterly* 60 (1981), 501–21.

Siebers, Tobin. *The Romantic Fantastic*. Ithaca, N.Y.: Cornell University Press, 1984.

Snow, Lotus. "The Disconcerting Poetry of Mary Temple." *New England Quarterly* 31 (1958), 312–39.

Spenser, Edmund. *The Faerie Queene*. In *The Poetical Works of Edmund Spenser*. Ed. E. de Selincourt. London: Oxford, 1912.

Stallman, Robert. "The Houses that James Built—*The Portrait of a Lady*." *Texas Quarterly* 1 (1958), 176–96.

Stock, Irvin. "Hawthorne's Portrait of the Artist: A Defense of *The Blithedale Romance*." *American Literature* 47 (1975), 21–36.

Stoehr, Taylor. "Hawthorne and Mesmerism." *Huntington Library Quarterly* 33 (1969), 33–60.

────── . *Hawthorne's Mad Scientists*. Hamden, Ct.: Archon, 1978.

Stone, Donald David. *Novelists in a Changing World*. Cambridge, Mass.: Harvard University Press, 1972.

────── . *The Romantic Impulse in Victorian Fiction*. Cambridge, Mass.: Harvard University Press, 1980.

Stouck, David. "The Surveyor of the Custom-House: A Narrator for *The Scarlet Letter*." *Centennial Review* 15 (1971), 309–29.

Stowe, William. *Balzac, James, and the Realistic Novel*. Princeton, N.J.: Princeton University Press, 1983.

Stowell, Peter. *Literary Impressionism: James and Chekhov*. Athens, Ga.: University of Georgia Press, 1980.

Stubbs, John C. *The Pursuit of Form: A Study of Hawthorne and the Romance*. Urbana, Ill.: University of Illinois Press, 1970.

Sundquist, Eric, ed. *American Realism*. Baltimore, Md.: Johns Hopkins University Press, 1982.

Swann, C. *"The Blithedale Romance:* Translation and Transformation, Mime and Mimesis." *Journal of American Studies* 18 (1984), 237–53.

Taylor, Gordon. "Chapters of Experience: *The American Scene." Genre* 12 (1979), 93–116.

Thorburn, David. *Conrad's Romanticism*. New Haven, Ct.: Yale University Press, 1974.

Tintner, Adeline. *"Paradise Lost* and *Paradise Regained* in James's *The Wings of the Dove* and *The Golden Bowl." Milton Quarterly* 17 (1983), 125–31.

Toulouse, Teresa. "Spatial Relations in 'The Old Manse.'" *ESQ* 28 (1982), 154–66.

Trachtenberg, Alan. *"The American Scene:* Versions of the City." *Massachusetts Review* 8 (1967), 281–95.

Trilling, Lionel. *The Liberal Imagination*. New York, N.Y.: Anchor-Doubleday, 1953.

———. *The Opposing Self*. New York, N.Y.: Viking, 1955.

Tuttleton, James. *The Novel of Manners in America*. Chapel Hill, N.C.: University of North Carolina Press, 1972.

Tuve, Rosemond. "Spenser and Medieval Romances." In *The Faerie Queene: A Casebook*. Ed. Peter Bayley. London: Macmillan, 1977.

van Deusen, Marshall. "Narrative Tone in 'The Custom-House' and *The Scarlet Letter." Nineteenth-Century Fiction* 21 (1966), 61–71.

Van Ghent, Dorothy. *The English Novel: Form and Function*. New York, N.Y.: Rinehart, 1953.

van Dyke, Carolynn. *The Fiction of Truth: Structure of Meaning in Narrative and Dramatic Allegory*. Ithaca, N.Y.: Cornell University Press, 1985.

Van Leer, David. "Roderick's Other Serpent: Hawthorne's Use of Spenser." *ESQ* 27 (1981), 73–84.

Veeder, William. *Henry James—The Lessons of the Master: Popular Fiction and Personal Style in the Nineteenth Century*. Chicago, Ill.: University of Chicago Press, 1975.

Waggoner, Hyatt. "Art and Belief." In *Hawthorne Centenary Essays*. Ed. Roy Harvey Pearce. Columbus, Ohio: Ohio State University Press, 1964, 167–195.

———. *The Presence of Hawthorne*. Baton Rouge, La.: Louisiana State University Press, 1979.

Ward, J. A. *The Search for Form: Studies in the Structure of James's Fiction*. Chapel Hill, N.C.: University of North Carolina Press, 1967.

Weinstein, Philip. *Henry James and the Requirements of the Imagination*. Cambridge, Mass.: Harvard University Press, 1971.

Wessel, Catherine Cox. "Strategies for Survival in James's *The Golden Bowl." American Literature* 55 (1983), 576–90.

White, Allon. *The Uses of Obscurity*. London: Routledge and Kegan Paul, 1981.

Williams, Ioan, ed. *Novel and Romance*. New York, N.Y.: Barnes and Noble, 1970.

Wilson, John. Review of "The Entail." Blackwood's Magazine 13 (1823).

Wilson, R. B. J. *Henry James's Ultimate Narrative: The Golden Bowl*. St. Lucia, Queensland: University of Queensland Press, 1981.

Winner, Viola Hopkins. *Henry James and the Visual Arts*. Charlottesville, Va.: University Press of Virginaia, 1970.

Winston, Robert. "Paulding's *The Dutchman's Fireside* and Early American Romance." *Studies in American Fiction* 11 (1983), 47–60.

Winters, Yvor. "Maule's Well, or Henry James and the Relation of Morals to Manners." In his *In Defense of Reason*. Denver, Colo.: Allen Swallow, 1937, 300–343.

Yeazell, Ruth Bernard. *Language and Knowledge in the Late Novels of Henry James*. Chicago, Ill.: University of Chicago Press, 1976.

Ziff, Larzer. "The Artist and Puritanism." *Hawthorne Centenary Essays*. Ed. Roy Harvey Pearce. Columbus, Ohio: Ohio State University Press, 1964, 245–69.

———. "The Ethical Dimension of 'The Custom-House.'" *Modern Language Notes* 73 (1958), 338–44.

Index